Fifth International
Sakharov Hearing

PROCEEDINGS

Fifth International Sakharov Hearing

PROCEEDINGS

April, 1985

Edited by Allan Wynn
Associate Editors: Martin Dewhirst,
Harold Stone

ANDRE DEUTSCH

Editors' note

Chapters 2–32 of this book reproduce (with some brief additions and updated information) the Proceedings of the Fifth International Sakharov Hearing, which took place in London on 10–11 April 1985. The three items which appear as Appendices were originally presented to members of the Executive Committee of the Hearing as background information. The editors feel they deserve a wider readership. Chapter 1 was written in 1986.

We have not aimed for total consistency in the transliteration of personal names. Many people who have left the USSR for the West now spell their names according to personal preference and/or the linguistic norms of the country in which they have settled.

First published 1986 by
André Deutsch Limited
105-106 Great Russell Street
London WC1

British Library Cataloguing in Publication Data

International Sakharov Hearing (5th :
   1985 : London)
   Fifth International Sakharov Hearing.
   1. Civil rights——Soviet Union
   I. Title   II. Wynn, Allan   III. Dewhirst,
   Martin   IV. Stone, Harold
   323.4'0947   JC599.S58

ISBN 0–233–98050–4
ISBN 0–233–98051–2 Pbk

Phototypeset by Falcon Graphic Art Ltd
Wallington, Surrey
Printed in Great Britain by
Billing & Sons Ltd
Worcester

Andrei Sakharov Campaign

The Sakharov Hearings have acquired a substantial history. The first Hearing took place in Copenhagen in 1975, the second in Rome in 1977, the third in Washington in 1979 and the fourth in Lisbon in 1983. Their purpose is to foster the cause of human rights, the cause for which Andrei Sakharov has sacrificed his freedom.

The Fifth Hearing concentrated on the development of the human rights situation in the USSR in the ten years since the signing of the Helsinki Final Act.

The preamble of the Helsinki Final Act, which was signed on 1 August 1975, states *inter alia* (Principle VII): 'Recognising the close link between peace and security in the world, and the need for each participant to make its contribution to the strengthening of peace and security by the promotion of fundamental rights, economic and social progress and the well being of all peoples, the participating States will respect human rights and fundamental freedoms including freedom of thought conscience, religion or belief for all without distinction as to race, sex, language or religion.

'They will promote and encourage the effective exercise of civil, political, economic, social, cultural and other rights and freedoms all of which derive from the inherent dignity of the human person, and are essential for his free and full development.

'In the field of human rights, the participating States will act in conformity with the Charter of the United Nations and the Universal Declaration of Human Rights and the International Covenant on Human Rights by which they are bound.'

Principle X of the Helsinki Final Act pledges the participating States to conform with their legal obligations under international law while exercising their sovereign rights to determine their laws and regulations.

The Fifth International Sakharov Hearing considers the evidence relevant to these commitments made by the USSR and, in the light of the evidence, also considers the future of the Helsinki accords.

ALLAN WYNN

CONTENTS

CHAPTER 1

Andrei Sakharov: A Tribute

ALLAN WYNN

Andrei Sakharov is regarded by many as the most important human rights activist of this century. His epic struggle to humanize the power of the Soviet state has captured the world's imagination. The Sakharov Hearings, of which the London Hearing is the fifth, are meant to further the cause of mankind's struggle for human rights and to serve as a tribute to Sakharov, whose life and work are briefly outlined below.

Academician Andrei D. Sakharov, born in 1921, the son of a physicist, graduated from Moscow University in 1942. Soon after, he began work on cosmic rays at the Lebedev Institute in Moscow under Professor Igor Tamm. After defending his doctoral thesis, he worked on the theoretical aspect of thermonuclear reactions. Although he made important observations in this field, the frequently made claim that he was the 'father' of the Soviet hydrogen bomb is thought by scientists to be an exaggeration. (Sakharov himself makes no such claim.) Sakharov's greatest scientific achievement was to devise the theoretical basis for controlled nuclear fusion — the tokamak, a development which may rank in importance one day with man's discovery of how to make fire.

Sakharov's standing in Russia was enhanced because he was the first Soviet scientist of world renown whose achievements owed nothing to tsarist or foreign training. Elected to the Soviet Academy of Sciences at the age of 32 (its youngest member), he received many honours; he was on three occasions awarded the Stalin Prize alone. With his election to the Academy came many material rewards.

Sakharov's transition from a privileged member of the Soviet élite to a reviled 'dissident' began gradually. In 1957, realizing the danger to the environment of radioactive contamination, he began to campaign against atmospheric nuclear tests. His advocacy is credited with persuading Khrushchev to agree to the Partial Test Ban Treaty of 1963. Soon other social topics engaged him: he criticized the Soviet educational system, calling for less indoctrination and more freedom of expression; he condemned the intrusion of political ideology into science, as typified by the Lysenko controversy, which made a laughing stock of Soviet genetics.

But it was the growing evidence of the re-introduction of Stalinism after Khrushchev's ouster which transformed Sakharov, a reticent man, from committed scientist into active dissident. (He has, of course, continued his scientific research, so far as circumstances have permitted.)

With Khrushchev's revelation of Stalin's crimes at the 20th Communist Party Congress in 1956, the Soviet people were promised a new era of moderation, tolerance and, above all, legality. The rights of Soviet citizens guaranteed by the constitution were to be protected. The days of arbitrary arrest and punishment were over. For a few years, the Soviet people had reason to believe that the central communist power was undergoing a humanist reformation. The publication of Solzhenitsyn's *One Day in the Life of Ivan Denisovich* symbolized the new mood. Writers, poets, artists and thinkers began to deviate from the strait-jacket of 'Socialist Realism'. A few mildly satirical books by Yuli Daniel and Andrei Sinyavsky were published abroad. But by 1965 the reformation was over — Khrushchev had been deposed and Leonid Brezhnev and his associates made it clear that they wanted no more 'liberal nonsense'. Sinyavsky and Daniel, after trials so crudely rigged that there was a world-wide outcry, were given heavy labour-camp sentences.

If the trial of Sinyavsky and Daniel had made a deeply painful impression in the West it provoked a strong protest among the growing dissident community in the USSR who saw clearly what it portended. In the absence of any democratic institutions through which the voice of the people can be heard, writers have always had a special role in Russian life. Only writers can ask the questions and express the agonies of millions. In the Soviet Union, it has been mainly writers who were the chief witnesses to oppression and the chief protesters against it – Gorky, Mayakovsky, Mandelshtam, Akhmatova, Pasternak and, finally, Solzhenitsyn.

Prior to the 23rd Congress of the Communist Party in 1966,

when it was widely rumoured in Moscow that Brezhnev intended a full rehabilitation of Stalin, Sakharov joined with twenty-four leading figures in science and art in warning Brezhnev against this move. Brezhnev drew back. Thereafter, Sakharov identified himself increasingly with the small and diverse group of dissidents who were striving to secure broader democratic rights for the Soviet people and, above all, to prevent the re-introduction of Stalinism.

In 1968, a brilliant essay by Sakharov began circulating in Russia in *samizdat*. It was soon published unofficially abroad under the title 'Progress, coexistence and intellectual freedom'. In it, Sakharov advanced two basic theses: the division of mankind threatens it with destruction, and intellectual freedom is essential for the survival of human society. He stated that the principal dangers which confronted mankind – thermonuclear war, mass hunger, destruction of the environment, the unforeseeable consequences of rapid technological change, and the stupefying effect of mass culture — could be averted only by universal cooperation under conditions of intellectual freedom. He totally rejected the Marxist view that only universal communism could solve the problems of humanity. On the contrary, he stated that freedom of thought and expression was an essential precondition for the development of a rational, stable and democratic society. Above all, he warned that no autocratic government could be relied upon to keep the peace. The prevention of nuclear war demanded that all authority be made responsible to public opinion.

Sakharov also warned that a nuclear war would be an unmitigated disaster for mankind, that a limited nuclear war would inevitably escalate into a total war, and that there was no possibility of evolving an effective defence against a massive nuclear attack. A nuclear war would simply be a means of mutual suicide. Therefore it was inadmissible to consider the use of nuclear weapons under any circumstances.

Realizing that to prevent the use of nuclear weapons meant that it would be necessary to prevent war between the superpowers, Sakharov addressed himself to the best ways of preventing such a war. First, he concluded that there should be a 'convergence' of the two great economic systems — socialism and capitalism. The first step in this process should be the extension of civil rights for the Soviet population. He urged the superpowers to recognize the rights of all people to self-determination and to regard both revolution and counter-revolution as forms of aggression, and proposed that the nations cooperate with a view to reducing the economic imbalance in the world. Above all, he urged an end to the exploitation of every local difficulty with the object of de-stabilizing the situation and extending spheres of influence. (For a fuller account of Sakharov's views on disarmament and the avoid-ance of nuclear war see Appendix III.)

With the signing in August 1975 of the Helsinki Final Act with its promise by all the signatories to 'respect human rights . . . freedom of thought, conscience, religion or belief' (Principle VII) many people within the USSR and beyond felt that there was to be a new beginning, a new liberal era.

One of the provisions of the Helsinki Final Act was that compliance with its human rights provisions could be monitored by the citizens of its signatories. Shortly after, citizens' groups were formed in Moscow and several other major cities in the USSR for this purpose. The authorities viewed this development with growing displeasure, and finally cracked down. Practically every known member of a Helsinki 'watch' group was eventually imprisoned, confined to a psychiatric hospital, compelled to emigrate or sent into exile.

All this time, Sakharov was at the forefront of the Soviet human rights movement. His activities caused increasing annoyance to the authorities but his position as an Academician protected him to some degree. (He had been deprived of his security clearance and access to secret scientific work since 1968.)

Sakharov periodically spoke very frankly to the Western press on many subjects but especially on the question of 'détente'. He warned that a rapprochement with the Soviet regime before it had adopted meaningful measures of democratization would be a danger for mankind. It would strengthen the totalitarian forces within the USSR and weaken democracy outside it. Sakharov continued, at the same time, to advocate a 'true détente' — a process whereby increasing democratization within the USSR and increasing socialism outside it would bring about the 'convergence' which he still saw as the only hope for a peaceful future. The key to this process, Sakharov believed, lay in the field of human rights. He considered that disarmament alone would not bring peace. Only world-wide respect for human rights could do that.

In 1980 Sakharov was exiled by administrative decree to the closed city of Gorky. The purpose was to cut off his contacts with the outside world. But he was able to maintain some links through his wife, Elena Bonner, until she too was confined to Gorky in 1984.

Despite his isolation, Sakharov continued to address himself to international and human rights problems with characteristic fearlessness and bluntness, indifferent to the consequences to himself. Nothing typifies his approach so much as the open letter he wrote to Professor Sidney Drell in response to the latter's Danz lecture (University of Washington Press, 1983). Sakharov's letter was published in the journal *Foreign Affairs* in June 1983.

Sakharov reiterated that nuclear war would destroy mankind and therefore must be prevented. He argued that nuclear weapons could not be regarded as a deterrent to an attack by conventional weapons. (Mutual suicide is not a means of defence.) Therefore the West, inferior in many respects to the East in conventional weapons, must urgently increase its conventional strength before commencing serious negotiations for nuclear disarmament. (The Soviet media described this as an incitement to seek military superiority over the USSR.) Sakharov explained that the Soviets' powerful silo-based inter-continental missiles were first-strike weapons which gave the Soviet Union a destabilizing advantage over the USA and threatened peace. He urged that the USA continue the policy of building MX missiles, stating that only when the Soviet leaders perceived that their present nuclear superiority over the USA had gone, would they seriously negotiate on nuclear arms reduction.

In a letter in October 1983 to the Sorbonne, where he had been invited to address a meeting of Nobel Laureates, Sakharov said:

The restoration of parity in conventional weapons is necessary; it is the realistic road to the renunciation of nuclear weapons which threaten our existence. During a transitional period, until parity in conventional weapons is achieved, the West, *and possibly the USSR in certain categories,* will still have to add to its nuclear arsenal. These additions will assure the stability of nuclear parity and spur the successful conclusion of disarmament negotiations.

It would not be difficult to imagine the furious reaction to this statement in the USSR, especially with the deletion of the key words underlined.

The Drell letter caused anger beyond the USSR. During Sakharov's hunger strike in May 1984 Mgr. Bruce Kent, of the British Campaign for Nuclear Disarmament, refused to sign a petition on behalf of Sakharov on the grounds that Sakharov had supported the MX programme and opposed a nuclear freeze. He refused to accept that Sakharov might know more than any member of CND about how to negotiate an ultimate reduction of nuclear weapons. Indeed, Sakharov believes that it might be necessary to carry on the arms race for another fifteen years before both sides achieve evident parity; only then would they be likely to agree to meaningful arms reductions. (Gorbachev's latest proposal suggests a fifteen-year period for reducing nuclear arms.)

Sakharov has never abandoned his essential thesis — without a wide extension of human rights in the USSR, meaningful disarmament will not occur. For disarmament requires mutual trust which, in turn, requires freedom of information and communication, freedom to travel and to emigrate.

Mikhail Gorbachev has stated to *l'Humanité* that Sakharov cannot be permitted to leave the country on the grounds that he possesses vital state secrets. Apart from the fact that Sakharov has been excluded from secret scientific work for twenty years, had he wished to betray state secrets, he had ample opportunity to do so before his banishment to Gorky. Gorbachev has also stated, ominously, that Sakharov has 'done things which were contrary to what was right and proper', without specifying what these things are.

Sakharov's courage and dedication to the cause of human dignity and freedom have justly earned him the Nobel Peace Prize (1975) and the characterization of him as 'the conscience of mankind'. The proceedings of the Fifth International Sakharov Hearing do more than pay tribute to him — they demonstrate that the cause to which he has made such a unique contribution and for which he has endured so much suffering is being continued and will continue until it prevails.

CHAPTER 2

The Fifth International Sakharov Hearing·

SIMON WIESENTHAL

This Hearing is being held in the name of a man who has become a symbol. The name of Andrei Sakharov is respected by millions of people not only in the USSR but throughout the world.

Dr Sakharov relinquished all the privileges accorded him by the Soviet system in order to speak out on issues of human rights. In 1980 he was exiled to the city of Gorky.

When Dr Sakharov continued to inform the free world of the Soviet abuse of human rights — mainly through the agency of his wife, the dissident Elena Bonner — this isolation was intensified and Elena Bonner too was compelled to live in Gorky.

The Soviet authorities hope the world will forget Andrei Sakharov and Elena Bonner but they are wrong. The free world has not forgotten them and Dr Sakharov's thoughts are now common knowledge in the West. We must do everything in our power to relieve the isolation of Dr Sakharov and his wife.

This Hearing will deal with all kinds of human rights problems which are close to the heart of Andrei Sakharov. It is our hope that the Sakharov Hearings will assist in alleviating the plight of this courageous man and result in a greater understanding of the ideas for which he has had to pay so dearly.

CHAPTER 3

Helsinki, Ottawa and the London Sakharov Hearing

EFREM YANKELEVICH

In four months' time the tenth anniversary of the signing of the Helsinki Final Act will be commemorated. The Soviet leaders are nostalgic for the détente of the 1970s. As indicated by a recent Politburo statement, the Soviet representative at the commemoration ceremony will in all probability speak positively about peaceful coexistence and cooperation and about Soviet compliance with the Helsinki accords.

I hope the Western leaders are preparing for this contingency. We may still have enough time to decide whether or not détente is still alive, what was wrong with the old détente, whether we want a new one and, if so, for what purpose.

If we agree to a détente, would it be the détente of the 1970s — the détente conceived by the West to remedy the inability to sustain the traditional policy of containment? The détente maintained to preserve the Alliance? The détente inspired by our perception of military–political realities? The détente driven by fear?

Would it be the détente advocated by Andrei Sakharov? A détente whose main purpose is the gradual 'opening' and liberalization of Soviet society? Andrei Sakharov has advocated his concept of détente since 1968. By 1973 he had begun to feel uneasy about the détente offered by Henry Kissinger and Willy Brandt:

. . . my basic premise still holds true, namely that the world faces two alternatives — either gradual convergence, with democratization within the Soviet Union, or increasing confrontation, with a growing danger of thermonuclear war. But reality has turned out to be trickier, in the sense that we now face a very specific issue: Will rapprochement be associated with the democratization of Soviet society or not? This new alternative, which at first sight may seem a halfway measure, better than nothing, in fact conceals within itself a great internal danger.

He argued that:

> ... As long as a country has no civil liberty, no freedom of information, and no independent press, then there exists no effective body of public opinion to control the conduct of the government and its functionaries. Such a situation is not just a misfortune for citizens unprotected against tyranny and lawlessness, it is a menace to international security ...

Is it unrealistic to hope that internal evolution in the USSR could change, in the long run, the nature of East–West relations? Is it unrealistic to believe that this evolution could be encouraged or shaped by outside pressure?

After all, the 'Sakharov doctrine' — the indivisibility of peace and human rights — was reflected in the Final Act and was practised, with varying degrees of vigour and consistency, at least within the framework of the 'Helsinki process'. Why then have we witnessed a dramatic deterioration of the human rights situation in the USSR as compared with the first years of the Helsinki accords?

Is it too early to judge the results of the 'Helsinki process'? Were the Helsinki accords an inappropriate vehicle for the expression of human rights concerns? Is the deterioration as profound as it appears to be? Can external pressure work and, if so, why has it not been working for the last six or seven years?

These are some of the questions that will be addressed by the Fifth Sakharov Hearing. In 1975 the USSR could hardly have been expected to abide by the broad human rights provisions of the Final Act. At any rate, it had not abided by the International Covenants on Human Rights which it had ratified two years earlier and which it had pledged again in Helsinki to respect. However, one could have hoped for a minimal compliance with the accords if only in the form of a demonstrable intention to comply. Indeed, for a period, the USSR did demonstrate such intent, most importantly by scaling down political persecution. Commendable behaviour — for which it never received much credit. Unfortunately, this period of restraint lasted only for about two years. Since then, it seems, the authorities have not felt constrained by their international obligations.

Who is at fault? The follow-up meeting in Belgrade? The Western desire for 'détente', whether human rights were respected or not? The Western determination to preserve the accords, come what may? Soviet fear of the spread of dissent?

All these matters are likely to be discussed at the forthcoming

Hearing. We also hope for a discussion on an even more controversial subject — the *future* of the Helsinki accords. What should be done about the Helsinki process, should it fail even to extract limited concessions in individual cases? Is there a brighter future ahead and, if so, how can it be best assured? Could a suspension or renunciation of the accords by the West encourage Soviet willingness for a new and better beginning?

There will soon take place another meeting which could change the course of this discussion — the meeting of human rights experts in Ottawa, which is being convened within the framework of the Helsinki process. This will provide a good opportunity for us to decide whether the Helsinki process works — whether the West can effectively insist on an improved observation of human rights in the USSR and whether the Soviet authorities are reasonable enough to accommodate at least some of the concerns expressed.

CHAPTER 4

The Sakharov Case and International Law

PAUL SIEGHART

Our meeting here today and tomorrow is not only one of protest; it is also one of celebration. True, the main reason why we are here is to add our collective public protest to the many others that have already rung out over the years at the manner in which the public authorities of the Soviet Union are treating one of their own citizens, the eminent physicist and Academician Dr Andrei Sakharov. But in making that protest, we also recognize and celebrate the courage, the integrity, the stand on principle, and the determination of this man; for without all these things he would not have evoked the persecution to which he is now being subjected. So we are here as much to salute a great man and his virtues, as to condemn the actions of his oppressors.

Sadly, great men and women who display such qualities constitute only a minute fraction of all mankind, so minute that they are often dismissed as cranks — or, especially in the Soviet Union, committed to psychiatric institutions as lunatics. But few though they are, they represent a central aspect of the human spirit — the search for truth, the struggle for freedom, and the insistence on the inherent dignity and worth of every human individual.

It is a striking fact that these standard-bearers of the human spirit, few though they are, are not confined to any particular nation, religion, tradition, or culture. They arise wherever there is oppression, persecution, deprivation, or exploitation of human beings by others of their kind. In that sense, Andrei Sakharov is not alone: he has spiritual brothers and sisters in South Africa, Libya, Uganda, and Zaire; in Cambodia, Iran, Iraq, Pakistan, and the Philippines; in Chile and El Salvador; in the other countries of the Warsaw Pact; and in our own liberal democracies also, even in quite recent times.

When people in the West protest about the treatment of Andrei Sakharov in the Soviet Union, they are commonly accused of adopting a 'capitalist' or 'bourgeois' stance, as if they were motivated only by anti-Soviet or anti-socialist sentiments. Perhaps that is true for a few, but for the great majority the accusation is quite false. There are many here today who, on other days of the year, protest with just as much fervour about events in the other countries I have just mentioned, for many of whose governments 'communism' — or even just 'socialism' — is anathema, and sufficient reason for locking up, or assassinating, those whom they suspect of sympathizing with it.

For today, concern for the victims of persecution need no longer be founded merely on moral conviction, religious belief, or political ideology; thanks to a very recent revolution in the international legal order, it can be founded on a quite new branch of international law — so new that it is still far too little known, which is why I must now explain it.

The international code of human rights law

Every society, large or small, must have laws in order to be able to conduct its affairs. Every modern nation-state therefore has its own internal laws, sometimes called 'national', 'domestic', or 'municipal' laws. But the world's nation-states also constitute a society among themselves, and that society too needs laws of its own. So, for many centuries, there has been a system of 'international' law, designed to regulate the relationships between sovereign states. But for most of those centuries, international law consistently refused to take any cognizance of national laws, or of the relationships between the public authorities of a state and its individual inhabitants. Indeed, the whole concept of national sovereignty meant that all such things were matters for the exclusive determination of each sovereign state, and could not be the concern of any other state or of international law.

This law dealt only with matters like war and peace between sovereign princes or nations, diplomatic relations, international shipping on the high seas, and similar things of concern to states in their relationships with each other. Its 'subjects' were sovereign princes and nations; though an individual could be the 'subject' of the domestic laws of a prince or a state, he or she could never be the subject of international law, in the sense of having any rights which that law could recognize. And, in the time-worn phrase, any foreign expression of concern for such things was dismissed as 'an illegitimate interference in the internal affairs of a sovereign state'.

That doctrine held almost absolute sway until well into our present century, and was frequently and successfully invoked by an endless procession of oppressive tyrannies. Ironically, it was finally toppled by two of the worst tyrants of our time — Adolf Hitler and Josef Stalin. The atrocities which they perpetrated against millions of their own citizens truly 'shocked the conscience of mankind', and helped to precipitate a world war of hitherto unprecedented dimensions and ferocity. But those atrocities also made the absolute doctrine of national sovereignty untenable in international law. We are apt to forget today that Hitler's persecution of Jews, gypsies, and others was conducted with full domestic legality, in accordance with laws enacted by a constitutionally elected legislature of the sovereign German people; and that Stalin's persecution of the *kulaks* was likewise justified with appropriate legal formulae. Plainly, the conscience of mankind could no longer tolerate a state of affairs in which international law, the highest rung on the ladder of man-made laws, could accept such monstrous national laws as legitimate, simply because they were beyond its concern. Something had to be done to ensure that, in future, mere national *legality* could not be enough to validate even the most monstrous Acts of State. Somehow, an international standard of *legitimacy* had to be installed, by which one could assess the conduct of a national government not only in its external affairs, but in its domestic ones also.

And so, in the course of a few brief decades, there was emplaced in the world's international legal order an elaborate structure of what we now call 'human rights law', comprising the Charter of the United Nations and the Universal Declaration of Human Rights; the twin International Covenants; the European and American Conventions; and a whole mass of more specific and detailed treaties dealing with different aspects of human rights, several of them establishing international organs with jurisdiction to interpret and apply them, either generally or in specific cases. The revolutionary effect of all this on the previously hallowed doctrines of international law was well expressed by Professor Sir Hersch Lauterpacht when he wrote, as long ago as 1950, that 'the individual has acquired a status and a stature which has transformed him from an object of international compassion into a subject of international right'.

In installing this new code of international law, the world's nations of course had many precedents from their domestic legal systems. Battles for individual liberty, autonomy, equality before the law and due process of law, freedom from torture and slavery, freedom of conscience, freedom of speech, and many other civil liberties and civil rights, had been fought and won in many countries over the centuries. There had been a steady evolution of catalogues of civil rights from the English Magna Carta of 1215 to the American Bill of Rights of 1791. The industrial revolution, and the political philosophy of socialism which its excesses evoked, had also created a second generation of welfare rights, such as rights to health, education, housing and social security. The material therefore lay ready to hand for the construction of a universal code of individual human rights and fundamental freedoms, agreed upon by the international community, and to be respected by all states. And the code guarantees these rights 'to all . . . without distinction of any kind, such as race, colour, sex, language, religion, political or other opinion, national or social origin, property, birth or other status'.

For our purposes today, what is most important about this new code is that it is universal, and has come into being by the consent of the international community, comprising nations of every political and economic system, every stage of development, and every religious and cultural tradition. Until it came into force, what were 'human rights' — and, indeed, whether there were any — remained a matter of legitimate dispute, on which different people could come to quite different conclusions depending on their religious, ethical, political, or ideological convictions. Indeed, human rights could scarcely be discussed apart from politics or morality.

I have met Soviet international lawyers of the older generation who still take this view, for the Soviet Union is a very conservative country. But, in fact, they are behind the times: today, this is no longer so. What human rights now *are* is conclusively determined by the content of the international code, and any violation of that code by the public authorities of a nation that is bound by it becomes a matter of *legitimate* concern for all other nations and their inhabitants, so that their protests can no longer be dismissed as 'an illegitimate interference in the internal affairs of a sovereign state'.

I should perhaps mention, at this point, the Helsinki accords. Famous though they are, they are not a binding treaty in international law; what underpins them are the human rights treaties to which most of the Helsinki states have adhered, but some of which only entered into force quite recently, after the accords were signed. Because these treaties are still so new, there has barely been time to study in any detail the conformity of different nations with their provisions. Indeed, the first such study has only just been completed by two of your Patrons — Professor J. M. Ziman and Professor J. H. Humphrey — and myself. It is a detailed study of the observance and violations of the human rights of scientists in the thirty-five participating states of the Helsinki accords, which it has taken us over three years to complete, and we sent the typescript to the publishers, the Oxford University Press, only just over a fortnight ago.[1] (Perhaps I might take this opportunity to acknowledge the generous support given to this project by the Airey Neave Memorial Trust in the form of an award for research into freedom under the law, without which we should certainly not have been able to undertake such a daunting task.)

The code and the Sakharov case

Let me then resume the central thread of my argument. If we protest here today about the manner in which the public authorities of the Soviet Union are treating Andrei Sakharov, it is not because we prefer a 'capitalist' economic system to a 'socialist' one; or because we happen to be Christians, Jews, Muslims, humanists, or atheists; or because we have been brought up in a liberal tradition which some decry as 'bourgeois'. The Soviet Union was one of the original signatories to the Charter of the United Nations. She took a full part in the drafting of the twin UN Covenants which form the main components of the new global code — the International Covenant on Civil and Political Rights, and the International Covenant on Economic, Social and Cultural Rights. She was a party to the adoption of their texts in 1966; she signed them both on 18 March 1968; she ratified them both on 16 October 1973; and she became legally bound by them when they entered into force in 1976. (Indeed, it was her close ally Czechoslovakia which had the distinction of depositing the thirty-fifth instrument of ratification which finally brought them into force.)

Accordingly, the treatment of any Soviet citizen by the public authorities of the Soviet Union is today a matter of international *law*, which can be objectively assessed by interpreting and applying the provisions of the UN Charter, the Universal Declaration of Human Rights, and these two Covenants, independently of any personal views one may hold about morality, politics, economics, ideology, or indeed anything else.

Lawyers may not always be the most popular of our professionals, but in matters like these they have a vital role to play. For example — and leaving aside altogether the obvious violations of his internationally guaranteed right to freedom 'to seek, receive and impart information and ideas of all kinds, regardless of frontiers . . . through any media of his choice' — we know that at the centre of Dr Sakharov's present sufferings lies his internal exile to Gorky. Others here today know far more than I do about Soviet domestic law, and will be able to tell us whether it even formally provides for the institution of internal exile; whether it provides procedures for imposing it which give the subject of the condemnation adequate rights, on a basis of equality with his accusers, to put forward his defence in the course of a fair and public hearing by a competent, independent and impartial tribunal established by law, from which neither the press nor the public may be excluded save only in quite exceptional circumstances; and whether any such procedures were followed in the present case.

What I do know is that, in the absence of any of these things, the imposition of this exile on Dr Sakharov constitutes a violation of the Soviet Union's obligations under international law. For example, Article 9 of the Universal Declaration of Human Rights provides that 'no one shall be subjected to arbitrary exile'; Article 12(1) of the International Covenant on Civil and Political Rights provides that 'everyone lawfully within the territory of a state shall, within that territory, have the right to liberty of movement and freedom to choose his residence'; and this Covenant — as well as guaranteeing the right to freedom of expression which I have already mentioned — is full of other detailed provisions designed to prevent precisely the kind of arbitrary harassment and persecution which has been Andrei Sakharov's fate over these last few years.

So far as I know, Dr Sakharov has been accused of no crime, let alone convicted of one. So far as I know, he has not been guilty of any breach of administrative regulations. So far as I know, he constitutes no threat to national security, public order, public health or morals, or the rights and freedoms of others. So far as I know, the steps which have been taken against him have never been sanctioned by any court, or tested before any court. If I am wrong in any of these things, then it is high time we were told why, and given chapter and verse for it, so that we can see whether the Soviet authorities have any answer to our protests.

All this is fit stuff for lawyers, and boring stuff for the layman; so I shall not bore you further with it. But I need to say one last word about the rule of law. Many important things changed in Russia in 1917, but many others that are also very important did not. Internal exile was not a new invention of Communists, Bolsheviks, or Marxist-Leninists: the tsars had practised it for centuries before. Indeed, one of the principal complaints about their system of government was that it was an oppressive bureaucratic tyranny, which is precisely the complaint levied against the Soviet Union today.

When Russians complain to me at meetings like these about the dreadful things that are happening in their country, I always ask them what the Soviet Constitution and Soviet domestic law have to say about these things, what the courts do about them, and what has happened to 'socialist legality'. Then they are apt to give me a pitying look, and to say: 'Don't waste our time with all this legalism — all we want is freedom for our people.'

In that dismissal, I hear echoes of the Marxist thesis that laws only serve the interests of the ruling classes, and that politics and power are the only determinants of human progress and well-being. Let me retort, as forcibly as I can, that freedom cannot exist except under the rule of law; that the law is there to protect the weak from the strong, the poor from the rich, the stupid from the clever, and the citizen from the state; that the laws of the Soviet Union are now constrained by the paramount code of international human rights law; and that the best way in which we can salute Academician Andrei Sakharov and celebrate his outstanding civic virtues is by concentrating our efforts on the establishment of the rule of law in his country, in conformity with the international legal obligations by which she has been bound these last eight years and more.

Note
[1] Published in 1986 under the title *The World of Science and the Rule of Law.*

Paul Sieghart

CHAPTER 5

Changes in Soviet Criminal Legislation since the Helsinki Final Act

DINA KAMINSKAYA

Observing the principle of stability of the law is one of the most important conditions for maintaining genuine law and order in a country. An analysis of Soviet criminal legislation over the last few years demonstrates that this principle has not been observed in the USSR.

On 21 September 1981 the RSFSR Supreme Soviet adopted two decrees on the criminal liability of service and trade workers. Each decree extended the scope of the criminal law by establishing new crimes, namely extortion and the concealment of scarce goods.

On 11 October 1982 the RSFSR Supreme Soviet Presidium adopted a decree amending the law on criminal liability for vagrancy and leading a parasitic way of life (parasitism). The terms of deprivation of freedom and corrective labour were increased from one year to two and the range of individuals who could be prosecuted for these crimes was extended. Whereas the law in its previous wording provided for criminal liability for vagrancy and parasitism only if these were systematic or of long duration, the new wording of the law lacked these two provisos. An analysis of Soviet judicial practice reveals that the amended law on parasitism accords the authorities greater opportunities for the prosecution of dissidents.

On 15 December 1983 the USSR Supreme Soviet Presidium adopted a decree substantially amending and supplementing the law on criminal liability for crimes in the military sphere. Liability for actions previously regarded as only disciplinary offences was introduced. The terms of punishment for certain crimes in the military sphere were increased substantially. The law relating to violations of military discipline and relations between soldiers was amended fundamentally.

The most serious — indeed, sinister — changes in Soviet legislation in the last few years were introduced in 1984. On 11 January 1984 the USSR Supreme Soviet Presidium adopted a decree introducing into the All-Union Law on State Crimes a new article, 13-1, establishing liability for passing to foreign organizations or their representatives information constituting an official secret. Criminal liability provided henceforth not only for the divulging of information of general state significance but also for divulging information of a departmental character.

The 11 January 1984 decree also amended Article 7 of the Law on State Crimes (this corresponds to Article 70 of the RSFSR Criminal Code). The scope of liability for anti-Soviet agitation and propaganda was extended significantly. The scope of the second part of this article was also extended.

The above decree introduced significant amendments in the Law of Criminal Liability for Actions Disorganizing the Work of Corrective-Labour Institutions. In its new wording this law placed prisoners in a position of total dependence on the camp and prison administration, providing the authorities with the opportunity to take harsh measures against those who defend their rights, i.e. dissidents for the most part.

Thus Soviet criminal legislation introduced since the signing of the Helsinki Final Act demonstrates one tendency — that of widening the scope of the law and increasing the severity of the penalties.

CHAPTER 6

Recent Changes in Soviet Legislation: Administrative Law and Educational Reforms

LOUISE I. SHELLEY

The past two years have seen an expansion of the scope and jurisdiction of law and increasing intervention in, and regulation of, the lives of Soviet citizens. This trend has been noted in criminal law, but changes in criminal law and the Corrective Labour Code affect only a small proportion of the Soviet population — criminals, deviants and political dissenters. The recently introduced RSFSR (Russian Federation) Administrative Code[1] and the educational reforms, however, affect the entire Soviet population, showing the force of law as an agent of control. These legislative changes have reduced contact with foreigners, increased controls over daily life, and redirected the educational objectives of the population. To understand the impact of these new laws, it is necessary to be familiar not only with the legal provisions but also with the context in which these laws were introduced. Fortunately for observers, the changes were not merely announced in the newspapers but were accompanied by significant comment in Soviet workplaces and the media.

Administrative law changes

A similar evolution is occurring in both administrative and criminal law. In both areas of the law new activities are being subjected to regulation, and increasing penalties are being imposed on prohibited conduct. Soviet citizens are now being subjected to harsher penalties for acts that were only recently considered permissible, and acts that were initially subjected only to administrative penalties are subsequently being criminalized. For example, the antiparasite laws (legislation that penalizes individuals who refuse to work), which were first introduced in 1961 in the RSFSR as administrative measures, were criminalized in 1970. Recently, increased criminal sanctions have been imposed against 'parasites'. Consequently, it is important to understand recent developments in administrative law not only to be fully aware of the increasing regulation of daily life but also to foresee future trends in criminal legislation.

Controls on contacts with foreigners

A decree of 25 May 1984 established administrative penalties for Soviet citizens who violate rules concerning the stay of foreigners or stateless persons.[2] This administrative act followed the revision to the Criminal Code in January 1984 which made it a state crime to transmit information constituting a work-related secret to foreign organizations. The introduction of these laws in early 1984 provided both administrative and criminal law with vehicles to reduce contact with foreigners.

The May decree established fines for Soviet citizens who provide foreigners with 'housing or means of transportation or . . . other services in violation of the established regulations'. It may also be applied to individuals who are helping Jews and others who have renounced their Soviet citizenship in the hope of leaving the Soviet Union. These individuals, who are in limbo and have no viable means of financial support, are dependent on the assistance of others. This legislation provides a financial disincentive to helping either foreigners outside of official channels or those who are stateless within their own country.

While the possible penalties that can be imposed under this decree involve sums of only ten to fifty roubles, the decree has had a much more far-reaching impact than the force of the legislative provisions may suggest. While little publicity has been given to the enforcement of this decree, there are strong indications that many Soviet citizens have been avoiding foreigners since the decree was introduced. Why has a decree that carries only administrative penalties had such an impact on the behaviour of Soviet citizens?

The principal reason is that many Soviet citizens perceive the decree as more threatening than its penalties suggest. This may be because a major propaganda campaign on the imposition of the law was conducted at workplaces throughout the country, an unusual legal educational measure for a brief administrative decree. Secondly, as many Soviet citizens are aware that there exists much unpublished legislation in the USSR, many may believe that there is more to the decree than has been announced. Thirdly, many individuals remember the arrests of Soviet citizens under Stalin for contact with foreigners; they may choose to avoid foreigners now, fearing that increasingly repressive legislation may make them liable for prosecution later.

The RSFSR Administrative Code

In June 1984 the first Administrative Code for the RSFSR was adopted and on 1 January 1985 it went into effect. As the Fundamental Principles of Administrative Law were adopted for the USSR,[3] it must be assumed that separate codes will soon be adopted by each of the union republics. The formalization and systematization of the administrative laws provide some added protection for Soviet citizens, but the introduction of this major piece of legislation provides for greater regulation over the daily lives of private citizens. As similar codes are adopted throughout the USSR, many forms of conduct that were previously handled informally will now be subject to regulation and established penalties.

The code helps to strengthen the authority of law enforcement agencies to maintain order and to control and regulate public services, allocation of housing, and commerce in collective farm markets. A total of 152 articles of the RSFSR Administrative Code define acts that are subject to administrative penalties. The penalties range from administrative warnings, fines of up to 100 roubles, corrective labour for up to two months' duration, and detention not exceeding fifteen days.

The proscribed acts span a wide variety of activities, including hunting, fishing, operation of vehicles, petty speculation, minor hooliganism, contraband, drunkenness and fire safety. The administrative articles are distinguished not only by their encompassing nature but also by the very subjective nature of the acts that are subject to administrative penalties. This provides officials with tremendous latitude in law enforcement. The encompassing nature of these legal provisions and their intrusion into private life are demonstrated by such acts as those concerned with 'leading a juvenile to drunkenness by parents or other individuals' (Article

163), 'receiving poached game' (Article 190), and 'negligent care of the land' (Article 50).

While the code provides citizens with certain increased protections by allowing them the choice of appeals to the higher authorities or to the procurator, the representation of legal counsel, and the right to a translator at administrative hearings, it provides little restraint on the action of officials. Only Article 141 provides a fine for officials who violate the procedures for determining the eligibility of citizens for better 'living space'. Furthermore, the police (*militsiya*) have been granted increased authority to detain citizens and inspect their persons and property.

The introduction of an administrative law code, while providing greater clarity in the enforcement of the law, expands and formalizes control over the Soviet population. While subordinate to the criminal law, the scope of the Administrative Code is so broad as to regulate the lives, and limit the activities, of a significant proportion of the population.

Educational reforms

The far-reaching school reforms adopted in the spring of 1984[4] may lead to major changes in the structure of Soviet society. The legislation passed recalls in many respects the educational measures adopted under Khrushchev to involve youth in Soviet production and to proletarianize Soviet education. These educational measures affect students of all ages, but their most long-term effects are on the teenage population, many of whom will now be denied the possibilities for upward social mobility through the educational system.

While the complex reforms contain many provisions, the legislative changes of most concern to the present discussion are the following:

(1) the exclusion of large numbers of individuals from institutions of higher learning;
(2) the linking of schools in long-term relationships with enterprises in their areas;
(3) the provision of a free youthful labour force for Soviet industry;
(4) the increased control over youth's exposure to ideas: 'A reliable barrier

must be set up to block the infiltration of unprincipled, vulgar, and base spiritual works into the milieu of young people';

(5) the heightened discipline in schools: 'Provisions must be made in them for enhancing school children's responsibility for the quality of studies and observance of study, labour and social discipline';

(6) the financial control over youth's earnings: 'Some of the money earned by students should be placed at the disposal of the school collective';

(7) the promotion of Russification: 'Fluency in the Russian language must become a norm for young people graduating from secondary educational establishments'.

Soviet education has always been an important means of disseminating the views of the authorities to the population. The above-listed educational reforms emphasize the indoctrination function of education. Furthermore, they seek to limit the possibilities for free and independent thought by further restricting the exposure of youth to new ideas. The provision on the sharing of youth's earnings with the school collective represents an encroachment on the financial independence of Soviet youth. The goal of educating all youth in secondary institutions in Russian enhances the position of Russians in relation to other Soviet nationalities.

The Russian language requirement is not the only provision that will affect other national groups. The provisions on technical and vocational education will have a particularly pronounced effect on members of non-Slavic nationalities as well as on members of lower social economic groups. In the Asian republics, where there are few institutions of higher learning, residents of these republics will have little opportunity for education beyond high school. Many Caucasians and Central Asians will be assigned early in life to work and train for local enterprises in their communities. The same fate awaits Slavs residing in remote regions of the RSFSR. These different groups will be denied the possibilities for upward social mobility through the educational system. While the newspapers of the different Soviet republics and the RSFSR have been very critical of these measures,[5] measures which will ensure that children of lathe workers remain lathe workers, the leadership's response has been to emphasize the importance of the measures for the state. The state's need for skilled labour has thus been translated into legal measures that may deny educational opportunities for many who would desire another future.

Notes

[1] See *Vedomosti Verkhovnogo Soveta RSFSR*, no. 27 (1341), 5 July 1984.

[2] See Foreign Affairs Note, 'New Soviet legislation restricts rights, strengthens internal security', United States Department of State, Washington DC, July 1984.

[3] For a fuller discussion of administrative law see Hiroshi Oda, 'The system of administrative sanctions in the USSR', in F. J. M. Feldbrugge and William B. Simons (eds), *Perspectives on Soviet Law for the 1980s* (The Hague, 1982), pp. 181–96. For an analysis of the fundamental principles of administrative law see Jane Giddings, 'Administrative law in the Soviet Union: the new federal principles of legislation', *Review of Socialist Law*, vol. 8, no. 1 (1982), pp. 41–65.

[4] See *Pravda* 14 April 1984.

[5] For a discussion of the educational reforms see *Sovetskaya Rossiya*, 23 March 1984; *Kommunist*, no. 4 (1984); and *Trud*, 17 November 1983 and 15 January 1984. The *Trud*, 17 November article contains a discussion of the effect of the educational reforms on Central Asia.

CHAPTER 7

Repression through Criminal Law in the USSR

FERDINAND FELDBRUGGE

Soviet law nowadays requires that a person who is to be punished may be punished only under a published criminal statute. A criminal statute is any directive, general or specific, issued by a government (or quasi-government) agency which allows for the imposition of punishment or alters such an arrangement. Publication is insertion in an official gazette or notification in another manner making the text of the law available to the general public.

On the basis of these definitions there were very significant areas of unpublished criminal legislation during the Stalin era. Hundreds of thousands, if not millions, of persons were consigned to labour camps, or even sentenced to death, by special boards acting on the basis of unpublished administrative instructions. The prosecution of Soviet citizens as well as of foreign nationals accused of war crimes was based on an unpublished decree of 1943.[1] Even after Stalin's death there was at least one notorious case in which the death penalty was applied on the basis of an unpublished decree issued after the defendants had already been convicted.[2]

The present situation is, as we have said, that there is to be no punishment without a previous criminal statute allowing such punishment, and that such a statute is to be published. The first principle — no punishment without a previous criminal law — repeats a famous Latin maxim and is widely accepted throughout the world as having the character of a basic human right. As such it is included in the Universal Declaration of Human Rights (Art. 11, para. 2) and the International Covenant on Civil and Political Rights (Art. 15, para. 1). In a more elaborate form it is found in the Fundamental Principles of Criminal Legislation of the USSR in

Articles 3 and 6. The second principle — the publication of laws — is not as explicitly recognized; mainly, one presumes, because in most legal traditions the idea of secret laws is considered so odd that most legislators do not even bother to stipulate that laws should be made public, this being regarded as self-evident.

As I have indicated, no firm tradition to this effect exists in the Soviet Union. There is a Constitutional requirement (Art. 116) of publication of acts of supreme soviets, and major criminal legislation will normally be in this form. Such legislation may be amended by edict of a supreme soviet presidium. These edicts are subject to publication if they have general significance and also bear a normative character (Art. 3, USSR Supreme Soviet Presidium edict of 6 May 1980).[3] This would seem to include any edict which introduces, amends, or abolishes a criminal offence. At any rate, to my knowledge there have been no unpublished criminal laws in the strict sense during the last decade or so, i.e. at the present time, unlike in the Stalin era, Soviet law does not have recourse to unpublished criminal statutes.

On the other hand, criminal law has been used extensively as a means of repression of political opponents of the regime. How has this been done?

The most common and simplest technique is the use of vague terminology. Once a definition is sufficiently sweeping, the entire requirement of a previous criminal law is easily rendered meaningless. The government can always claim that undesirable behaviour constitutes a criminal offence; the law appears to have been drafted precisely for that purpose. The most notorious provision in this respect concerns so-called anti-Soviet agitation or propaganda, entailing a maximum penalty of seven years plus five years of exile, and in certain cases even a maximum penalty of ten years plus five years of exile (Art. 70 of the RSFSR Criminal Code). It is defined as agitation or propaganda conducted in order to undermine or weaken Soviet power, or the dissemination, for the same purposes, of slanderous fabrications which discredit the Soviet political or social system. This provision has proved to be a most effective instrument against any form of political criticism of the regime.

Another vaguely defined crime is *khuliganstvo*, the Russian version of hooliganism (Art. 206 of the RSFSR Criminal Code), 'intentional behaviour which grossly violates public order and expresses an obvious lack of respect for society'. This provision has also been used with great success, particularly against participants in unofficial demonstrations.

Closely related to the device of vaguely defined crimes is the use of umbrella definitions. By this I mean offences defined as violations of rules which are indicated only in a general manner. In such cases the question of publication arises again, because it is of little help to the citizen if the Criminal Code states that it is an offence to violate the rules on a certain matter and at the same time these rules have not been published.

Such rules are usually issued by the Council of Ministers or by individual ministers. Council of Ministers' decrees which have general significance or which bear a normative character are subject to publication.[4] Curiously, this requirement is stricter than the one governing the publication of edicts of the Presidium of the Supreme Soviet (general significance *and* normative character). There are no general rules prescribing the publication of rules issued by individual ministers.

Of course, the device of the umbrella provision, which allows for the punishment of the violation of rules which are to be defined elsewhere, is not typical of Soviet law and is not objectionable under all circumstances. But its acceptability should be subject to at least two minimum conditions: the rules to which the criminal law provision refers should be reasonably accessible to persons who are expected to obey them; and the definitions of offences which allow the imposition of more serious penalties should be unambiguous, which means that in such instances no umbrella provisions should be used. On both counts Soviet practice is defective.

I shall limit myself to three examples, all of which concern situations with clear political overtones.

Article 198 of the RSFSR Criminal Code refers to 'malicious violation of the rules of the passport system'. The principal rules of this, internal, passport system are presumably to be found in a decree of the USSR Council of Ministers of 1974 entitled 'Regulations on the Passport System of the USSR', and an accompanying decree of the same body, entitled 'On Certain Rules for the Registration of Citizens'.[5] The latter decree, as published, consists of four sections. A fuller version of the same decree, consisting of ten sections, of which sections 5–10 were marked 'not for publication', was published in *samizdat* form.[6] The most important element of this unpublished part of the decree concerned the prohibition against granting residence permits to persons who had served a sentence for any one of a number of specific crimes, including the most common types of political crimes. This prohibition applies to a number of towns and districts, to be listed by the USSR government. The result is that political dissidents who have served their sentences may be forbidden to return to their family residence, on the basis of an unpublished rule, if their place of residence happens to be on an also unpublished list of prohibited places. If they do not observe these restrictions they are committing a criminal offence.

The second example concerns Article 142 of the RSFSR Criminal Code — violation of the laws concerning the separation of church and state, and of church and school. The first thing to be noticed here is that, although the law speaks of 'laws' (Russian *zakony*, i.e. enactments made in the constitutional manner by the Supreme Soviet), the official construction provided by the Presidium of the Supreme Soviet of the RSFSR considerably widens the scope of the provision.[7] The Presidium explains that the violations of Article 142 embrace four categories of acts, all of them rather vaguely defined, such as 'the organizing and conducting of religious meetings, processions and other ceremonies which violate public order'. Another category of violations is defined as 'the organizing and regular conducting of religious education for minors in violation of the legally established rules'. Here again, incidentally, we find the dubious device of the Criminal Code, in its definition of a specific offence, referring to other rules, and the latter rules referring to further more detailed rules. It almost goes without saying that such further rules are usually not published, or at least not accessible to the general public, because they are printed 'for the use of officials only'. A copy of such a collection of rules concerning religious activities 'for official use only' became available in the West a few years ago through the good offices of Keston College, and shows very clearly how already at the level of official regulation the treatment of religion is extremely oppressive.[8]

My third example concerns the internal order of Soviet prisons and labour camps. On 10 October 1977 the then Minister of Internal Affairs of the USSR, the subsequently disgraced N. A. Shchelokov, confirmed the Rules of Internal Order of Corrective Labour Institutions.[9] These Rules have also not been published, but they are occasionally referred to in Soviet legal literature.[10] Copies of them have recently become available in the West. The Rules offer a fairly detailed picture of the daily routine and arrangements in Soviet penitentiary institutions. What primarily interests me now is the question of prisoners' rules of conduct and their possible connection with criminal law.

The Rules contain a long section entitled 'Rules of conduct of convicts', consisting of three parts — what is permitted, what is obligatory, and what is forbidden. What is permitted does not concern us, while the list of what is forbidden is, with a single exception, precise. The same cannot be said of the list of what is obligatory. The first duty it mentions is 'to observe strictly the rules of conduct and the order of the day, established in corrective labour institutions'. This can mean two things, one of which does not make sense — one of the rules of conduct is that one should observe the rules of conduct. The other meaning that can be read into it is that beyond the duties defined in the present rules of conduct, there are also other and more detailed rules of conduct, which may be established by the administration of the institution. I have no doubt that this is the real meaning of the rule, because this would conform to the model of repeated references in criminal code provisions from one set of rules to another set of rules, which we have already encountered more than once. The end result is always the same: the individual cannot be certain about his position in law because the authorities can usually charge him with the violation of certain rules which he did not and could not know sufficiently well. The most promising provision, from the point of view of the Soviet regime, which can be used against recalcitrant prisoners is Article 188–3 of the RSFSR Criminal Code, introduced in 1983 and entitled 'Malicious non-compliance with the demands of the administration of a corrective labour institution'. The full definition of the offence spells out that it refers only to *legitimate* demands of the administration and, additionally, that it covers 'other acts thwarting the administration in the fulfillment of its duties', committed by a person who had already been punished previously for disciplinary infractions by being placed in solitary confinement or prison.

There are many other examples in Soviet criminal law of provisions which refer to the violations of certain rules; such rules as, for instance, the Traffic Regulations of the USSR are often published and are normally widely and easily available. In a number of cases, however, of which I have given three examples, such rules are not available and have not even been published. The principle to which Soviet law subscribes — that a criminal law must be published, and published beforehand — is granted token observance, but is at the same time circumvented by the device of unpublished rules. It would be too much to say that this practice is aimed specifically at political opponents of the regime, but they certainly belong to its most obvious victims.

Notes

1 For further data on this subject see F. J. M. Feldbrugge, 'War crimes in Soviet criminal law', *Review of Socialist Law*, vol. 10, no. 4, pp. 291–302.

2 This matter is reported in detail in H. J. Berman, *Justice in the USSR* (Cambridge, Mass., 1963), pp. 86, 403.

3 *Vedomosti Verkhovnogo Soveta SSSR* (Gazette of the Supreme Soviet of the USSR), no. 20 (1980), items 374 and 375.

4 Cf. Law on the Council of Ministers of the USSR of 5 July 1978, Article 31, *Vedomosti Verkhovnogo Soveta SSSR*, no. 28 (1978), item 436.

5 Decrees of 28 August 1974, *Sobranie postanovlenty* (Collection of USSR Decrees), no. 29 (1974), items 109–110. Additionally, the Passport Regulations themselves make clear that there is also a third source of rules governing the passport system—further detailed provisions issued by the USSR Ministry of Internal Affairs. Of these nothing is known.

6 See L. Lipson and V. Chalidze (eds), *Papers on Soviet Law*, no. 1 (New York, 1977), pp. 183–7.

7 The Presidium of the Supreme Soviet (of the USSR as well as of the union republics) is constitutionally empowered to provide binding interpretations of the law. The RSFSR Presidium exercised this right in a decree of 16 March 1966, *Vedomosti Verkhovnogo Soveta RSFSR*, no. 12 (1966), item 22, 'Concerning the Application of Article 142 of the Criminal Code of the RSFSR'.

8 *Zakonodatelstvo o religioznykh, Sbornik materialov i dokumentou* (Legislation on Religious Cults: Collected Materials and Documents) (2nd enlarged edn) (1971). This collection was edited by the then chairman of the Council of Religious Affairs of the USSR Council of Ministers, V. A. Kuroedov, and Deputy Procurator General of the USSR, A. S. Pankratov.

9 Text published in *Review of Socialist Law*, no. 1 (1986).

10 See F. J. M. Feldbrugge, 'Soviet corrective labour law', in D. Barry, G. Ginsburgs and P. Maggs (eds), *Soviet Law after Stalin I, Law in Eastern Europe*, no. 20 (1) (1977), pp. 33–69, which contains a partial reconstruction of the Rules.

CHAPTER 8

The Fate of the Helsinki Groups and Participants in the Helsinki Movement in the USSR

LUDMILLA ALEXEYEVA

The underlying concept of the Helsinki Final Act is the indivisibility of international security and human rights. This concept emerged from the bitter experience of two world wars and the endless regional conflicts of our blood-soaked century. The credit for reaching this conclusion belongs to public opinion in the free world. The concept is engraved in the Universal Declaration of Human Rights. It took a further twenty years before the idea of human rights became the banner of an independent movement in the USSR. The *Chronicle of Current Events*, the bulletin of the human rights movement, first appeared in 1968. Its cover cited Article 19 of the Universal Declaration of Human Rights, which deals with the right to receive and impart information, regardless of frontiers.

The political significance of the movement which emerged in the USSR in the 1960s lay in the striving of the public for a dialogue with the authorities on problems of vital importance. Such a dialogue is the only possible beginning of cooperation between these two forces. Andrei Sakharov's well-known article 'Thoughts on progress, peaceful coexistence and intellectual freedom' constituted an offer of such cooperation. In addition, numerous individual and collective appeals and letters were addressed to the Soviet authorities. However, the only response the public received was repression. This reduced considerably the number of petitions to the authorities and stimulated appeals to public opinion in the free world. I have in mind first and foremost individual and collective appeals to the UN by the Initiative Group for the Defence of Human Rights in the USSR, which was created in 1969.

Public opinion in the free world is the natural ally of our

movement, whose moral values coincide with the traditional values of Western civilization. The political neutrality of human rights activists makes it possible for both right and left to support them.

The West did not remain deaf to the stream of information about the abuse of human rights in the USSR. Without pressure from the West, the repression might well have been harsher. Yet something was lacking: the governments of the democratic countries did not appeal to the Soviet government to observe human rights and its own laws, even though the West was vitally interested in this issue for the sake of its own security.

The USSR did pledge its support for the various international agreements on human rights. But it was the Helsinki Final Act which provided an opportunity to examine its compliance with these provisions.

Yury Orlov, the founder of the Moscow Helsinki Group, was bold enough to put into practice the opportunities offered by the humanitarian provisions of the Helsinki accords. In his view, the rights of citizens as set down in the humanitarian provisions of the Final Act were to be regarded as the minimum norm for relations between citizens and those governments which had signed the Final Act. This *modus operandi* was determined by the massive spontaneous response by Soviet citizens to the Helsinki accords, a response encouraged by the publication of the Final Act in Soviet newspapers. The Moscow Helsinki Group, founded on 12 May 1976, declared it would accept information from citizens regarding the violation of the humanitarian provisions of the Final Act, would compile documents based on these data, and would make them available to the public and governments of the states which were signatories of the Final Act.

The Final Act might have remained little more than a gesture had not the Soviet human rights movement adopted it as its banner. The Moscow Helsinki Group was the small seed from which the international Helsinki movement grew. When calling on the public to follow their example the members of the Moscow Helsinki Group had in mind primarily the democratic countries. The first response did not, however, come from abroad but from their fellow citizens in the non-Russian republics. Within a year, Helsinki groups had sprung up in the Ukraine, Lithuania, Georgia, and Armenia. Analagous groups were formed outside the USSR too, again not in the free world but in the Soviet bloc countries of

Poland and Czechoslovakia. Attempts to form monitoring groups were also made in the GDR, Hungary and Romania, but they were suppressed from the outset.

In summer 1976 the Commission on Security and Cooperation in Europe — also known as the Helsinki Commission — was formed under a Bill by Millicent Fenwick, a member of the US Congress. In early 1979 the American Helsinki Watch, which adopted the platform of the Moscow Helsinki Group, was founded. By 1982 similar groups had been formed in a number of European countries and they had affiliated to the International Helsinki Federation for Human Rights.

As the movement expanded it began to be noticed in the West, and the Western media referred to the human rights situation in the USSR far more frequently. Western radio stations broadcasting to the USSR also began to refer to this issue and awareness of the human rights movement grew among Soviet citizens and this, in turn, attracted new people.

Through compiling data on human rights violations from various sources, the Moscow Helsinki Group came to represent citizens from all walks of Soviet life and of various nationalities and religions, and it became a link between previously unconnected non-conformist movements. This cooperation provided an opportunity to resolve one of the USSR's most difficult problems — relations between the Russians and the non-Russian nationalities. Moscow human rights activists established cooperation with the Ukrainian, Lithuanian, Georgian, Armenian, Jewish, German, Meskhetian and Crimean Tatar national movements and with the religious movements of the Russian Orthodox, Catholics, Baptists, Pentecostalists and Adventists. They were instrumental in the first attempt to establish free trade unions in the USSR.

The human rights activists disseminated more widely throughout the world information about the human rights situation in the USSR. Documents prepared by the Moscow Helsinki Group were made available to participants in the Belgrade CSCE follow-up meeting in 1978. At the Madrid CSCE review meeting in 1980, 138 documents, along with documents prepared by other Helsinki groups, were made available to delegates.

By the time of the Belgrade meeting it had become clear that the Soviet authorities, faced with either the possibility of losing prestige in the West — even the benefits of détente — or the slightest weakening of control over their citizens, preferred the former alternative.

As previously, the USSR fails to fulfil its obligations under the humanitarian provisions of the Helsinki accords. Repression has increased sharply since 1980. Changes in the Soviet leadership have not influenced this trend. At the present time, the suppression of dissent is comparable in harshness to the Stalinist period. Most members of the Helsinki Groups have been imprisoned. Yury Orlov received seven years in labour camp and five years' exile. The persecution of dissenters is visibly demonstrated in the treatment of Andrei Sakharov and Elena Bonner. Three members of the Helsinki groups — Yury Lytvyn, Oleksa Tykhy and Eduard Arutyunan — have perished in prison. More than fifty Helsinki activists are now serving sentences in prisons, labour camps and exile. They include the eighty-year-old Oksana Meshko.

As we recall the tragic fate of those who have attempted to introduce openness into Soviet society — and this is a guarantee of mutual security for all of us — I ask that their names and the words of Andrei Sakharov be remembered:

In the international arena, it is impossible to trust a state that violates the rights of its citizens, rights guaranteed by international agreements and obligatory for each state that has signed them. It is impossible to trust a state where human rights are violated, if not behind an iron curtain, then at least behind a fairly solid one, so that the world learns about these violations only because there exists a movement for human rights. The closed nature of a society in and of itself is a violation of human rights and, by the same token, creates conditions for the violation of international security.[1]

Note
[1] See Andrei Sakharov, *Alarm and Hope* (London, 1979) p. 138 (translation amended).

CHAPTER 9

Changes in the Categories of Soviet Political Prisoners

CRONID LUBARSKY

My view — which may be regarded by some as heretical — is that there have been no substantial changes in the categories of Soviet political prisoners in the decade since the signing of the Helsinki Final Act. There have been only what may be described as small oscillations in the fundamentally repressive Soviet policy; neither the structure nor the scale of this repression has changed in substance. I should add that it is a very difficult matter indeed to ascertain, from the information available to us, whether real changes have occurred in Soviet repressive policy. Frequently it appears that the repressive measures have been reduced, but then it emerges that we have ceased to receive the relevant information.

On the basis of the information at our disposal, information gathered and published in *News from the USSR* in Munich for over seven years now, we must conclude that the level of repression has risen. The years 1978–9 were the turning-point — it was then that the aim of destroying the human rights movement became evident.

This onslaught on the human rights movement did not lead to any substantial increase in the number of those persecuted; rather, the repressive measures were aimed at activists already known in the West, activists who had believed that publicity about their cases in the Western media had secured them a degree of immunity. Sakharov is one example, but by no means the only one.

When we in the West demand that such and such a person be freed it is essential that we be aware of all the circumstances. Of course, it is of the greatest importance that every Soviet political prisoner be freed. But at the same time, despite the individual successes we have had, we must remain aware that there has been no improvement in the general position of human rights activists in the USSR. What we are seeing is, in effect, a commercial deal, bartering, negotiations, compromises, agreements or even — and I do not believe this but some people do — an act of clemency on the part of the authorities. Human rights cannot, however, depend on the disposition of the authorities at a given moment or on any material advantages which may accrue to them. In such circumstances, even an act of clemency is an act of injustice. Let us not forget the fate of the hundreds and thousands of unknown political prisoners in the USSR. No one is involved in silent diplomacy on their behalf. The fact that their names do not appear in the Western press does not mean that they are not suffering. The position with regard to human rights can be improved only if Soviet law is implemented in fact and not otherwise.

Let us deal with specific changes in the repressive structure. For example, it is noticeable that after the powerful campaign against the abuse of psychiatry that was conducted in the West, the number of political prisoners known to us who are in general or special psychiatric hospitals recently diminished by about 20 per cent. However, I have the strong impression that this drop occurred only because the persecution by psychiatric means of well-known activists was terminated. Let me take the example of Yuri Shikhanovich, who was recently sentenced to ten years in camp — previously he had been treated in a psychiatric hospital. In his case, the means of repression have been changed. Another example is that of Kukobaka, a dissident worker from Byelorussia who spent many years in psychiatric hospitals. After the campaign in the West against psychiatric abuse, Kukobaka was declared sane and he is now persecuted as a *sane* man![1]

I have a strong impression that those who remain unknown to the Western media continue to be no less subject to psychiatric abuse.

Certain changes in regard to persecution of the Jews may be remarked. Jews who demanded repatriation to their historic homeland of Israel were less subject to repressive measures during the first period after the signing of the Final Act. At the present time, however, the Jews are persecuted no less than others. But even these changes are not changes of substance. The impression that the Jews were not subjected to harassment and persecution in the mid-1970s is false as far as the most prominent Jewish activists were concerned. In reality, a large number of Jews who were especially active in the emigration movement were subject to repression even during the most 'blessed' time of détente, when it appeared that emigration was a relatively open option. The fact is that there never was a free emigration.

We have data for only about 10–20 per cent of all political prisoners in the USSR. The lists compiled by *News from the USSR* enable us to analyse the structure of the repression. Our data on about 900 political prisoners allow us to define fairly precisely who is subject to repression. Over the last few years the first two places have been held by two groups — those imprisoned for their religious beliefs and members of national movements. These two groups have held first and second places not only in the last few years but also over the last decade. Thus in 1982 about 30 per cent of all known Soviet political prisoners were participants in national movements, while 25 per cent were religious activists. In 1984 the order was reversed, with the religious activists coming out on top at 34 per cent and the national activists being reduced to about 24 per cent. Immediately after them came participants in the democratic movement, who in 1982 constituted 18 per cent — in 1984 their number grew to 20 per cent. As members of the democratic movement I have in mind not only the prominent activists including those in Helsinki groups and other human rights bodies, but also all those convicted for expressing general democratic demands in either written or spoken form. Often these are people mostly unknown in the West and it would be a good thing if their names were to appear in the Western media.

Next are the emigration activists. They comprise a stable category of about 15 per cent of Soviet political prisoners. They include, of course, members of the Jewish emigration movement and of the movement for repatriation to the FRG and all those who attempted to leave the USSR illegally in so far as they had no possibility of leaving legally.

What type of people comprise these groups? Who was subject to persecution more than others?

First are the religious activists. Here the leading place belongs to the *Baptisty-Initsiativniki*, i.e. those Baptists who refuse to register their church officially. About 20 per cent of all political prisoners belong to this category. One should, of course, bear in mind that these figures are in all likelihood distorted by the paucity of our information. The Baptists differ from many other groups in that they are particularly well organized and make a point of sending data on their activities to the West. The fact remains, however, that the Baptists are persecuted especially intensively.

In second place are the Pentecostalists, whose number has risen sharply in recent years because, it appears, they have intensified their movement for emigration after having concluded that they can no longer practise their beliefs in the USSR. During the two and a half years up to April 1985 the number of arrested Pentecostalists rose two-fold.

Seventh Day Adventists are subjected to almost as much persecution as the Pentecostalists. Unfortunately, we know very little about the fate of the Jehovah's Witnesses, although the number of arrests among them must surely be large. Jehovah's Witnesses are a hermetically sealed group in the USSR and there is scant information about them in the West. Hindus, as well as practitioners of yoga, are also subjected to repressive measures in the USSR. In the last two years the almost unbelievable proportion of 1.5 per cent of all known political prisoners have been yogis.

In recent years we have also become aware of the emergence of a relatively large group of Moslems who have been persecuted for maintaining unofficial Koran schools and distributing unofficial religious literature. It may be assumed that groups of this type were in existence before, but we did not receive information about them. It is also possible that there has taken place a renaissance of Moslem religious activity as a result of the general Islamic resurgence and possibly also of the events in Afghanistan.

The persecution of Russian Orthodox activists has also risen recently. However, as before, they constitute only a small proportion of religious groups persecuted — about 2.5 per cent. They are, for the most part, dissidents in one way or another within their own church.

Let us turn now to the national movements, which form the other large group to which I referred earlier. In first place, as before, are the Ukrainians. Their number has declined in the last two and a half years from 13 to 10 per cent. They are followed by the Lithuanians — about 5 per cent — and then the Estonians. The number of persecuted Estonians declined recently. This decline is not due to any reduction in repression but because the principal wave of arrests of Estonians took place two years ago and all the known activists of the Estonian national movement are now behind bars.

There has recently been a sharp increase in the number of Georgians arrested. This is possibly linked with the outburst of Georgian national consciousness and the more open activities of the Georgian patriots. We are probably dealing here with a real rise in the number of arrests in this republic. What happened two years ago in Estonia is now happening in Georgia.

Over the last year, and particularly in the last few months, the number of Jews arrested for involvement in the emigration movement has also grown. Members of the Jewish cultural movement are now subject to more intense repression.

Finally, mention must be made of a small but numerically stable group — 1 per cent — which comprises members of the socialist underground opposition, all kinds of Marxist and neo-Marxist groups, and of members of the workers' movement — also about 1 per cent.

We conclude on a particularly unpleasant note — the number of those convicted of acts of terror has grown two-fold. There are only a few individuals of this type but their existence is a reality.

What is it that unites all the dissenting groups we have been discussing? First and foremost, it is the independent nature of all the individuals concerned. At first sight, exponents of yoga would seem to have nothing in common with the human rights activists but the fact is that they *do* have something in common. The Soviet regime fears *any* independent ideology or behaviour and this fear is now extended even to groups which previously were tolerated. It is this hostility to *any* independent ideology that is the underlying feature of Soviet political repression.

Note
[1] Kukobaka is now serving a new sentence of seven years in a strict regime labour camp, to be followed by five years of internal exile.

CHAPTER 10

The Deterioration of Conditions of Political Prisoners in the USSR

GEORGY DAVYDOV

The suppression of all manifestations of resistance to the regime is the perpetual function of the Soviet punitive organs. Performing this function, however, even in circumstances in which little publicity is involved, entails considerable effort and an unavoidable loss of prestige, both where the Soviet population and Western public opinion are concerned. The primary objective of the punitive organs is clearly to prevent the free flow of uncensored information; once this has been achieved, protestors can easily be dealt with far from the public eye. Camps, prisons, exile, psychiatric hospitals — these are the principal means for suppressing resistance.

To gain a better appreciation of the essence of the changes in the conditions of political prisoners over the last decade, it is first necessary to give a general outline of the conditions in places of confinement. There is, of course, a difference between camps and prisons, a difference which is indeed substantial for a prisoner. But I intend to deal with the most general features of the life of prisoners in both camp and prison. When therefore, for the sake of simplicity, I use the word 'camp', I am referring to all places of confinement. Whenever I refer to specific conditions in a prison, this is indicated. Although I am concerned primarily with political prisoners, much of what I have to say is equally applicable to all prisoners.

Conditions of prisoners

We are concerned here only with the most basic aspects of camp life. Many other matters, for example the spiritual life of prisoners, are excluded from our discussion.

Inadequate food rations

Only a starving man can consume the poor-quality — or, rather, inedible — food that prisoners are given. The basic ration on which the vast majority of prisoners have to subsist is 15–20 per cent lower than that necessary to compensate for the energy they expend. Hunger is therefore the continuous lot of the prisoner. And we are not yet discussing penal rations!

The prisoner is constantly preoccupied with finding some way of supplementing his daily ration, however minimally. At the same time, he has to beware of 'infringing the regime' as the camp educationalists' favourite tactic is — to use a prisoners' expression — to 'hit at the stomach'. This means depriving the prisoner of the right to buy food in the camp shop with the very limited money permitted him by the regulations (this must only be money earned through his work in the camp or prison), or placing him on a lower, penal ration.

Poor clothing and shoes

In winter it is difficult for a prisoner to obtain any kind of warm clothing or to warm his unlined camp uniform himself. In addition, he has to be very wily indeed to get through the routine search where, under the pretext of 'infringement of type of clothing', an object may be confiscated and destroyed in front of its owner. Furthermore, an 'infringement' of this kind is punishable by deprivation of the right to buy food in the camp shop or of a visit, or by incarceration in a punishment cell. There are a minimum of two searches per day — on the way to work and on leaving work. The prisoner can also be searched individually. Searches are regularly held in the huts and workplaces.

Finally, there are sometimes zone inspections. The prisoners are ordered to assemble with all their belongings and are locked up in their quarters one by one. On these occasions, every single possession of each prisoner is inspected. The prisoner must also strip to his shorts. The number of possessions a prisoner may have in the camp is severely restricted; in an inspection, anything that exceeds this severe norm is confiscated. Before a prisoner can be passed by an inspection commission, the camp guards and officers go through the huts and work changing rooms with a fine tooth comb. Shoes, jackets, teapots, a poorly concealed second blanket — everything is piled up. Try protecting yourself from the cold by secreting a spare item of clothing!

A prisoner must always be completely buttoned up. For this reason, when summer comes he is particularly vulnerable to being caught 'infringing the type of clothing'. Should he be spotted by a guard sunbathing half-undressed, he will be punished. (In summer 1974, political zone no. 36 in Perm went on strike in protest against the beating up of political prisoner Stepan Sapelyak down a mine. Sapelyak was dragged off to the mine after having been found sunbathing after work in the living area.)

Unsuitable living quarters
Here one suffers from cramped conditions, stuffiness, lack of fresh air. In winter there is the cold to contend with. Naturally, you want to get close to the window, where the air is fresher and it is lighter; in winter you want to get close to the stove. But so does everyone else! In winter you throw a jacket over your decrepit blanket but when the guard does his nightly round he pulls the jacket off you 'for sanitary reasons' and you spend the entire night freezing and unable to sleep. If you are not punished for 'infringing the regime' you are lucky! (In a number of cells in Vladimir prison in the mid-1970s, prisoners went to bed without undressing but even putting their jackets over their blankets did not save them from the cold. The walls were covered in damp and in the morning puddles of water ran over the floor along the walls. And these were not punishment cells, but normal 'living' cells where a prisoner spends twenty-three hours a day for the entire period of his confinement!)

Medical 'assistance'
What sort of medical assistance is a prisoner to expect when there is no qualified personnel, no appropriate equipment or medicine, and when what there is is no longer usable? Even more to the point — what can be expected from a doctor who says he is 'a Chekist first and a doctor second'?

Medicine in the camp does not cure, it temporarily relieves an acute condition by internalizing the illness. The prisoners have a saying: 'If you want to be well, forget the camp hospital!' A prisoner must take great care not to catch even the slightest illness, for in the camp this illness can easily develop complications and become chronic.

Work

Any kind of work, even light work, is difficult for the prisoner, who has an inadequate diet, disgusting work conditions and high norms to fulfil. Every prisoner, of course, wants to do work to which he is most accustomed, but the work is chosen for him by the camp authorities and they pay no attention whatsoever to his inclinations, capabilities, or state of health. If you do not fulfil the norm you will be punished.

In my description of the life of the prisoner, I would like to stress what effort is demanded of him by the everyday exhausting battle to survive. The circumstances in which he finds himself, as it were, compel him to concentrate entirely on himself. This is in 'normal' conditions — but there is the penal regime too. Each prisoner faces the real and constant threat that he may be placed on penal regime. It is easy enough to understand why few prisoners protest openly in such circumstances. The fact is that prisoners' conditions are conceived, and effected, in such a way as to serve the aim of repression by transforming the overwhelming majority of prisoners into passive creatures obedient to the will of the authorities.

All the basic elements of camp life have, as it were, their penal equivalents. The half-starvation general camp ration has its penal equivalent — the energy expended by a prisoner on the so-called 'lower nutrition norm' is approximately 50 per cent in excess of the nutritious value of his diet. As for the punishment cell ration, this is no less than torture by starvation, as the energy expended is 55 per cent more than the diet received. In the punishment cell, poor clothing and lack of protection from the cold are also tantamount to torture. As for the prisoners' huts, they are unfit for habitation and have their equivalent in the punishment cell. Everything here is designed to ensure that suffering is the prisoner's overriding feeling. In the punishment cell there is no medical attention whatsoever. This is not the whim of the camp administration but in accordance with a decree of the Ministry of Internal Affairs.

And finally the work itself. In addition to 'Plan' work, there is purely penal work. This tends to be work of secondary importance unrelated to productivity targets. Norms on this type of work are many times greater, i.e. there is no norm as such, as the figures are entirely arbitrary — fail to fulfil them and you will end up in the punishment cell. There are also some jobs the prisoner does all he can to avoid. These are usually harmful or physically difficult. A prisoner may also be given such work as an unofficial punishment. Working in the camp prison or in a solitary confinement cell in these conditions eventually wears a man down.

These varieties of torture are all specially designed to crush those audacious enough to protest even in the camp. The undisguised arbitrary actions of the camp-prison administration serve a similar purpose. This system gives the administration *carte blanche* to deal with prisoners in any way they like and there is no limit, including physical torture, to the means they may employ.

Changes in prisoners' conditions since the Helsinki Final Act

Prisoners' general conditions have changed over the last decade, but not significantly. They have changed not because the authorities have become humanitarian — there remain the same half-starved existence, the same symbolic medical assistance, the same camp huts and overcrowded prison cells, the same slender camp uniform.

The Soviet authorities have accumulated considerable experience in keeping many millions of people in camps — under Stalin, in particular, when millions perished. Given the current labour shortage, they can hardly allow such an inefficient usage of the labour force to continue. Thus the relative stability of prisoners' conditions indicates that a bottom limit has been reached. And this extremely low level is, so to speak, the background against which the conditions of political prisoners have deteriorated in the last ten years.

This deterioration has assumed other forms too. For the sake of clarity, I have grouped changes in the position of political prisoners as follows: intensification of the information blockade; the attack on political prisoners' traditional means of self-defence; intensification of special means of suppression. It is worthwhile pointing out in this connection that in those sections which concern us, the Code of Corrective Labour has remained virtually untouched. On the other hand, decree no. 37 of the Ministry of Internal Affairs of 15 March 1978 introduced new regulations for internal order —

regulations which have a substantial bearing on the position of prisoners.

Intensification of the information blockade

(1) Correspondence There is no formal restriction of the number of letters a prisoner may receive. However, the number of letters he may *send* is restricted in accordance with the regime of confinement. In a general regime camp he can write letters without restriction of number; in a strict regime camp, he is limited to two letters per month; in a prison to one letter per month; in a punishment cell, he is forbidden to send any letters at all. There is also a very strict ban on what he may write about: anything having any bearing on the camp or prison is forbidden. All letters, both from and to the camp, are examined strictly by the camp censorship.

Only one formal change related to correspondence is known: in accordance with the new regulations, letters submitted to the camp authorities for sending, including those confiscated by the censors, are included in the limit prescribed by the Code of Corrective Labour. Previously, if a letter were confiscated, the prisoner could write another letter in its place and this to some extent acted as a check on the censor's arbitrariness. Now, a prisoner's correspondence may be intercepted at any time and for any period. This kind of threat invariably results in increased self-censorship.

A broad interpretation of the regulations is applied for the purpose of blocking correspondence. The fact is, however, that the regulations are themselves composed with a deliberate lack of precision, so that any letter, whether to or from a prisoner, may be confiscated at will. The most common pretexts for confiscating letters are that they are of 'a suspicious content' or 'contain coded expressions'. Should you ask what precisely is meant by these terms you will never receive a direct reply.

Giving a broad interpretation of the instructions is, so to speak, 'technical' arbitrariness, but overt arbitrariness exists too. Since the late 1970s, for example, it has been the practice not to pass letters containing complaints about one's state of health. In recent years, arbitrariness in regard to correspondence has been 'enriched' by depriving prisoners of the right to correspond as a disciplinary punishment. (This was the case with A. Verkhovsky in 1983 and V.

Senderov in 1984.) Sometimes deprivation of correspondence can be used for 'amusement' at the expense of a prisoner and his relatives. The mother of the Estonian prisoner of conscience, M. Niklus, for instance, received from her son a blank sheet of paper in an envelope.

Correspondence and visits are the only means of communication a prisoner has with his relatives and those dear to him, and they provide therefore the only possibility he has of learning how his case is proceeding. Intensifying the blockade on correspondence as well as applying psychological pressure on the political prisoner and his relatives deprives him of support from outside the camp, at the same time enabling the administration to do whatever it pleases in secrecy.

Thus the prisoner's right to correspondence, a right whose unconditional character is prescribed by decrees of the Ministry of Internal Affairs, has, in practice, been transformed into a conditional right by censorship and habitual arbitrariness. It should also not be forgotten that, since the latter half of the 1970s, letters from prisoners of conscience which have passed the camp censorship have been particularly sought for during searches of relatives and friends of the prisoner. During these searches the letters are confiscated.

(2) **Visits**   The Code of Corrective Labour distinguishes two types of visit — 'general' ones, which take place in the presence of a guard and last from two to four hours; and 'personal' ones, which are solely with close relatives and last from twenty-four to seventy-two hours. The number of visits is severely restricted and ranges from two 'personal' and three 'general' ones per year on general regime to two 'general' ones per year in prison. In the punishment cell and on strict regime in prison and in the camp prison, visits are forbidden.

But it is not the restriction on the number of visits that is the most important thing. It is the *conditional* nature of the prisoner's right to visits — i.e. the administration's right to deprive him of a visit — which constitutes a special kind of cruelty. I would describe this as legalized psychological humiliation, for depriving a prisoner of a visit is double-edged — it is directed not only against him but also his loved ones. On occasion, the administration adds its own particular ingredient – cancelling a visit when a prisoner's wife or mother has already arrived in the camp after having travelled a considerable distance.

There is also a ban on what may be said during visits. During a 'general' visit 'only domestic matters' may be discussed. Anything having any bearing on the camp, or the prison, or the prisoners in general is forbidden. Should this ban be violated, the visit is terminated.

Insulting, too, is the demand that only Russian be spoken during visits. The prisoner and his loved ones are not forbidden to use their native language in principle; in practice, however, the administration will interrupt the visit if Russian is not used. It is a desperately difficult situation if the prisoner's relatives do not know Russian.

Not only humiliating, but a cruel psychological torture, is the personal search, both before and after the visit, of relatives who have come for a 'personal' visit with a prisoner. The relative must strip naked and no indignities are spared.

The practice of depriving a prisoner of a visit illustrates the total arbitrariness of the administration. Should there be a disposition not to allow a visit to take place, a pretext will always be found to prevent it. There has been an increasing tendency in recent years to curtail the very institution of the visit itself. In accordance with the new regulations of internal order, the time a prisoner may be kept in a camp internal prison and on strict regime in prison is now calculated in such a way that the prisoner's next visit is cancelled. There have been an increasing number of cases in which one visit after another is cancelled so that a prisoner sometimes never sees his family for years on end. (A. Lavut, for instance, did not have a single visit during his three-year term.) Moreover, it appears that the administration now has the option to deprive a prisoner not only of a routine visit but of all visits during the year. Although we are aware of no normative act which extends to this degree the administration's right to deprive a prisoner of visits, *samizdat* sources indicate that some new regulation or other on this score has been adopted.

Thus the very principle of making the right to a visit conditional not only gives the administration a powerful lever of psychological pressure on a prisoner but is also a necessary pre-condition for preserving the secrecy of camp arbitrariness.

The attack on political prisoners' traditional means of self-defence

Prisoners of conscience have few means of self-defence — submitting complaints about the camp/prison administration, the hunger strike and the strike. The strike has always been regarded by the administration as a serious violation of camp regime and those participating in strikes have been severely punished. The other two means of prisoners' self-defence, the written protest and the hunger strike, have in the last ten years been subjected to unrelenting pressure.

The routine practice with statements and complaints was for a long time more or less as follows. The prisoner would submit a written protest either directly to the highest authorities or to the various levels of the Ministry of Internal Affairs and the procuracy. From there his protest would gradually descend lower and lower until he received a reply in the form of an empty acknowledgement (occasionally even a nonsensical reply) from the lowest levels of the hierarchy, the reply frequently containing the signature of the official against whom the complaint had been made. The lack of effectiveness of this form of protest was evident and it was correspondingly unpopular.

In the mid-1970s political prisoners adopted a new tactic — sending large numbers of statements to any number of Soviet organizations and, specifically, addressing personal letters to members of soviets at all levels. They also made sure of proceeding with their complaint from one level to another with the aim of seeking a reply of substance. The administration, arbitrarily, sought to nip this campaign in the bud but it was compelled by the prisoners to submit to the law, and the letters reached their destination.

Now the authorities were facing an unexpected problem: letters from the camps and prisons describing conditions in the camps and the administration's arbitrary actions were 'flooding' the country. There was a risk of a spontaneous, uncontrolled flow of information, that the means of repression might be exposed, and that unwelcome doubts might arise in the minds of those uninitiated in the punitive secrets of the authorities, and much more. Quickly realizing the potential danger of a legal flow of information from the camps and prisons, the authorities rushed to divert this stream into a smooth bureaucratic channel. In 1976 the Ministry of Internal Affairs, acting jointly with the USSR Procurator General, placed a restriction on the number of addressees to whom statements and complaints could be sent by prisoners.

'Divide and rule' is a major principle of Soviet punitive policy. When the new regulations for internal order were introduced in 1978, this principle was taken to its logical conclusion. Whereas previously not even a hint of any possibility of prisoners' self-defence had been allowed — even presenting collective protests was forbidden — decree no. 37 of the Ministry of Internal Affairs forbade the submission of complaints regarding another person. From then on, it was possible to protest only about one's own circumstances. The purpose of this ban was clearly to deprive the political prisoner of even the symbolic support of his fellow prisoners of conscience.

Apparently in the first half of 1984, there appeared a new regulation banning the last of the political prisoners' traditional means of self-defence — the hunger strike. This was now declared a violation of the regime punishable by penalties including incarceration in a punishment cell. The first victims of this instruction were Tatyana Osipova, who declared a hunger strike on 20 June 1984 at the Mordovian women's political camp — two days later she was placed in a punishment cell for fifteen days and nights; and, several months ago, the Pentecostalist Ivan Fedotov, who was thrown into a punishment cell at Syktyvkar camp for declaring a hunger strike.

Intensification of special means of repression

These means are aimed at those who still find the strength to protest. From a juridical point of view, they fall into two categories: those provided for in accordance with published laws; and those nowhere provided for, except in secret instructions, and therefore completely arbitrary.

Of those provided for by law, the principal ones are the prison punishment cell (in the camp its equivalent is the solitary confinement cell) and the strict regime in prison (its equivalent in the camp is the camp internal prison). The new regulations of internal order introduced in 1978 strengthened these penalties even further. Although as before one cannot remain in the punishment cell longer than fifteen days and nights, the term can now be extended repeatedly, each time for a further fifteen days and nights. Now, in principle, a person could be kept in a punishment cell for the entire term of his imprisonment. Here are two such cases. By April 1984 Ivan Kovalev had remained without a break for about nine months in the punishment cell at Perm political camp no. 35. Valery Senderov spent about seven months in a punishment cell in the same camp during the same period.

Extending the term of confinement in a punishment cell did not begin with the introduction of the new regulations. As early as 1975, there had been a number of cases in which political prisoners did not leave the punishment cell for a month and a half. Then, however, this means of torture was only just being adopted, and the text of the previous regulations was not as unambiguous as it is now. The torture by starvation and cold for months on end which exists now is, at the very least, deliberate undermining of the prisoner's health and, in effect, constitutes protracted, deliberate murder.

The regulations for incarceration in a punishment cell, and correspondingly for strict regime in prison, have also been made more severe. Now the term of incarceration in a solitary confinement cell for prisoners on these regimes is not included in the time spent in a punishment cell. It is now also possible to extend the term of confinement in a punishment cell and to cancel visits and parcels.

The most important of the non-regime methods of repression is physical violence, both on the part of the camp or prison administration or that of prisoners acting for the administration. Those interested in the fate of political prisoners in the USSR will be aware of the existence of the so-called 'press cells'. These are cells in which specially chosen criminals rob, beat up, maim, or rape recalcitrant prisoners. In recent years, physical violence has been applied systematically to prisoners of conscience. In the political camps and at Chistopol prison the guards themselves, led by the officers, frequently beat up political prisoners.

Criminals are incited against the political prisoners who are dispersed throughout the camps. The 'press cells' are frequently used, the object being to make the prisoner renounce his convictions. In investigative prisons, 'press cells' are used to break the political prisoner during investigation, and to make him sign whatever is necessary and renounce his views and any form of resistance to the authorities.

The non-freeing of prisoners when their term of imprisonment is complete and convicting them on new charges is another means of 'legal' treatment of political prisoners. In the 1980s the authorities used this method seven or eight times more frequently than in the second half of the 1970s. Furthermore, while previously it had been necessary to fabricate a case with the aid of provocations and false witnesses, with the amendment in 1983 of Article 188 of the Criminal Code this method became, in effect, a disciplinary penalty.

The case of Vladimir Poresh demonstrates how easy it is now to extend a term of imprisonment. The charge against Poresh under Article 188–3 of the Criminal Code of the RSFSR was based on the following:

(1) Transferring correspondence from one exercise yard to another. The correspondence itself was not confiscated and it was never proven that this was what was transferred.
(2) Refusal to work. In protest against the treatment of political prisoner S. Grigoryants, whose arm had been broken by the guards, Poresh refused, together with other political prisoners, to work for two weeks.
(3) Slandering the administration. Poresh wrote a protest against the beating up by the guards of a prisoner. This prisoner confirmed during investigation that he had been beaten up.
(4) Insulting the administration. When the prison governor decided that a number of prisoners should receive 350 instead of 450 grams of bread per day, Poresh accused him in a statement to the procurator of stealing bread from the prisoners.

On 23 October 1984 Poresh was sentenced to three more years in strict regime camps.

Deterioration in the position of political exiles

Political exiles are scattered throughout the huge expanses of Siberia, the Far East, Central Asia and Kazakhstan, and the north-eastern European part of the USSR. Although there have been no juridical changes in the position of exiles during the last decade, their situation has deteriorated significantly. All kinds of pressure is applied by the authorities. Tatyana Velikanova, who is now in exile in Kazakhstan, writes: 'The exile has the right . . . to choose where he wishes to live within the confines of a *rayon*. But they [the authorities] have the right to choose a "suitable" *rayon* and a "suitable" apartment and are able to make you do "suitable" work'.

Some of the means of exerting pressure on the political exile are as follows:

pressure through work and living accommodation;
pressure on the exile's relatives;
pressure of the local population against the exile by disseminating false rumours about him or publishing special articles in the local press;
the threat of physical violence;
the planting of informers and *agents provocateurs*;
the fabrication of a new case against him.

Conclusions

Although many of the devices used to achieve a deterioration in the conditions of political prisoners may appear new to us, they are not so in fact. Some of them are known to have been used on previous occasions, while others are normal practice. What really is new is the systematic and deliberate manner in which these devices are being used.

In general terms, the arbitrariness of the camp administration constitutes, as it were, the accumulated experience of cowing those who refuse to submit. It could easily be legalized and introduced on a large scale should the need arise.

Such measures as prolonging the term of confinement in a punishment cell indefinitely, transferring the practice of violent treatment of prisoners from criminal camps to political camps, the non-freeing of prisoners and, finally, legalizing some aspects of the arbitrary actions of the camp authorities, are all designed to create a feeling that there is no defence against the threat of physical violence and extension of the term of imprisonment. The object of all these new measures is, in my view, to break those political prisoners who refuse to submit and, if necessary, to destroy them physically. Publicizing these actions impedes the realization of this aim. It is for this reason that the information blockade has been intensified at the same time.

We can even give the date when the overall directive for suppression was adopted — it was in 1975, when the Helsinki Final Act was signed. This is clear from a statement by Degtyarnikov, chief of KGB operations with responsibility for the Perm political camps. In October 1975 he told a prisoner of conscience: 'We have now got the sanctions we have been after for a long time. As in 1952' (see *Chronicle of Current Events*, no. 39).

Some of the results of this directive are as follows. In the last fifteen years one can observe a consistent rise in the number of political prisoners who have died a 'natural death' in the camps. A particularly alarming year was 1984, when almost one in every hundred of those on the well-known list of political prisoners died, as against an average of almost one in every 200 for 1980–4. The average age of prisoners of conscience who died a 'natural death' over the last fifteen years has dropped equally consistently. In 1984 it was 55.4 years. These figures provide further evidence for the systematic deterioration of the conditions of prisoners of conscience. But the conditions in special psychiatric hospitals are especially severe: political prisoners who have died in these institutions have been on average ten years younger than those who perished in all places of imprisonment — 42.3 as against 53 years.

CHAPTER 11

The Church in
the USSR – Prospects under
the New Leadership

MICHAEL BOURDEAUX

Since the earliest days of Soviet power, the state has used a
combination of Draconian legislation and force going well beyond
the bounds of legality in its struggle against religion. While the
basic laws have not changed that much over the years, implementation has varied considerably in harshness. Religious persecution
remains one of the most distinctive traits of Soviet communism, a
feature which has been exported in various forms to every communist country.

As early as January 1918, the Council of Peoples' Commissars
issued a decree taking away the Church's right to own property and
prohibiting any institutional teaching of religion to those under the
age of 18. This law, together with Stalin's restriction in 1929 of the
number of churches the state was willing to register, as well as the
banning of any religious activity outside the premises of those
churches, mosques, or synagogues, constitutes the core of the
system which has remained in force ever since.

Tens of thousands of Church leaders, local and national, were
arrested and imprisoned already in Lenin's day. Under Stalin, the
meagre protection that registration would seem to provide was not
available in practice, as the churches were closed down in their tens
of thousands. During the purges of the 1930s central administration of Church life ceased and scarcely a priest or pastor remained
actively at his post in an open church. The Russian Orthodox
Church virtually ceased to exist as an institution (though evidence
of its vigour underground is still coming to light).

By a curious irony of history, it was the Nazi invasion of the
USSR in June 1941 which led to a dramatic upturn in the fortunes
of the Church. Stalin, caught totally unprepared for the war,

needed to muster help from wherever he could and the Orthodox Church was an effective focus for rallying patriotism. Those clergy who would commit themselves to loyalty to the regime returned to their parishes, where many churches re-opened. Behind German lines, too, there was a perhaps even more significant religious revival, in so far as the Nazis saw that the churches could nurture the latent anti-Soviet feelings of the population.

After the war some of these improvements became institutionalized. The state permitted the Church a central administration — the Moscow Patriarchate — which was permitted to publish a small journal. Theological education, discontinued nearly thirty years earlier, began again, albeit in restricted form. Some monasteries re-opened, as did approximately 20,000 Orthodox churches, including those in the territories which fell under Soviet rule for the first time in the wake of the retreating German armies. The number of churches and clergy would still have needed to be perhaps five times as great to fulfil the needs of the population throughout Soviet territory.

Up to this time the Catholic Church had been only a small minority but, owing to acquisition by conquest, it became an important presence in all Western areas, its vigour being that much greater because its leadership had not been liquidated during Stalin's purges of the 1930s.

These massive changes came about without any alterations whatsoever in the provisions of Soviet law.

In the postwar period, both before and after Stalin's death in 1953, the rulers had more important priorities than continuing the anti-religious struggle. Stalin was nevertheless able to distract himself sufficiently from rebuilding the economy to attempt to break the power of the Church in the newly-acquired territories. Men and women in all leading positions (and many others) were deported from the Baltic states to Siberia, which badly affected the Lithuanian Catholics, as well as Latvian and Estonian Lutherans. In the Western Ukraine, the position was even worse, with the liquidation in 1946 of the Eastern-rite Catholic Church, which had consisted of no less than 4 million members. The ostensible reason for this was that it had identified itself with Ukrainian nationalism and was therefore anti-Soviet. The only way to avoid physical persecution was to join the Russian Orthodox Church, which took over those Catholic church buildings which remained open. The symbol of resistance was Archbishop (later Cardinal) Iosyf Slipyj, the most senior of hundreds of clergy who were imprisoned. Eventually, in Khrushchev's time, the Vatican persuaded the Kremlin to relent in this one limited instance and the Archbishop went to Rome, where he became the symbol of Ukrainian resistance for over twenty years until his death in 1984.

Locked in a struggle for succession after the death of Stalin, the Kremlin permitted the Church its best few years since the Revolution, a situation which changed rapidly once Khrushchev had established himself firmly in office. A knowledge of the devastation of Church life resulting from this renewed persecution is a prerequisite of any understanding of the present situation. Any concessions granted in the form of the occasional re-opening of churches should be set against the mass closure of Orthodox and Baptist churches in the Khrushchev period; the increase over recent years in the number of Orthodox seminarians should be set against the closure of five of the eight remaining seminaries in the early 1960s. Monasticism barely survives and the recent return to the Church of a prominent monastery is mainly intended to provide merely a better headquarters for the Moscow Patriarchate and has no bearing on monastic life as such.

The decline in the Church's fortunes twenty years ago evened out after the fall of Khrushchev. A certain stability appeared to be the norm and government agencies exhibited greater flexibility in dealing with the religious question. Yet astute observers noted no cessation of the Communist Party's public commitment to the elimination of religion from Soviet society. Rather, direct assault had been replaced by a war of attrition on the principle of 'two steps forward, one step back'.

The state kept a tight rein on Church appointments during these years. A new leadership emerged among both Orthodox and Protestants which accepted, at least in public, the new *status quo*, while working behind the scenes for small concessions. From 1961, when the Russian Orthodox Church was permitted to join the World Council of Churches, Soviet Church leaders became engaged in an elaborate pattern of world-wide diplomacy, which provided, at least in theory, a certain safeguard against the excesses of persecution. At the same time, the state was able to make considerable political capital out of the Church pronouncements which constantly justified Soviet international policies, including such controversial issues as the invasion of Afghanistan in 1979.

There was, however, one major change which the state could not, or did not, control up to 1979. This was the emergence of truly independent movements within virtually every denomination in the Soviet Union. The 'Church of Silence', as it has been called, had found its voice. In no way was this development due to any 'liberalization' on the part of the authorities. Rather, it was a reaction to Khrushchev's persecution, in the realization that the concessions of the postwar years were in immediate danger of disappearing altogether.

These movements gained ground rapidly among Protestants and Catholics, though very much more slowly among the Orthodox, before meeting a determined attempt to stamp them out from 1979 onwards. Under the impact of this new campaign, the number of Christian prisoners has risen sharply and in order to continue at all much of the activity has had to go underground. This new repression began during Brezhnev's declining years and could even have been due to the grip already being exerted by his successor, Yuri Andropov, who had extensive experience of the effects of religious and dissident activity during his long years as head of the KGB. In his single year as party leader, Andropov initiated legislation which was potentially, or actually, devastating to religious believers. The infringing of camp discipline could now lead to the re-sentencing of prisoners immediately they had served out their sentences. Performance of religious acts, even private prayers, has come under this rubric, so many Christian prisoners are serving extended sentences with no definite prospect of release. It is now also technically illegal to pass to foreigners any information not officially available. Those expressing the new 'voice' of the churches are greatly at risk in this, although the full effects of this 1984 law are still to be felt.

Konstantin Chernenko was also a moving force in the anti-religious campaign. In June 1983, when in charge of ideological matters, he attacked the growing influence of religion on the young and especially their links with the world outside. This was the first time for many years that a top Kremlin leader had spoken out on the subject. At an earlier stage in his career, learning his political craft in Moldavia in the 1950s, Chernenko had almost certainly been involved in the war of attrition against the Orthodox Church in an area where religion was at its strongest, this republic having been annexed from Romania during the Second World War. Chernenko's appointment was yet another stage in the deterioration of the situation of the Church since 1979. From the last days of Leonid Brezhnev to the accession of Mikhail Gorbachev, the number of Christians known to be in prison for alleged infringements of the anti-religious laws has risen from just over 100 to around 400 (and possibly many more, of whom we know nothing).

For many Soviet authors religion is a problem in the same class as corruption, drunkenness and bad harvests, to be tackled and eliminated. Should Gorbachev prove an efficient executor of this dogma, the Church can hardly fail to suffer. This in itself should make us cautious about joining in the euphoric treatment of Gorbachev characteristic of much of the media, while privileged foreign guests to the Soviet Union should be more reserved in their praise for some of the cosmetic 'improvements' in the religious situation vaunted by regime spokesmen over recent years.

Despite the problems facing the Church there has been a very real growth in religious faith that has affected most Christian denominations over recent years, as well as the Jewish and Muslim communities. There are exceptions, such as the Lutherans in Estonia and Latvia, who have lost considerable ground, in part because of the weaknesses of their leadership compared with that of the local Baptists and Methodists. Overall, however, the situation is one in which far more young people than at any time since 1917 are being influenced by religion.

The Russian Orthodox Church

It is impossible to estimate the number of Russian Orthodox believers in the Soviet Union today. Church sources have given figures varying from 30 to 50 million, with the most reliable estimate being 35 to 40 million, that is, approximately one-seventh of the population.[1] It seems that young or middle-aged converts replace those who die and that, from the official viewpoint, this necessitates further repression.

There are no reliable figures for the number of Orthodox churches open after the war, but approximately 20,000 is the figure most often quoted. Certainly at least half of these were closed during the Khrushchev period, and the decline continued, though less dramatically, afterwards. By 1974 figures compiled secretly (but which later leaked out) by the Government's Council for Religious Affairs indicated 7,500, of which 'about one thousand were formally listed, but not in use'. Since then a few churches have opened here and there, while instances of equally isolated closures, such as at Rechitsa (Byelorussia) in 1979, have been documented.

According to the law, a group of twenty believers is sufficient to petition the authorities for the right to open a church. However, there are many instances of sizeable towns with no churches open, where such groups have been trying in vain to utilize the legal machinery for years.

The venerable monastic tradition of the Russian Orthodox Church has been devastated. There are 6 monasteries and 10 convents, the only ones remaining out of 69 in 1958 and many hundreds before 1917. Not one exists east of Moscow, and there are 14 in the non-Russian Soviet republics, leaving only 2 (Zagorsk and Pskov) on Russian soil. The Council for Religious Affairs gave a figure of 1,273 religious for 1970, of whom three-quarters were nuns. The position of all these institutions is vulnerable as they have at present no guaranteed existence under the law.

Thousands of monks and nuns were thrown out onto the streets when their institutions were closed in the 1960s, but their fate has been lost to view. Occasionally, the veil is lifted, as with Sister Valeriya Makeeva, who was arrested in Moscow in April 1979 (just at the time when the Church was coming under sharper attack again) and accused of engaging in an illegal trade. She had been making small religious artefacts, such as belts embroidered with quotations from the Psalms, and selling them at a moderate price to believers. She was placed in a penal psychiatric hospital and subjected to enforced injections which paralysed her right arm. Sister Makeeva was released only in 1982, after prolonged publicity about her case in the West.

Since the mid-1960s, there have been a number of attempts to bring out into the open the various restrictions on general religious activity and the many violations of the liberty of individuals and congregations, not only for internal discussion and petitioning of the Soviet government but also to present them before the court of world public opinion. We can do no more here than touch on the outlines of this campaign, which was initiated by Frs Nikolai Eshliman and Gleb Yakunin in 1965. The latter is still a key activist and is currently serving a ten-year sentence. Aleksandr Solzhenitsyn claimed that their careful documentation of illegal measures against the Church influenced him in his own fight to win the right to publish his works.

After ten years of silence decreed by the Patriarch of Moscow (under pressure from the secular authorities), and during which many others took up their pens to write a spate of documents, Fr Gleb Yakunin began to be active again. In the autumn of 1975 he addressed a detailed and impressive appeal to the Fourth Assembly of the World Council of Churches meeting in Nairobi. Believing (wrongly, as it turned out) that he had a substantial section of world Christian opinion behind him, he founded the Christian Committee for the Defence of Believers' Rights, which compiled the most complete documentation ever on all aspects of the Church in the Soviet Union. In August 1979, as an indication of a renewed determination by the state to suppress all kinds of dissent, Fr Yakunin was arrested and sentenced to ten years in prison and exile.

Meanwhile, a new generation of young people was becoming committed to the Orthodox faith. They gave firm expression to the lack of teaching and feeling of community within the confines of Church activity permitted by the law. When, however, they sought to enlarge the means of expression, they too fell foul of the forces of repression. One such group which sought to explore their faith regardless of official restrictions was the Christian Seminar, whose founder, Aleksandr Ogorodnikov, wrote:

In the Russian Church the parish is not like a brotherly community where Christian love of one's neighbour becomes a reality. The state persecutes every manifestation of Church life, except for the performance of a 'religious cult'. Our thirst for spiritual communion, religious education and missionary service runs up against all the might of the state's repressive machinery.[2]

No one has described better the present situation of the Church in general in the Soviet Union. For his enterprise, Ogorodnikov was arrested in 1979 and sentenced to eleven years' imprisonment, a fate which itself seems to sum up current Soviet policy. Despite this persecution, the 6,500 or so churches are full to overflowing and their priests faithfully carry out such pastoral work as they can under difficult conditions.

The Baptists

Including the Evangelical Christians and Baptists, Mennonites, Pentecostalists, Lutherans and several smaller groups, there are in the USSR several million Protestants. The total number is impossible to compute, not least because so many of them form unregistered communities. They have spread into the remotest corners of the country in the last half century, partly because of the continuing arrests and deportation of their members.

In no other religious community in the Soviet Union are the extent and consequences of state interference in Church affairs more apparent than among the Baptists. In 1961, in one of the most devastating acts of Khrushchev's anti-religious campaign, the authorities compelled the official body, the All-Union Council of Evangelical Christians and Baptists, to accept new regulations limiting the rights of the Church to evangelize, even in the context of official services. The failure of the Baptist leadership to offer effective resistance to these measures led to the emergence of an independent opposition group, the *Initsiativniki*, or Reform Baptists. Although the new regulations were not enforced for long, the damage was done and its effects persist to this day. On the one hand, the opposition group showed a high degree of organization and determination in the face of what is now almost a quarter of a century of relentless oppression. On the other hand, the All-Union Council managed in a curious way to win for themselves certain democratic rights and concessions unimaginable at the time the split began.

Why then does the schism persist? The main reason is that the state has never allowed reformers the breathing space to talk as man to man with the registered Baptists. At no time since 1961 has the *Initsiativniki* leadership been able to come out into the open. Their top leaders, together with hundreds of local activists, have had one period of imprisonment after another. One of the co-founders of the movement, Gennady Kryuchkov, has been in hiding from the police ever since he completed a three-year term of imprisonment in 1969. The other key founder, Georgy Vins, was imprisoned with Kryuchkov after the same trial in 1966, then released, but was sentenced again in 1974, this time to a term of ten years' imprisonment, halfway through which he was summoned to Moscow and put on an aeroplane. Only when he was in the air did he know that he was bound for the USA as an involuntary exile, and that a secret deal with the American government had been concluded. Under impossible conditions, the *Initsiativniki* have kept in contact with each other, operated secret printing presses and sent abroad a stream of information about the conditions in which they live. Much of this information was collected by the Council of Prisoners' Relatives, the first organization of its kind in a communist country.

One of the most successful Soviet propaganda campaigns of postwar years has been the blackening of the name of the Reform Baptists on the international scene. Countless times the Soviet authorities, and sometimes even registered Baptist leaders themselves, have described them as trouble-makers, people with a 'martyr complex', power-seekers, criminals who have received their just desserts for persistent law-breaking. In fact, there is nothing they wish to do more than to register their communities and live a quiet legal existence. After their conference in Tula in 1969 it became their official policy that they should do so. But all this has been in vain. With the exception of one or two isolated congregations, Soviet policy has consistently been to refuse their request for registration and then to punish them for not being registered. What is remarkable is not that they are fanatical, but how restrained and forgiving of their enemies they are after having endured so many years of brutality.

At the same time, the Reform Baptists seem to have drawn away the brunt of persecution from their registered brethren; this has had the effect of giving the latter a breathing space which they have been able to use to improve their position. They are not insincere when they point to some improvements in recent years — a few more churches registered, a few more Bibles printed, a better opportunity to participate in international movements and to be in contact with Baptists in other parts of the world.

No such benefits accrue to the Pentecostal community, whose position is analogous to that of the Reform Baptists, even to the extent of having won the concession of the registration of a handful of congregations in recent years.

The Catholics

The last decade has seen more developments among Soviet Catholics than among any other section of the religious community. This is due not least to the impact of the election of a Polish Pope, who is correctly seen by Soviet Catholics as someone who understands their situation and wishes to improve it. There are four main bodies of Catholics in the Soviet Union: in Russia and Central Asia, in the Ukraine, in Lithuania, and in Byelorussia.

Many of those scattered throughout Siberia and Central Asia reached their present place of residence through exile or deportation, especially during the Stalin period, and they include a considerable number of Poles and Germans. Only in recent years has news of this Catholic diaspora begun to seep out to the West.

There was the Polish priest Fr. Wladyslaw Bukowiński, who renounced the opportunity to return home after the Second World War in order to spend the last thirty years of his life ministering in Central Asia. The only time he was not on the move during the thirteen years he spent in prison for working as a priest without the state licence which was never granted him. Towards the end of his life he obtained permission for a visit to Poland. Here he met the future Pope John Paul II, who persuaded him to write his memoirs, a beautiful story which has since been published.[3]

We know less of Fr. Iosif Swidnicki, aged 47, who was arrested in December 1984 in the Siberian city of Novosibirsk. He is also of Polish origin, but lived in Latvia. Unable to gain entry to the tiny theological seminary there, he studied and was eventually ordained secretly in 1971. Moving to Siberia, he found a fruitful field for ministry among the 2 million ethnic Germans (descendants of eighteenth-century colonists) and eventually obtained a licence to work as a priest in the mid-1970s, at a time when anti-religious policies were being less severely implemented than at present. Until very recently, the huge city of Novosibirsk had no Catholic church; only in 1984, after many years of campaigning, was the community granted permission to use one. Although there is no bishop in Siberia to oversee appointments, Fr. Swidnicki somehow received the call to go there. Yet, having registered the community, the authorities arrested Fr. Swidnicki in December 1984 and in the following May he was sentenced to three years' imprisonment in a labour camp.

The largest single Catholic community in the USSR are the

Ukrainian Catholics of the Eastern Rite, or Uniates. Although this Church was forcibly liquidated in 1946, there are at present some 4 million adherents, making it the largest 'catacomb' Church in the Soviet Union. For years it was known that the Ukrainian Catholics were holding their own as an illegal body, but the information available in the West was fragmentary. Then, in 1982, undoubtedly influenced by the election of a Polish Pope, they began to present their case to the Soviet government and to the world in a more decisive way. On 9 September, Iosyf Terelya, a layman who had already spent eighteen of his thirty-nine years in prison and psychiatric hospital as a result of his religious activities, announced the formation of an Initiative Group for the Defence of the Rights of Believers and the Church. This was an act of incredible bravery in view of the savage treatment, not stopping short of murder in some instances, which had recently been handed out to various other Christian groups who had tried to defend their Churches in a similarly organized fashion. Moreover, the authorities had some precedents for treating the Ukrainian Catholics in a particularly severe way.

The sole aim of the Initiative Group, said Terelya, was to legalize the Ukrainian Catholic Church. He wrote to the Central Committee of the Ukrainian Communist Party:

Despite the prognoses of some Party members, we are living, growing and triumphing. The trials and persecution suffered by Catholics in the Ukraine have strengthened us even more in the faith and have given us the opportunity to sound the depths of God's providence. I can state without exaggeration that there is nothing greater than to die as a Catholic in a communist prison.[4]

Three and a half months later Terelya was back in detention, though to date his prophecy of martyrdom has not been fulfilled.[5]

Far from being terrorized into silence, the Ukrainian Catholics have recently become more determined. In January 1984 (although it took over a year for the text to reach the West) the Ukrainian activists began to produce a clandestine journal, the *Chronicle of the Catholic Church in the Ukraine*, of which nine issues have so far appeared. In content it is similar to the chronicle produced by Lithuanian Catholics from 1972 onwards, although its strong defence of persecuted religious groups other than Catholics is of particular significance.

After a year in prison, Terelya was released and immediately elected chairman of the Initiative Group, though the first issue of the *Chronicle* noted that the authorities were preparing a new case against him. He himself wrote:

We are hunted and without rights. They have taken away everything from us – our Church and our schools. We are constantly persecuted, we exist only as a work force in the labour camps as far as the authorities are concerned. Why then do we need Soviet passports?[6]

According to the third issue of the *Chronicle*, over 900 people surrendered or burnt their passports in early 1984, a remarkable act of civil disobedience. The same issue reprinted a letter of support from Ukrainian Catholics to Lech Walesa and Polish Solidarity (a bridge which, if established, would cause more than a little anxiety amongst the Soviet leadership).

Issue no. 2 of the *Chronicle* provides firm evidence of the growth of this catacomb church, stating that in the Transcarpathian region alone, eighty-two priests had graduated from secret seminaries and been ordained over the previous three years. We know of similar underground seminaries in Lithuania.

The end of the Second World War saw the Soviet Union in illegal possession of the Baltic republic of Lithuania, from which it had suffered no aggression. The Roman Catholic Church there has proved remarkably durable, both in membership and structure. A united population has kept open a higher percentage of its churches than elsewhere — 574, that is, about 50 per cent of the prewar number — and the number of students in the seminary, while still far too small, has doubled to sixty in recent years. Moreover, the authorities have proved unable to elevate a compliant leadership to head the Church. Indeed, the true situation of the Lithuanian Catholics has been thoroughly documented by the clandestine *Chronicle of the Lithuanian Catholic Church*, which has appeared at regular intervals since 1972 and which the authorities have proved unable to suppress. The persecution in Lithuania has often been violent. Fr. Bronius Laurinavičius, a key member of the Lithuanian Helsinki Monitoring Group, was murdered in 1981, while the leaders of the Catholic Committee for Believers' Rights (linked to the similar group founded by Fr. Gleb Yakunin in Moscow) are undergoing lengthy prison sentences.

At the same time, there have been further improvements in the institutional life of the Church, such as the elevation of Bishop Liudvikas Povilonis to the rank of Archbishop and the consecration of Juozas Preikša[7] as his auxiliary. Even more significant is the return of Bishop Sladkevičius from exile after years of pressure from believers. There are now seven active Lithuanian bishops, more than at any time since the Soviet take-over. They include Bishop Steponavičius, who is formally banned from office but remains active none the less, and is frequently subject to criticism by the Soviets for carrying out his episcopal duties.

If one includes perhaps 40 million Muslims and a relatively small number of observant Jews, there are probably not far short of 100 million religious believers in the Soviet Union, that is, over a third of the population. Clearly, Mikhail Gorbachev wishes to cultivate a favourable public image and a sure way of doing this would be to introduce a better deal for believers. Although there is no real indication that he is likely to do so, the continued expansion of religious influence in Soviet society means that the day cannot be far distant when the leadership will have to seek some means of conciliation rather than confrontation.

Notes

[1] The question of the number of Orthodox believers is discussed in more detail in Jane Ellis, *The Russian Orthodox Church: A Contemporary History* (London, 1986), pp. 173–7.

[2] Aleksandr Ogorodnikov, Letter to Philip Potter, General Secretary of the World Council of Churches, 27 July 1976 in *Religion in Communist Lands (RCL)* vol. 4, no. 4, Winter 1976, pp. 45–7.

[3] W. Bukowiński, *A Priest in Russia* (London, 1982). A slightly longer version is available in Polish, *Wspomnienia z Kazachstanu* (Paris, 1979).

[4] Iosif Terelya, 'Declaration to the Central Committee of the Ukrainian Communist Party', undated (probably 1982–3). English text in *RCL*, vol. 11, no. 3, Winter 1983, pp. 290–1. A selection of Terelya's writings can be found in Andrew Sorokowski (ed), *For my Name's Sake: Selections from the Writings of Iosif Terelya* (London, 1986).

[5] Terelya was arrested on 8 February 1985 and on 20 August 1985 sentenced to seven years' camp and five years' exile.

[6] *Khronika Katolicheskoy tserkvi na Ukraine, no. 1*, (Arkhiv samizdata, no. 5371, p. 10) (Munich, 1984).

[7] Appointment reported in *Keston News Service 219*, 21 February 1985.

CHAPTER 12

Emigration from the USSR, 1975–1985

SIDNEY HEITMAN

Since the end of the Second World War, 400,000 citizens of the USSR have emigrated to the West in what is today called the 'Third Soviet Emigration'. This exodus comprises chiefly three ethnic minorities: 286,000 Jews, 100,000 Germans and 50,000 Armenians. The vast majority of emigrants left during the 1970s. Since the end of that decade, emigration has been reduced to a mere trickle, stranding thousands of persons in the USSR who still wish to leave but are no longer permitted to do so.

The origins of the 'Third Emigration' go back to the early postwar years. As part of the massive population resettlements after the Second World War, 23,000 Soviet Jews and 22,000 Soviet Germans were reunited with relatives in the West. These emigrants were mainly elderly or infirm individuals of no interest to the Soviet state, and their transfer was considered a special dispensation, not a precedent. Soviet law now, as then, does not provide for emigration from the USSR *per se*.

These transfers ended when East–West relations deteriorated over the 1968 Soviet invasion of Czechoslovakia, but the initiation of détente at the beginning of the 1970s led to a new wave of emigration. Between 1970 and the end of the decade, thousands of Soviet Jews, Germans and Armenians — this time persons of all backgrounds and ages and even entire families — were granted exit visas.

Of the many questions this movement raises, I want to deal here with only three: (1) What accounts for the rise and decline of Soviet emigration in the 1970s?; (2) What is the present Soviet policy towards emigration?; and (3) What are the prospects of a revival of emigration in the near future?

The rise and decline of Soviet emigration

The rise and decline of Soviet emigration in the 1970s can be explained by two sets of factors: internal pressures — the specific causes and precipitants of emigration; and Soviet motives for relaxing and then re-imposing emigration restrictions.

Internal pressures

These have to be considered separately for each of the three emigrant groups.

Jewish emigration   The reasons for Soviet Jewish emigration are particularly interesting because the Jews were the first and largest group of emigrants, whose success inspired the other two nationalities to emulate them.

In 1970 the 2.1 million Soviet Jews were a predominantly urban minority without a geographic base or structural supports for their traditional culture. Those who lived on the periphery of the USSR generally preserved more of their religious and cultural heritage than those who were scattered among the major cities of central Russia. Most had become Russified, but not assimilated, for their identity as Jews was reinforced by their Jewish consciousness, their distinctive treatment and their internal Soviet passports.

Many were well educated and disproportionately well represented in academic, scientific and artistic professions, but they were barred from attaining the highest positions — a fact of Soviet life that Jews had learned to live with. Emigration from the USSR as an escape from antisemitism was simply unthinkable.

Two events in the late 1960s changed this, however. One was the rise of a particularly virulent wave of antisemitic persecution; the other was the Israeli victory in the 1967 Six-Day War, which stirred Jewish pride in the USSR and revived a dormant Zionist movement.

The relaxation of internal Soviet controls in the early 1970s that paralleled improved relations with the West, and the mobilization of world Jewry on behalf of the threatened Soviet Jews prompted many of them to seek to emigrate from the USSR. Surprisingly, the Soviet government concurred by granting exit visas in increasing numbers on the grounds of 'family reunification' to circumvent Soviet law and discourage others from seeking to leave.

The first emigrants, primarily traditional, religious Jews, resettled in Israel. In the second half of the 1970s, Jewish emigration changed its character and direction when more assimilated Jews joined the exodus, not only to escape antisemitism, but also to seek greater personal and economic opportunities in the West. These emigrants resettled mainly in the United States.

By the time emigration was restricted again, a total of 286,000 Jews, or more than 10 per cent of the Soviet Jewish population, had emigrated from the country, but an estimated 350,000 to 500,000 others who also wanted to leave were no longer able to do so from the turn of the 1980s. Today, Jewish emigration averages fewer than 100 persons per month, compared with more than 51,000 emigrants in the peak year of 1979.

German emigration Soviet German emigration has some parallels to that of the Soviet Jews. The 2 million ethnic Germans in the USSR are also an unassimilated minority with a strong national consciousness but no geographic base since the Second World War when they were suspected of mass treason and brutally deported to forced labour camps. After the war they were dispersed in western Siberia and Central Asia. Like the Jews, many Germans are Russified but not assimilated, and they also look to an ancestral 'homeland' in West Germany. They also experience ethnic discrimination due to a lingering prejudice in the USSR against things German since the Second World War.

They differ, however, in that they are content with their economic status in the agricultural, industrial and service jobs that they fill. Their disaffection stems from the failure of the Soviet government fully to exonerate them of the charge of wartime treason, and its refusal to return them to their original homes in European Russia and restore their prewar political autonomy. They also complain of religious restrictions and obstacles to preserving their traditional language and culture.

Emigration was also unthinkable for the Soviet Germans — until the exodus of Soviet Jews inspired many to emulate them by claiming relatives in West Germany whom they wanted to rejoin. In the liberalized climate of détente and the new West German *Ostpolitik*, the Soviet government concurred. Before restrictions were again imposed in the early 1980s, a total of 100,000 Soviet

Germans had left the USSR, but an estimated 100,000 (some say up to 1 million) others were left behind.

Armenian emigration   Armenian emigration has no parallel to that of Soviet Jews and Germans for, on the whole, the status of Armenians in the USSR is good by Soviet standards. They have a separate union republic; enjoy linguistic, cultural and religious autonomy; have a high standard of living; and, until recently, could freely receive foreign visitors and even travel abroad.

Contrary to the alienation felt by Soviet Jews and Germans, Armenians in the USSR (and throughout the world) consider Soviet Armenia their current national homeland and, whatever their feelings about communism, they remember with gratitude that the USSR defended their forebears from Turkish attacks and created the Armenian republic in the 1920s.

Why then do they wish to emigrate? Those who have left the USSR and would do so today are almost entirely newcomers to Soviet Armenia. They were among thousands of former Soviet citizens who responded to a call by the government of the USSR after the Second World War to return to their homeland and help to rebuild it. Two hundred and fifty thousand Armenians from the Middle East, Europe and America immigrated to Soviet Armenia, where they were granted Soviet citizenship and helped to start new lives. It was they who were largely responsible for the postwar Armenian economic and cultural renaissance that transformed the sleepy republic into perhaps the most prosperous region of the USSR.

But there were problems. The newcomers had difficulty adjusting to the backward conditions which they found; they were shunned by the local Armenians; and they were barred from top positions in their professions and the government by jealous native authorities.

Although many of them prospered in the postwar economic boom, they knew they could do better in the West. When emigration for Jews and Germans was eased, disaffected Armenians also applied to leave. Under the cover of family reunification, 50,000 Soviet Armenians left the USSR, chiefly for the United States. When emigration was cut back in the 1980s, an estimated 200,000 — equal to the entire original immigrant community — still wanted to leave.

Motives of the Soviet authorities

What accounts for the Soviet authorities' concurrence with the wishes of the emigrants, considering the absence of a legal basis for emigration, the historical Soviet antipathy to emigration, and the risk that other disaffected groups might also seek to emigrate? The most honest answer to this question is that we really do not know. There are some indications, but no certainty. Concerning the Jews and Germans, three factors suggest Soviet motives. These are: certain internal developments; American and West German diplomacy; and international public opinion.

Internal Soviet developments include the general relaxation of political controls that accompanied détente, and heightened pressure by Soviet Germans and Jews for the right to leave. Both groups circulated petitions, staged demonstrations, sent appeals to Soviet and foreign officials, stormed embassies, held press conferences, and engaged in other forms of activism and civil disobedience to publicize their causes. Surprisingly, the Soviet government not only tolerated such behaviour, but allowed Jews and Germans to emigrate in increasing numbers.

Détente also held out the prospect of increased trade, credits, technology, scientific exchanges and security from the West, for which the United States and West Germany demanded preferential treatment for Soviet Jews and Germans as a *quid pro quo*. Both sides openly used emigration as a bargaining chip, the United States and West Germany taking every opportunity to extract concessions, the Soviet Union trading callously in humans for material gain.

The influence of Western public opinion on Soviet emigration policy is difficult to gauge. There is reason to believe, however, that wide press coverage, the activities of human rights organizations, demonstrations before Soviet embassies in Western capitals, and parliamentary appeals and denunciations all helped to liberalize Soviet emigration policy for a time. When Brezhnev began to fail and tougher leaders took over behind the scenes in the late 1970s, however, the Soviet government grew increasingly indifferent to foreign public opinion, even to criticism from European communist parties.

The reasons the Soviet government permitted Armenians to

emigrate are more difficult to explain. Unlike the Jews and Germans, the Armenians have no homeland outside the USSR and no foreign government working for them. Although the United States offers them a sanctuary, it does not intervene actively on their behalf with the Soviet government. There is not even an Armenian lobby in Washington or other foreign capitals. Indeed, the American–Armenian community deplores and discourages the emigration of their countrymen from the USSR in the belief that it weakens and discredits the only national homeland they have. The ironic fact that those who deplore and discourage are all comfortably established in America will go without comment.

Some explanations have been suggested for the Soviet government's leniency towards Armenian emigration for a time. These include benign neglect of the Armenian republic under Brezhnev; the desire to be rid of trouble-makers who might stir up others or embarrass the USSR; an effort to camouflage Soviet bending to Western pressure on behalf of Jews and Germans by also allowing Armenians to join in the reunification of families; and the Soviet government's courting of Armenian goodwill against a time when Soviet Armenia might become strategically important during a possible conflict with Turkey or trouble in the turbulent Middle East.

Whatever the reasons, Soviet policy towards all three emigrant groups changed radically after 1979. Exit quotas were sharply reduced; visa procedures were made extremely difficult; and persistent applicants were dealt with harshly to discourage them and others.

Accounting for this was undoubtedly the general tightening of political controls behind the scenes during Brezhnev's last years, when hard-liners, in particular Andropov and Gorbachev, emerged to leadership positions. Playing into their hands were the failure of détente to deliver the benefits it had promised; the worsening of East–West relations by the NATO decision to deploy American missiles in Europe; the Soviet invasion of Afghanistan; the Polish crisis; the failure of the United States to ratify SALT II; the election of publicly avowed anti-Soviet leaders in the United States and West Germany; the American boycott of the 1980 Moscow Summer Olympics; and other such events in the renewed cold war.

By the early 1980s, détente was dead and emigration all but at a standstill. Charges against the Soviet Union that it was violating its legal obligations to facilitate emigration and family reunification were answered with, alternately, flat denials; the claim that all who wished to had already emigrated; the assertion that emigration was an internal Soviet matter of no concern to outsiders; and advice that critics should put their own house in order before pointing fingers at the USSR.

Present status and future prospects of emigration

To conclude — what is the present status of Soviet emigration and its future prospects? I fear neither is good. Emigration quotas reached their lowest level since 1970 in 1984 and the first three months of this year indicate the decline is continuing.

The recent thaw of the new cold war has not yet affected emigration. In the 1970s, the Soviet government would often 'lubricate' forthcoming important meetings or conferences by increasing quotas of emigrants. This did not happen in advance of the current discussions between the USSR and the West concerning arms control, trade, technology transfer and scientific exchanges, among others. The West did not require a *quid pro quo* of larger emigration quotas, and the USSR would not have given it in any case. Emigration has a lower priority today for both sides than in the 1970s.

It is unlikely that the Soviet government will, in any case, return to a policy of liberal emigration. Past losses of skilled and productive workers have had an impact on the Soviet economy. Emigration runs against the grain of Soviet authoritarianism, which is not likely to lessen under the new Soviet leaders. And there is a danger that the demand to emigrate may spread to other disaffected groups in the USSR.

In sum, the prognosis is not hopeful for the near future. This is a judgement based on long study of this subject — although I earnestly hope I am wrong.

Table 1
Emigration from the USSR, 1950–1985[a]

Year		Jews	Germans[b]	Armenians[c]	Total
1950–69		23,000	22,150	–0–	45,150
1970		1,027	342	–0–	1,369
1971		13,022	1,145	–0–	14,167
1972		31,903	3,420	75	35,398
1973		34,933	4,493	185	39,611
1974		20,695	6,541	291	27,527
1975		13,451	5,985	455	19,891
1976		14,325	9,704*	1,779	25,808
1977		16,831	9,274	1,390	27,495
1978		28,993	8,455	1,123	38,571
1979		51,547*	7,226	3,581	62,354*
1980		21,471	6,954	6,109*	34,534
1981		9,860	3,773	1,905	15,538
1982		2,700	2,071	338	5,109
1983		1,320	1,447	193	2,960
1984		908	910	88	1,906
1985	Jan.	61	39	5	105
	Feb.	88	28	4	120
	Mar.	97	33	5	135

* Peak year.
[a] Sources include Jewish, German and Armenian ethnic organizations, and United States and West German government statistics. There are variations in the figures reported by different sources; the numbers here are a composite of the different versions.
[b] These figures do not include several thousand emigrants who have resettled in East Germany. The precise number is not known; some of them are believed to have re-emigrated later to West Germany and are counted in official statistics as emigrants from East Germany.
[c] These figures represent only Armenians who resettled in the United States and for whom there are official records – the vast majority of those who left the USSR. An unknown number also resettled in other countries. Estimates within Armenian circles of total Armenian emigrants range as high as 45–50,000.

CHAPTER 13

Soviet Propaganda and the Dissidents

VLADIMIR TOLZ

Soviet media attacks on dissidents are frequently linked to specific punitive actions. On the one hand, the intention may be to justify an action which has already occurred. This is because Soviet citizens may have become aware of it from independent sources — for example, Western radio broadcasts, *samizdat*, rumour — and interpreted it in a manner not desired by the authorities. On the other hand, the propaganda attacks may be linked to an action about to be undertaken. This occurs only in rare cases where an action may appear particularly unjust (for example, the one against the Russian Social Fund for Assistance to Political Prisoners, or the one against Dr Sakharov which began in May 1984). In these rare cases, a secondary aim of the propaganda is to influence Western public opinion.

Soviet propaganda attacks on the dissidents have been inextricably linked to the rise of the human rights movement in the USSR. Until the mid-1960s the Soviet authorities seldom faced any internal ideological or political challenge. As the human rights movement developed, however, information about dissent became increasingly accessible to the Soviet population. At the present time, while the overwhelming majority of Soviet citizens may never have read a *samizdat* work, many of them are none the less aware, to some extent or other, of the views of the dissidents on many issues. Western radio stations have done a great deal to disseminate this information.

Correspondingly, Soviet propagandists have been unable to restrict themselves to using such clichés as the 'anti-Soviet' or 'anti-socialist' activities of 'renegades'. Their task has been made all the more difficult in that many of the human rights activists claim that the right to dissent is fully in accordance with Soviet law. As for the authorities, they have shown themselves unable to enter into polemics with the dissidents — perhaps for the very reason that it was precisely such a dialogue which the dissidents were seeking. The authorities responded with propaganda intended to intimidate potential dissenters and to create in the consciousness of the masses the stereotype of the 'villainous dissident'.

Soviet propagandists use a number of clichés to create this image. One of these is the dissidents' alleged links with 'fascism'. The link is sometimes made directly, as in the case of the prisoners Svyatoslav Karavansky, Daniil Shumuk and Bohdan Chuiko. But more often than not it is made by innuendo. In such cases, the dissident is linked by association with persons described by Soviet propaganda as Nazi collaborators. Here are three examples:

(a) Cardinal Slipyj is shown embracing Dr Sakharov's grandson. As Slipyj succeeded Sheptitsky who, according to Soviet propagandists, collaborated with the Nazis, the implication is that Sakharov too is linked to the Nazis.
(b) According to Soviet propaganda, Radio Liberty and Radio Free Europe employ 'Hitlerites' who provide information about human rights activities in the USSR. Thus the implication is that the human rights activists must have at least a 'spiritual link' with the 'Hitlerites'.
(c) The Russian Social Fund assists prisoners alleged to have collaborated with the Nazis. The implication is clear . . .

A second thesis of Soviet propaganda against the dissidents is their alleged collaboration with foreign intelligence services, imperialism and Zionism. Yuri Andropov attributed the entire phenomenon of human rights activism in the USSR to this thesis:

The existence of the so-called 'dissidents' has become possible only thanks to the fact that the opponents of socialism have enlisted to their cause the Western press and the diplomatic, intelligence and other special services. It is hardly a secret that 'dissent' has become a sort of profession which is generously paid in foreign currency and other pickings and that in essence [dissidents are paid] in a manner very similar to how the imperialist special services pay their agents.[1]

Since around the second half of the 1970s, any concrete instances of dissent — Helsinki groups, unofficial activities by religious activists not sanctioned by the authorities, the now all-too-rare statements by Andrei Sakharov — have been said to result from the machinations of the 'Western special services'. Moreover, any foreigner who takes an abiding interest in the struggle for human rights in the USSR and speaks out on behalf of dissidents is described as an 'agent' or 'resident' of one or the other intelligence services and of 'imperialism' and Zionism (which Soviet propagandists hold to be identical to fascism).

Clearly, concrete examples of the alleged espionage of dissidents have to be furnished: the cases of Anatoly Shcharansky and, more recently, that of the Russian Social Fund for Assistance to Political Prisoners are two of the most frequently occurring examples of this genre.

It is not my concern to analyse the effectiveness of Soviet anti-dissident propaganda. It should, however, be said that we have evidence — from the Soviet media, *samizdat* and independent Western sources alike — that the claim that the dissidents are agents of foreign intelligence services is not found convincing by the Soviet public. For this reason, the image of the 'villainous dissident' has had to be supplemented by reference to his alleged immorality. So, for example, dissidents are portrayed as greedy and mercenary; parasites unwilling to work yet enjoying a higher standard of living than others on account of the foreign currency they receive; drunkards and libertines with criminal links, for example, speculators, thieves, swindlers, hooligans, sympathizers with terrorism.

Dissidents are also frequently depicted as people without a specific profession and only half-educated. Thus, for example, Yuri Orlov's professorial title is never mentioned: he is described simply as a 'scoundrel'. When, in the case of, for example, Dr Sakharov, the issue of academic qualifications cannot be avoided, it is 'neutralized' by reference to his 'retirement from scholarly activity', 'creative impotence', and the like.

The dissident's motivations must be distorted too. Besides having a mercenary character, he is said to be prey to overweening social ambition and, of course, to display a consuming hatred for his own country and people. Occasionally, he also suffers from a psychiatric disorder or some variety of mental inadequacy (although these motifs appear less frequently now owing to the success of the Western campaign against the Soviet abuse of psychiatry for political ends).

In addition to these generalized clichés, there have recently appeared a number of motifs related to individual instances of dissent. Thus the Russian Orthodox writer A. E. Levitin-Krasnov has been described as an adherent of Catholicism with the clear aim of casting doubt on the sincerity and genuineness of his religious beliefs. It is likewise claimed that Solzhenitsyn denounced his friends to the security organs.

Particular attention has been paid recently to searching for more effective forms of anti-dissident propaganda. The most 'promising' lines at the present time are various forms of 'documentary' propaganda which are intended to augment the impression of authenticity. Quotations from letters by dissidents, occasionally in distorted form, have been published, as well as 'confessions' by individuals who have been convicted and have recanted (for example, Regelson, Kapitanchuk, Kuvakin, Repin, and others). Interviews have appeared too (for example, with Repin, Yakovlev's aborted interview with Sakharov).

The genre of the television documentary film is increasingly common, for example, 'Catchers of Souls', 'Operation "Wedding" ', 'Conspiracy against the Land of the Soviets'. Soviet propagandists also respond to Western radio broadcasts by publishing anti-dissident materials borrowed from foreign communist publications, reference to the communist nature of the original publication usually being omitted. Attacks on dissidents also appear in *belles-lettres* and in the cinema.

The signing of the Helsinki Final Act stimulated human rights activism in the USSR and this evoked an intensification of media attacks on the dissidents. These attacks carry contradictory messages. On the one hand, they deny any genuine basis for the existence of dissent in the USSR; on the other hand, they claim that the dissidents pose a threat to the very existence of the USSR. The Helsinki provisions on the wider exchange of information, which is sought by most dissidents in the USSR, are officially welcomed while, at the same time, demands are put forward to introduce legislation which will undermine these principles. Attacks on human rights activists are now replete with references to the supposed flourishing of these rights in the USSR and their wholesale violation by the Western states which signed the Final Act. Occasionally, Soviet propagandists cast doubt on the value of specific provisions of the Final Act, for whose implementation the dissidents are fighting. For example, it is claimed that 'freedom' of emigration for the reunification of families gives rise only to an increase in the number of divided families.

Note
[1] *Pravda*, 10 September 1977.

CHAPTER 14

The Jamming of Western Radio Broadcasts

KEITH EDWARDS

Short-wave broadcasting

The discovery in the 1920s that transmissions in the short-wave bands could be heard over vast distances has led to the development of one of the most highly competitive uses of the radio frequency spectrum ever known. Successful international broadcasting necessitates the use of a medium capable of delivering strong signals over a very large area in the most cost-effective manner. Whereas medium-wave transmissions may be heard up to a distance of some hundreds of kilometres under favourable conditions at night, short waves can reach audiences with cheap short-wave receivers at ranges of many thousands of kilometres.

These signals reach the audience by being bounced off the ionosphere, a layer some three hundred or so kilometres above the earth consisting of electrically charged particles which acts like a mirror and reflects the signals back to the reception area on the earth's surface.

To ensure that the strongest possible signal is delivered to the reception area each short-wave broadcasting transmitter must be connected to one of a number of highly directional antennas. Instead of radiating the signal in all directions these antennas concentrate most of the radiated energy into a narrow beam. The effective radiated power can then be a hundred times the transmitter power. The beam will be steered and the best elevation angle will be selected to deliver the strongest signal via the ionosphere to the reception area. The result is one of the most cost-effective means of delivering signals to a large geographical area.

In some Western countries which have a plethora of media

outlets short waves have taken a back seat. In most parts of the world, however, the radio audience far exceeds that for television, and for the immediate future short-wave radio seems set to remain the only viable way of broadcasting across frontiers. This will apply as much to developed as to undeveloped and to Western as much as to Eastern ideologies. Pressure from the developing countries to achieve more equitable access to the short-wave bands is a clear indication of the importance they attach to the use of this medium.

Today, the short-wave bands are crowded as never before, with some 25,000 transmission hours every day. Even in these congested conditions audience research shows that reception of the BBC External Services is still increasing; there is now a total of some 120 million listeners. The Board for International Broadcasting claims a total daily audience of more than 20 million for the jammed Russian services of the VOA, BBC, Radio Liberty and Deutsche Welle. That listening on such a scale continues clearly illustrates that short-wave broadcasting is very much alive. The jamming found in all of the bands today indirectly causes congestion worldwide in addition to its more direct effect of rendering reception of those programmes against which it is aimed more difficult.

Jamming techniques

Any jamming operation must follow certain readily definable techniques. There are two fundamentally different technical approaches that can be used for jamming broadcasts on short wave, namely 'sky wave' and 'ground wave'.

'Sky-wave' signals

'Sky-wave' signals, arriving in the reception area after reflection from the ionosphere, will have maximum signal strength at a distance of typically 2,000 km or more from the transmitter. Jamming transmitters using this technique therefore need to be sited at a considerable distance from the reception area where the jamming signals are to be concentrated. High-gain transmitting antennas similar to those used at the broadcasting station must be employed to bounce the jamming signals off the ionosphere. Transmitters at such a jamming station may be used to 'lay down' signals in different reception areas at different times of day provided there is a sufficient number of antennas to beam signals in the required directions. This technique has the same advantage as the broadcasting station in delivering signals to a large area. It is, however, also like the broadcasting station, at the mercy of the daily and seasonal variability of the ionosphere. If the jamming is to be effective, several stations will be necessary at different distances and each must have a number of transmitters capable of operating over the range of frequency bands used for short-wave broadcasting. There will be certain times of day when this technique is of limited effectiveness. One example is referred to as the 'twilight immunity' period. Under this condition, Western stations can continue to use higher frequency bands than the 'sky-wave' jammers, whose signals will no longer be reflected via the ionosphere from the stations within the USSR. By a fortunate coincidence this effect is most pronounced during late afternoon and evening, through the sun's maintaining its influence on the ionosphere for longer to the west of the USSR. Other advantageous propagational openings may also exist: for example, transmitters located nearer the Equator can operate on much higher frequencies than the jammers operating in the USSR.

Both transmitter power and antenna system complexity will be comparable with that of a short-wave broadcasting station. The technique is thus expensive in both capital and running costs.

'Ground-wave' signals

'Ground-wave' signals reach the receivers like those from a medium/long-wave or VHF/FM transmitter and are strongest near the transmitting station; signal strengths decrease with increasing distance from the transmitter.

This technique is used for local jamming. The strongest signals will usually be those reaching the receiver by line of sight, more closely analagous to the VHF/FM case than to medium or long wave. Thus the higher the elevation of the transmitting antenna, the greater will be its range, and jamming stations are therefore more likely to be sited on high buildings or hills overlooking cities. The effective range of such jammers may be some tens of kilometres, dependent upon power, antenna height, topography, etc.

One local jammer can, however, jam only one incoming frequency and therefore many jammers will be needed to counter up to thirty or forty frequencies carrying Western radio broadcasts in Russian. It has been observed that it may take some time for these jammers to be realigned on different frequencies at the beginning of transmissions. The interval of a minute or two needed for these changes may account for some of the stories attributed to selective jamming.

While relatively low-power transmitters can be used for local jamming, the total number of such jammers will be very large when account is taken of the fact that most cities of any significant size have a jamming centre and more than one jamming transmitting station may operate in the larger cities in the USSR. Clearly a control system of some complexity must be in use to direct the attention of the jamming stations to those incoming transmissions most needing attention.

Changes in jamming techniques

Certain changes in jamming techniques have been recognized during the last few years. These have been concerned with the technical characteristics or the type of noise made by the jammer rather than any significant change in its power. Jammers are now more usually modulated with some type of noise where formerly they carried a distorted Russian programme. The noise is rather more effective as a jamming signal; it also has the secondary advantage of creating less interference to the adjacent frequencies. A jammer has a very considerable advantage over the broadcast transmitter; much lower power is needed because it can concentrate all the available power in the creation of interference, whereas most of the power in the broadcast transmitter is in the carrier wave needed to facilitate reception on cheap receivers. Thus increases in audibility can be obtained only by relatively large expenditures in either, or both, capital and operating costs.

A 'ground-wave' jammer can make reception of the frequency on which it is operating very difficult indeed within its rather limited range. Outside that area its effectiveness will diminish. Other frequencies will be receivable both inside and outside that area.

Reception under jamming conditions

However intense the effort, no jamming system can be totally effective throughout a large country such as the USSR. Nor, for that matter, can a broadcasting service which is being jammed claim that it can be received other than with varying degrees of difficulty.

Habitual listeners to short-wave services tend, however, to be quite reconciled to some of its problems. Instead of radios which are left tuned to a favourite station they know the six, or twelve, or even more places on the dial where they can find the station or stations of their choice. Only those who have a need to listen can appreciate just how competent even the non-technical can become in finding the best reception. The competence of those motivated to try and listen under these very difficult conditions must never be underestimated. It has been my experience that travellers who may well have an even greater motivation may still be much less successful through lack of experience of the local conditions, and they frequently do not stay in one place long enough to learn.

For success in this search even the experienced listener has to rely on the broadcaster's ability to offer a full range of transmitted frequencies for a choice to be made to cater for both diurnal and day-to-day changes in reception conditions. Under jamming conditions, at certain times of day, there are likely to be more relatively interference-free signals in the higher-frequency bands, such as the 19, 16 or 13 metre wave bands or the 15, 18 or 21 MHz frequency bands. It is an unfortunate fact that only relatively few of the radio receivers available in the USSR include these higher-frequency bands in their tuning range. The best the broadcaster can do is to transmit signals in every frequency band capable of delivering competitive signals and to encourage listeners to equip themselves with receivers that can take advantage of every opportunity.

Other choices in the listener's hands may be the choice of type of receiver and experimentation with its position in the room or apartment. Certain receivers are fitted with small loop antennas which have some directional properties. Most listeners will know that on long and medium waves the strength of the received signal will vary as the receiver is rotated. It is not so well known that there are some short-wave receivers which exhibit the same behaviour on some, if not all, of their short-wave ranges. Radios are frequently placed in the most convenient position for use. It does not follow that this will also be the best place for short-wave reception. Signals are almost invariably stronger out in the open; thus a window position facing the wanted transmitting station on the opposite side of the building from the jammer is a good starting point. The signal strength of the local jammer may well exhibit considerable differences in strength over a distance of a few metres. If this behaviour is found, it is likely to be quite different in different frequency bands.

Comparison of jamming in 1975 and 1985

The change in the jamming situation between 1975 and 1985 reflects the general increase in tension between East and West during that period. Jamming of BBC, VOA and Deutsche Welle Russian services had ceased in September 1973, recommencing in August 1980. Jamming of Radio Liberty, of some of the services of Radio Free Europe and certain other broadcasts had continued throughout this period without interruption. Heavy jamming of Western broadcasts in Polish, using jammers outside Poland, began during the political crisis in the winter of 1981–2.

The resumption of jamming in 1980 increased by about 25 per cent the number of frequency hours in the short-wave bands that were jammed. The jamming of Polish language broadcasts which began in December 1981 led to a further increase of about 10 per cent of the new total. The resulting nearly 40 per cent increase in the number of daily frequency hours being jammed broke through an important threshold. Whereas during 1975 about one-half of the frequencies in the four frequency bands from which listeners might wish to choose at a given time had been subject to jamming interference, by 1982 up to 80 per cent of these same frequency bands were being affected by jamming in the European area.

Studies by a number of organizations have demonstrated that jamming is confined neither to the European area nor to those broadcasts against which the jamming is principally aimed. Short-wave broadcast reception was found to be degraded by jamming in every populated continent. While the extent of the problem diminished with increasing distance from the jamming transmitters, it has become clear that jamming is not solely a 'European' or an East-versus-West problem but a world problem.

Appendix

Summary of the chronology/history of jamming

1918 First recorded use of jammer by the Germans to interfere with telegrams between Paris and Petrograd.

1920 Various jamming operations against the USSR, Radio Vatican and Germany.

1936 Italy jams Abyssinian and BBC Arabic broadcasts.

1936–9 Jammers used by both sides during Spanish Civil War.

1939–45 Germany, Italy and Japan use jamming extensively.
USSR jams broadcasts in Russian from Germany.
France jams broadcasts in French from Germany.

1946 USSR and Spain begin jamming one another.

1948 USSR begins jamming VOA.

1949 USSR begins jamming BBC.

1950–1 USSR and East Europeans begin jamming VOA and RFE broadcasts to Eastern Europe.

1953 USSR begins jamming Radio Liberty Russian broadcasts.

1956 China begins jamming VOA broadcasts in Chinese and English.
Britain jams Greek broadcasts to Cyprus.

1959 USSR stops some jamming during Khrushchev's visit to USA.

1960s France and Cuba use jamming.

1963 USSR stops jamming BBC and VOA in June.

1963 Romania stops jamming BBC, VOA and RFE in July.

1964 Hungary stops jamming BBC, VOA and RFE in February.
Czechoslovakia stops jamming BBC and VOA in April.

1968 USSR resumes large-scale jamming of most Western broadcasts in August, and of Kol Israel soon afterwards.

1973 USSR jamming of BBC, VOA and DW ceases in September.

1980 USSR jamming of BBC, VOA and DW resumes in August.

1981 Jamming of Polish broadcasts from transmitters in the USSR begins in December.

Major pauses in jamming

From June/July 1963 until August 1968.
From September 1973 until August 1980.
Jamming of Radio Liberty continued without interruption during these periods.

CHAPTER 15

Soviet Postal Restrictions*

VLADLEN PAVLENKOV

In 1979–82, due to a series of measures implemented by the authorities, very few things could be sent through the mail from the USSR to the rest of the world. Such articles as natural fabrics, leather or wooden souvenirs, became prohibited items (while televisions and radios, articles which were not needed in the West, were allowed). Limitations were placed on the sending of records and books, by the levying of export duties and the necessity of receiving special approval from the authorities; many books were completely excluded from mailing permission. When mailing any package abroad, the sender must present his passport, and he is limited to sending only one parcel per year. In addition, the package can only be sent from the postal agency closest to the place of residence.

In order to limit the parcels sent to their citizens as of 1 August 1984, the Soviet authorities have refused to accept duty pre-paid packages. This had been allowed since 1956, when agreements were made between the *Vneshposyltorg* agency and private Western companies located in various parts of the world. This action resulted in serious losses of convertible currencies by the USSR (as much as 10–15 million dollars according to our estimates; some estimates are two to three times higher), and demonstrated the importance that they place on limiting foreign contacts.

The USSR, however, has not had the effrontery to terminate completely direct mailing of parcels. This would violate agreements between governments, as opposed to those made with individual private companies. But steps have been taken by the authorities to limit such activities even more. In September 1983 the Soviet Union significantly increased customs duties for the recipients of international parcels. The fees for most articles were increased by two to three times, thereby becoming too excessive a financial burden for the receiver and forcing him to request that his friends and relatives stop sending these parcels. (For example, duty on new corduroy trousers — 50 roubles; sheepskin coat — 250 roubles; 1 kg of instant coffee — 15 roubles.)

In addition, the Soviet authorities have demonstrated an increasing tendency towards flagrant violations of postal regulations, such as theft of articles, or returning parcels to the sender without due cause. This is particularly directed at those individuals whom the authorities have designated as 'untrustworthy', i.e. dissidents, 'refuseniks', relatives of political prisoners, and so on. These are also the people who are the first to have their letters intercepted. But in the last two to three years, this tendency has affected the average citizen as well. Soviet postal violations were thoroughly analysed in the Freedom of Communications report *Postal Communications between the USA and the USSR and How to Improve Them*, which was included in the records of US Congressional Hearings of October 1983. Moreover, the number of Soviet violations has increased, particularly in 1984. About 60 per cent of some 180 respondents answered that delivery of mail to the USSR and back in comparison with the preceding two years had deteriorated.

Increased surveillance

Direct measures of intimidation are taken by Soviet officials against those who are maintaining postal contacts abroad and their supporters. Soviet citizens are often called to appear before the KGB, Party or other Soviet organizations, where they may be threatened with the loss of employment in their professional field, or a reduction in their wages, and even criminal prosecution. In 1984 additional amendments were included in the Soviet Criminal Code, allowing for measures designed to isolate Soviet citizens from foreigners inside the Soviet Union, and relating to contact with those living abroad.

Until recently, parcels from other countries could be picked up at various post offices within Moscow, Leningrad and other major cities (though not at all post offices, as in the West). But by spring

1984, only three post offices in Moscow continued to provide this service (some sources say that there is now only one location left: the Central International Post Office at 40 Warsaw Boulevard). Clearly, this was done for the purpose of keeping a closer tally on who is receiving parcels and in what volume; so that officials would know which individuals needed to be 'worked on'.

Having described the overall situation, it must be mentioned that in spite of increasing pressure from the authorities further to isolate the Soviet people from the West, there exists within the country a strong resistance to such attempts. Because much has changed in the country since the Stalinist era, forcing people to succumb to a state of fear-induced ignorance and loss of human dignity is not easy. Though they are denied an opportunity directly and democratically to improve their conditions of life, the best among them are resisting with persistence the re-introduction of Stalinist standards. Fighting for their right to maintain ties with relatives and friends abroad is an example of this resistance. Understandably, those who are capable of such resistance, whether in such areas as postal rights or other social causes, are not great in number; these individuals should be helped in every possible way.

Note
* This contribution has appeared in *Soviet Analyst* (London), vol. 14, no. 13. (26 June 1985).

CHAPTER 16

The Non-Russians in Defence of their National Rights

BOHDAN NAHAYLO

Although Mr Gorbachev's approach to the various domestic problems he inherited is still not entirely crystallized, it may be said with
a certain degree of confidence that he is unlikely to change course as
far as the crucial area of Soviet nationalities policy is concerned.
His predecessors, Brezhnev, Andropov and Chernenko, grasping
the long-term disruptive potential of centrifugal forces in what is
the world's largest multinational state, endorsed the intensification
of an unprecedented assimilatory programme of linguistic and
cultural engineering aimed at creating the new Soviet man in the
Soviet Russian image.

Gorbachev's patron, former KGB chief Yuri Andropov, formally
restored to the Soviet political agenda the highly charged Leninist
concept of 'fusing' (*sliyanie*) the many disparate nations of the
USSR into a Russian-speaking 'Soviet people'. In December 1982,
on the sixtieth anniversary of the formation of the USSR, Andropov, the then newly emerged Soviet leader, declared that the
ultimate goal of the Party's nationalities policy was not simply 'the
drawing together (*sblizhenie*) of the nations but their fusion'. In
May 1983 the Soviet leadership approved a whole range of
additional measures to increase and improve the already substantial
level of the teaching of Russian in the non-Russian republics.
Fluency in Russian was described as 'an objective necessity and
requirement of every citizen'.

The significance of these developments appears to have been
largely missed in the West. This is not altogether surprising given
the West's largely Russocentric perspective, which has not only
obscured the national tensions inherent in the Soviet system and the
nature of Moscow's policies towards its subject peoples, but has

also resulted in an incomplete understanding of the struggle for human rights in the USSR.

At the heart of the matter is the unequal relationship of the Russians, who constitute barely half of the USSR's population of some 270 million, to the numerous other peoples. Although the Soviet state is nominally based on a 'free and equal partnership' of the constituent nationalities, the majority Russian nation has always been dominant. Despite the federal structure, decision-making remains concentrated in Moscow and the Russian language and culture are predominant.

It is important to recall a number of historical details. On coming to power, the Bolsheviks reconquered the vast non-Russian areas which had broken away from Russia after the disintegration of the tsarist 'prison of nations' in 1917. But force alone was not enough to guarantee the cohesion of the fledgling Soviet state. Lenin realized the need to win the trust of the non-Russians and urged his colleagues to keep Russian chauvinism in check, respect local languages and cultures, and refrain from carrying out forcible Russification. In fact, for most of the Soviet period little more than lip service has been paid to his behest.

Under Stalin, the Russian nation was extolled as superior in every way, the Russian imperial past was rehabilitated and Russification of the national minorities was carried out. There was a respite in the mid-1950s when Khrushchev relaxed controls in the nationalities sphere and announced a return to Leninist principles. At the end of the decade, however, he changed course and inaugurated a new wave of Russification in the guise of promoting Russian as the 'common medium of intercourse and co-operation among the peoples of the USSR'.

The official euphemism for Khrushchev's assimilatory policy was 'fusion', a process Lenin had argued would not be completed until the distant future when communism had been achieved. The widespread resistance to this scheme — in 1965 in Ukraine the literary critic Ivan Dzyuba wrote a devastating Marxist critique of Moscow's nationalities policy, aptly entitled *Internationalism or Russification?* — brought reassurances from Khrushchev's successors that talk of 'fusion' was premature. Although the basic policy was left unchanged, during the Brezhnev era the term 'fusion' appeared for the most part only in specialized academic journals.

During the 1970s, because of demographic trends and the

growing national assertiveness of the non-Russians, the nationalities problem loomed as one of the most intractable and critical issues facing the Soviet leadership. The realization that the Russian share in the Soviet population was falling and that the non-Russians would soon constitute a majority raised considerable psychological and political anxieties. Moreover, urgent practical problems connected with the role of the Russian language had to be faced.

At present, around 40 per cent of the non-Russians have little or no knowledge of Russian.[1] Many of them belong to the Turkic nationalities of the traditionally Muslim regions of Central Asia and the Caucasus. Soviet demographers foresee that by the turn of the century, between one in four and one in five Soviet citizens will have a Muslim background. All this has serious ramifications for the Soviet economy and military. There is a chronic shortage of manpower in the European parts of the USSR and Siberia, while Central Asia has a rapidly growing labour surplus. The problem is compounded by the extreme reluctance of the Central Asians to leave their homelands and migrate north in search of employment. At the same time, Soviet military planners are confronted with the unsettling prospect that within a relatively short period approximately one in three draft-eligible young men will come from a Muslim people. Already the Soviet armed forces are having to integrate large numbers of mostly non-Russian speaking Central Asian conscripts into ethnically mixed units.

During Brezhnev's final years, in a race against time, the Soviet leaders embarked on a highly ambitious scheme to accelerate the integration and homogenization of the non-Russians. Camouflaged in internationalist rhetoric, its goal was to create a new Soviet citizen in the Russian image. Where possible, the national identities of the national minorities were weakened. In the case of the seemingly unassimilable Central Asians, Georgians and Armenians, the objective was to ensure that they become proficient in Russian and remained docile.

The main feature of this strategy has been the prescription of the language, culture and history of the 'leading' Russian nation as the basis of a new historical community — 'the Soviet people' — which the Soviet leadership insists has been forged from more than a hundred nationalities. The Ukrainians and Byelorussians, who as Slavs are linguistically closest to the Russians, and who make up a crucial 20 per cent of the Soviet population, are intended to form part of the Slavic core of this entity. With their assimilation the preponderance of a 200-million strong 'Russian' bloc in the USSR would be assured.

The displacement of local languages by Russian has been a key element in this campaign. In practice, as protesters have frequently pointed out, no attempt has been made to achieve genuine bilingualism. Russian is presented as the language of learning, culture, science and progress, while others — living languages spoken by the vast majority of the populations — are treated as provincial and increasingly superfluous. The 25 million Russians living in the USSR but outside of Russia proper, moreover, have not been pressured to learn non-Russian languages.

In 1978 major legislation was introduced to expand and intensify Russian language study at all levels of education in the non-Russian republics. For the first time the compulsory teaching of Russian was extended to kindergartens and nurseries. The highly sensitive nature of the 1978–9 measures was indicated by the fact that the Soviet authorities have still not published the text of the legislation. Nevertheless, details have become known from secret official documents smuggled out of Lithuania and Estonia.

It is important to bear in mind that Russification is seen by the non-Russian nationalities not simply as a problem of language but as the thin end of the assimilatory wedge. In addition to the pressures on the national languages, restrictions are placed in practice on the cultural development of the non-Russian people. The supposed flourishing of the cultures of the non-Russians is, in fact, controlled by the application of the formula 'national in form, socialist in content'. There is also the serious problem of the distorting and falsification of the histories of the non-Russians. In essence, these are presented in terms of the farcical formula of the 'longing' of the given non-Russian people for union with Russia (or the USSR, as the case may be). Only after the 'union' took place can the given nation be said to have enjoyed its finest hour. Even conquest by tsarist Russia has been presented as a 'progressive' feature.

What occurred in the Ukraine in the early 1970s is illuminative. In 1972–3 Moscow intervened directly to put an end to a vigorous revival of Ukrainian cultural and social life and carried out the most extreme purge of its type in the post-Stalin period. Scores of nationally minded people were imprisoned, ostensibly for 'anti-Soviet agitation and propaganda'. Even the Party chief in the republic, Petro Shelest, was removed and later publicly denounced for laxity on the national question.

In a detailed analysis of the consequences for the Ukraine — one of the most important *samizdat* documents dealing with Soviet nationalities policy — the Ukrainian philologist and dissenter Yuri Badzyo characterized the national predicament of the Ukrainians as a 'state of siege'. He concluded his work, *The Right to Live*, as follows:

The official ideology of the 'internationalization', 'rapprochement' and fusion of nations, and the historiographic concept of the history of Ukraine, leave the Ukrainian people virtually no room for free movement, either forward or backward. They block our access to the future and to the past. And those who have actually created this predicament beat over the head anyone who rises above the level of planned national extinction, anyone who tries to tell the truth about the reality of the Ukrainian nation or — God forbid! — tries to evaluate the overall picture on an all-national historical scale according to political criteria.

Badzyo paid the price for speaking out. In 1979 he was arrested, convicted of 'anti-Soviet agitation and propaganda' and given a twelve-year sentence of imprisonment and internal exile.

Not surprisingly, there have been numerous and widespread protests in recent years against the new wave of Russification. Lithuanian dissidents have described it as 'denationalization with an iron fist', while their Ukrainian counterparts have coined the term 'ethnocide'. In Georgia, Estonia and Lithuania mass demonstrations have taken place. Underground journals and leaflets have condemned 'Russian chauvinism' and called for the 'decolonization' of the 'Soviet Russian empire'. The regime has responded by sentencing scores of critics of its nationalities policy for up to fifteen years, ostensibly for 'anti-Soviet agitation and propaganda'.

If the non-Russian, dissident human and national rights campaigners have been the most forthright in attacking Moscow's nationalities policy, representatives of the national élites of the non-Russian republics have also voiced their serious concern. In 1980, 365 Georgian and 40 Estonian leading intellectuals signed open letters addressed to the authorities. The Estonians made the following proposal:

Every Estonian within the boundaries of the Estonian SSR possesses the self-evident right to an Estonian-language secondary and higher education and to use Estonian in spoken or written form in the conduct of business. We think that a legislative confirmation of this principle by the Supreme Court of the Estonian SSR would go a long way towards normalizing the present unhealthy situation.

The protestors concluded by stating that they wanted Estonia 'to become and remain a land where not a single person will suffer insults because of his or her mother tongue or ethnic origin'.

In Armenia, the thorny issue of Russification was raised at a congress of the Writers' Union. In Byelorussia, a leading scholar implicitly challenged the entire nature of Soviet nationalities policy on the pages of the press, arguing that 'nations are forever'. Numerous other examples of this type of resistance on the part of non-Russians can be found.

Despite this opposition, the Soviet authorities have continued with the same policies. One insubstantial gesture alone was made to reduce the sensitivities of the national minorities. In his speech in December 1982, Andropov included an ambiguous warning about national arrogance and disrespect for other nations. Warnings were also issued soon afterwards to writers not to become carried away with Russian nationalist themes and — for the first time in a decade — a number of dissident Russian nationalists were imprisoned for overstepping the mark. On the other hand, apart from signalling the intensification of the existing course of nationalities policy, Andropov launched fresh campaigns against non-Russian nationalism in several republics.

The latest 'additional measures' to promote the knowledge of Russian represent an unparalleled all-out drive designated to boost the strong assimilatory pressures which the non-Russians have had to face for most of the Soviet period. A classified document of the Ministry of Education of the Ukrainian SSR dated 29 June 1983, which reached the West through unofficial channels, revealed that, among other things, teachers of Russian were to be given preferential treatment. Their pay scales were to be raised by 16 per cent, and financial assistance to trainee teachers specializing in Russian language and literature increased.

More recently, there has been a significant development which may indicate what lies ahead. On 26 February 1984 the newspaper *Sovetskaya Estonya* published a remarkable article by the ethnographer M. Guboglo. Guboglo argued for a further diminution of the role of the non-Russian languages. In view of the fact that educated people are supposed to know Russian, why, he asked, did so much inferior literature continue to be published in the national languages, why were Russian films dubbed into the national languages, and so on. The publication of such a statement in a republic where the language issue has been particularly acute must surely have had the backing of very senior officials.

To complete the general picture of current Soviet nationalities policy, it is necessary to mention several other important aspects. First, alongside this Russificatory drive, an officially promoted anti-semitic campaign, poorly disguised as anti-Zionism, was evident during 1984–5. With the virtual termination of Jewish emigration from the USSR and the harassment and imprisonment of unofficial Jewish cultural activists, this propaganda offensive was indicative of probably the most difficult period Soviet Jewry has had to face since the last years of the Stalin era.

Secondly, the situation of several entire peoples forcibly deported by Stalin remains as tragic as ever. In the treatment of the Crimean Tatars, for instance, a discriminatory and, at times, racist, policy is blatant. Crimean Tatars seeking to return to their historic home-land are forcibly expelled from the region and their homes demolished. Campaigners for the rights of the Crimean Tatar people continue to be imprisoned.

Thirdly, I should also mention the plight of the Ukrainian Catholics, the largest banned denomination in the USSR. There has been a marked resurgence in their activities in the 1980s but, forty years after their Church was officially 'liquidated' by Stalin, they remain a 'catacomb church'.

I hope that this overview of recent Soviet nationalities policy makes it more understandable why for non-Russian human rights campaigners, the notion of human rights is inseparable from that of national rights.

Note
[1] Derived from Ann Sheehy, 'Language Affiliation Data from the Census of 1979', Radio Liberty Research 130/80, 2 April 1980.

CHAPTER 17

The Ukrainian Helsinki Group

NINA STROKATA

In 1975, on the first day of the Conference on Security and Cooperation in Europe, political prisoners in Perm labour camp no. 36 held a one-day hunger strike. Their objective was to express doubt as to whether the USSR would fulfil what have since become known as the Helsinki accords and, at the same time, to attempt to attract world attention to their pessimistic prediction. The prisoners included a number of individuals who were later to become members of the Ukrainian Movement to Further Observance of the Helsinki Accords, most notably Vitaliy Kalynychenko.

The Ukrainian journalist Vyacheslav Chornovil wrote at that time to US President Gerald Ford from a labour camp in Mordovia. Chornovil, who also was later to join the Ukrainian Helsinki Group, noted in his letter that the Soviet leaders had linked détente directly with the suppression of dissent in the USSR.

The subsequent persecution of the members of the Ukrainian Helsinki Group demonstrates that these human rights activists were accurate in their assessment.

The Ukrainian Helsinki Group was prevented by police surveillance from meeting with all its members present even once. Those who attempted to gather in the home in Kiev of the Group's leader were set upon by 'hooligans', and the police refused to investigate.

In the Group's first year of existence four of its ten charter members were sentenced. Nevertheless, new members, including prisoners in labour camps, joined. With the intention of nipping their hopes in the bud, the authorities resorted to well-tried repressive measures. By the end of 1979 six members of the Group found themselves in the West. But with the exception of these six — plus Leonid Plyushch — no Ukrainian dissident was permitted to leave. Lev Lukyanenko and Ivan Kandyba, for instance, were later sentenced to fresh terms of imprisonment.

Punitive medicine was also used. Oksana Meshko and the two Sichkos (father and son) were threatened with incarceration in a psychiatric hospital. Anna Mykhailenko, who had not joined the Group formally but was a sympathizer, has been imprisoned in a psychiatric hospital since 1980. Nor has the authorities' use of punitive medicine been limited to the abuse of psychiatry: restrictions imposed by the authorities on medical care led to the death of Oleksiy Tykhy in a labour camp.

The deaths of Mykhaylo Melnyk, who was still free, and of Yuriy Lytvyn in a camp are the result of the criminal aggressiveness of the Soviet authorities towards all who hoped to persuade them to implement the Helsinki accords.

The main instrument used by the authorities against the dissidents in the Ukraine between 1977 and 1980 was character assassination: baseless allegations, such as hooliganism, resistance to the police, attempted rape and possession of drugs were made. One-third of the Group's members who were sentenced were accused of crimes of this type. Some, such as Yaroslav Lesiv and Vasyl Sichko, have twice been accused of such offences.

Using criminal charges in this manner gives the authorities a further advantage — they can put the dissident in a camp for common criminals. In these camps it is a simple matter to recruit 'witnesses' for the purpose of levelling new charges, whether 'criminal' or political. According to Soviet law, the levelling of a new political charge provides an opportunity for a sentence of fifteen years. This ploy was used in the cases of Vasyl Ovsiyenko and the late Yuriy Lytvyn, and it will be used in the case of Mykola Horbal.[1] [Vasyl Stus, who was tortured while the indictment was being drawn up, died in a special regime labour camp on 4 September 1985.]

Let us also remember those who publicly recant. They do so only under circumstances which are unique and they too should be regarded as victims of repression. Their number includes one of the founding members of the Ukrainian Helsinki Group.

There is also the case of Bohdan Rebryk, who joined the Group when he was still a prisoner. After he had served out his sentence he was not permitted to live in the Ukraine and was compelled to return to his place of exile.

The Initiative Group for the Defence of the Rights of Believers and the Church, which was founded in the Ukraine in 1982, not long ago came to a decision to join the Helsinki movement. This is an outstanding event in the struggle of the Ukrainians to observe the Helsinki accords. I would, however, like to draw attention to the fact that the group's leader, Vasyl Kobrin, was arrested at the end of 1984. In March 1985 he was sentenced to three years' imprisonment in a general regime camp. Also, Iosyf Terelya, a founding member of the Initiative Group for the Defence of the Rights of Believers and the Church, was arrested in February 1985. [In August 1985 he was sentenced to seven years' strict regime in a camp and five years' exile.] Nadia Sylenko, who had come into contact with some of the members of the Ukrainian Helsinki Group, was arrested in early 1984.

My perception of the global campaign of corruption waged by Moscow and of the ineffectiveness of the Belgrade and Madrid CSCE review meetings causes me to doubt the utility of pursuing the Helsinki process. But it is for the sake of those who have fallen victim precisely because they supported this process that I believe it must continue, and it is my fervent wish that the freedom-loving participants in the Helsinki process find in themselves the force to resist. I appreciate that the tactics and the traditions of diplomats and dissidents do not necessarily coincide; yet can any of us have confidence in international security if we do not find a way to protect those who have suffered for having put their faith in international agreements?

Note

[1] Horbal (a poet, as was Stus) was indeed resentenced in this way on 10 April 1985, when he was given an extra eight years' imprisonment in special regime labour camp plus three years' internal exile.

CHAPTER 18

The Baltic States

MARITE SAPIETS

The basic concern of the movement for human rights in Estonia, Latvia and Lithuania over the last ten years remains the forcible incorporation of these countries into the USSR in 1940. The groups which have emerged in all three countries calling on the Soviet government to grant national, human and religious rights — as well as a few short-lived, all-Baltic associations — have met an unyielding response. In recent years, repression has increased and longer sentences have been more frequent for human rights activity.

The strongest and most active national human rights movement is in Lithuania. One reason for this is the almost inseparable link between national feeling and the Catholic Church, a situation somewhat similar to that in Poland.

The Lithuanian Helsinki Monitoring Group (founded in 1976) and the Catholic Committee for the Defence of Believers' Rights (1978) have engaged in almost parallel activity. The Helsinki Group consisted largely of Catholic believers and one of its members was always a priest. It has concentrated more on questions of national independence, psychiatric abuse and persecution of dissidents in the Baltic states and among national minorities in the USSR as a whole, also protesting against the exile of Andrei Sakharov to Gorky. However, many of its documents, like those of the Catholic Committee, were concerned with state discrimination against religious believers in Lithuania and interference in Church affairs, for example, the exile of two bishops.

The Soviet authorities acted far more swiftly against the Lithuanian Helsinki Group than against the Catholic Committee. Viktoras Petkus, who had already served sixteen years in camps, was arrested in 1977 and sentenced to three years in prison, seven years in camps and seven years in exile. Tomas Venclova and Eytan Finkelshteyn were given permission to emigrate. Following the death of Fr. Garuckas his successor, Fr. Laurinavičius, met with a road accident in 1981 in suspicious circumstances. Of those who later joined the Helsinki Group, three — Jurevičius, Skuodis and Vaičiunas — were imprisoned in 1980–1, Statkevičius was sent to a psychiatric hospital, while Balys Gajauskas (who joined in 1978) was already a long-term political prisoner serving a fifteen-year sentence. With the death of Ona Lukauskaite-Poškiene in 1983, the activity of the Lithuanian Helsinki Group effectively came to an end.

The Catholic Committee lasted longer as an organization because it consisted of priests. The Soviet authorities seem to have been unwilling, during the period from 1973 to 1982, to imprison Catholic priests, though a large number of active lay Catholics were imprisoned throughout the 1970s and 1980s for their association with the Committee and with Catholic unofficial journals. The reason for this comparative restraint lay in the considerable public support the Catholic Committee had, both among the laity and the clergy. The Catholic Committee's criticism of the Law on Religious Associations as unworkable and contrary to the Constitutional guarantee of religious freedom and separation of Church from state, was supported by 522 out of 711 Lithuanian priests — a situation without parallel in any other denomination or Soviet republic. The willingness of Lithuanian Catholics to sign petitions on religious matters — over 148,000 signed a petition asking for the return of a confiscated church in Klaipeda — was also unparalleled. The Catholic hierarchy did not cooperate with the state, refusing to condemn the Catholic Committee. Lithuanian *samizdat* journals, which combined national and religious feeling to a great extent, had a significant following, especially the *Chronicle of the Lithuanian Catholic Church* (now in its sixty-fifth issue) which printed all the Catholic Committee documents. The authorities also had the problem of unofficial Church institutions, which existed beside the officially recognized ones — the 'secret seminary' and the diocesan priests' councils established in 1980. The 'secret seminary' was recognized by the hierarchy and its ordained graduates were accepted by parishes, despite the fact that they had no state registration. The priests' councils were elected and included members of the Catholic Committee.

In 1982 the Soviet authorities yielded to the appeals of the Catholic Committee on one point — Bishop Sladkevičius was allowed to return from exile to the diocese of Kaišiadorys. This was, however, the point at which a clampdown began on the Catholic Committee itself and other unofficial groups. Two members of the Committee, Fr. Alfonsas Svarinskas and Fr. Sigitas Tamkevičius, were arrested and given sentences totalling fifteen years each (1982–3). Two other members were forced by police pressure to resign. Although the Committee had increased slightly in number, the members decided it would be better for the organization to become anonymous and go underground. The KGB continues to harass the former members, however. A campaign has also started against the priests trained in the unofficial seminary — Fr. Jonas Matulionis was sentenced to three years in camps in 1985 for 'impersonating a priest'. According to the Council for Religious Affairs in Lithuania, such priests are to be considered 'vagrants'.

There has been a firm refusal on the part of the Soviet authorities to yield to large-scale petitions — there has been no positive reaction in the case of the Klaipeda church and, when a petition with 123,000 signatures calling for the release of Frs Svarinskas and Tamkevičius was delivered to the Procurator General in Moscow, his reaction was to tell those who brought it: 'Fr. Svarinskas is an enemy, so are you and all believers.'

It seems clear that the authorities' next move will be against the priests' councils, as they are the only independent organizations left untouched in Lithuania.

The situation in Estonia and Latvia is quite different and it has been far easier for the authorities to repress dissent where it appears. A far smaller proportion of the population is Estonian (64 per cent) or Latvian (53 per cent) as opposed to the growing numbers of Russian immigrants. Neither country has a strongly unifying factor comparable to the Catholic Church in Lithuania. The only unifying factors among the national human rights activists have been their language and culture. Among the population in general there is less willingness to become openly involved with dissent — many protest letters and petitions in these two republics are anonymous — and less *samizdat* circulates (though it certainly exists).

Variously entitled organizations appear from time to time and issue *samizdat* letters or petitions, but they are less substantial and their membership less clear than the Lithuanian groups, undoubtedly because the reaction of the authorities is well known. In Estonia appeals and open letters have been issued by the Estonian Democratic Front and the Estonian National Front (1978), by eighteen scientists (1978) and forty intellectuals (1980), and by an Estonian peace group (1983); in Latvia documents have been issued by the Latvian Independence Movement, the Latvian Democratic Youth Committee (1975–6), by seventeen Latvian sportsmen condemning the Moscow Olympic Games (1980), and, of course, by individuals in both countries. Social democratic groups are known to exist and occasionally individuals are tried for belonging to or 'organizing' them — as is the case of the Latvian, Juris Bumeisteris (sentenced to fifteen years for 'treason' in 1981) and the Estonian, Veljo Kalep (sentenced to four years' imprisonment in 1981). The issues important to the Estonian and Latvian human rights activists are above all national — the right of their nations to self-determination, and calls for free elections under the auspices of the UN and for an end to forcible Russification and increasing militarization in the Baltic states. In almost all documents these issues are linked with the implementation of human rights as cited in the republics' constitutions, the Universal Declaration of Human Rights and the Helsinki Final Act. There is, however, some distrust expressed of the provisions of the Helsinki agreement, as being merely paper promises if they are not backed up by the Western countries involved. Western naiveté is mentioned more than once.

Members of the Estonian Democratic Front, such as Mäti Kiirend, Kalju Mättik and Sergei Soldatov, and of the Latvian Democratic Youth Committee, such as Janis Veveris, have received sentences of from three to six years. Some individuals, for example Jurgis Skulme and Zanis Skudra, have been sentenced almost arbitrarily (to two-and-a-half years and fifteen years respectively) for writing a letter to UNESCO giving information about a strike in Riga or photographing ruined churches.

However, the activity most disliked — and suitably punished — by the Soviet authorities is that of all-Baltic committees or associations. Viktoras Petkus's long sentence was partly due to his attempts to set up an Estonian–Latvian–Lithuanian committee which would co-operate on national issues. The requests put forward by recent open letters signed by Balts from all three countries — forty-five in 1979, twenty-one in 1980 and thirty-eight in 1981 — were particularly unpalatable to the Soviet authorities. A 1979 'memorandum' called for a public declaration by the Soviet government that the Molotov–Ribbentrop pact was now void, thus allowing the Baltic states self-determination by withdrawing their troops; a 1980 letter condemned the Soviet invasion of Afghanistan comparing it with that of the Baltic states; the last letter called for the establishment of a nuclear-free zone in the Baltic area. The organizer of the 1979 letter was said to be Mart Niklus, one of the signatories, now serving a sentence of ten years in camps and five years' exile despite his ill-health (he has radiculitis). His 'crime' was seen as especially grave on account of his co-operation with Lithuanian dissidents. Jüri Kukk, another Estonian, who signed the 1980 letter and wrote another condemning the Olympic events in Tallinn, was given a two-year sentence but he succumbed to camp conditions and died in Vologda in 1981. The 1981 letter, which was supported by Sakharov and other Russian dissidents, together with the Estonian peace group's declaration in 1983, has led to a large number of searches, detentions and arrests in the last few years. Four Estonians were sentenced — one (Enn Tarto) to fifteen years — in 1983–4, as well as four Latvians — Ints Calitis, Lidija Doronina, Janis Rožkalns and Janis Veveris. Some of them had not signed the documents in question but were connected with the unofficial Baptist Church or with unofficial peace groups.

Human rights activism in the Baltic states reached its highest point in the late 1970s; it was influenced by the Helsinki Final Act to a greater or lesser degree. How far the Final Act influenced the Soviet authorities in this domain is debatable. Certainly by the 1980s its impact in the official sphere was minimal. At the present time, *samizdat* documents contain occasional invocations of the humanitarian provisions of the Final Act as well as criticism of the West for its feebleness and gullibility.

CHAPTER 19

Soviet Persecution of the Crimean Tatars

AISHE SEITMURATOVA

Following the barbarous expulsion of the Crimean Tatars from the Crimea in 1944, the Soviet government adopted a number of legislative acts designed to liquidate the Crimean Tatars as a people. Even such a formality as a residence permit was used by the government against the Crimean Tatars: on 26 April 1978 the Ministry of Internal Affairs of the Uzbek SSR issued instruction no. 221 which said *inter alia*, that 'Tatars who formerly lived in the Crimea are forbidden to leave Uzbekistan . . .' On 15 August 1978 the Council of Ministers of the USSR issued a decision 'On strengthening the passport regime in the Crimean *oblast*'. Although the decree makes no reference to the Crimean Tatars, its application has clearly shown that it is directed against them.

In the winter of 1978–9 the authorities expelled a large number of Crimean Tatar families from the Crimea. In February 1979 Academician Sakharov, protesting against this illegal act, appealed to members of the Presidium of the USSR Supreme Soviet, calling upon 'the highest organs of power in the country to intervene and . . . rectify not only those lawless acts already committed but also the historic injustice perpetrated by the Stalinist administration thirty-five years ago against an entire people'.

Decision no. 700 of the USSR Council of Ministers of 15 August 1978 describes this action as a 'temporary measure'. However, it continues to operate even to this day. In the Crimea there are at the present time hundreds of Crimean Tatar families who have not been permitted to live in their own homes for over ten years. For example, Adzhimelek Mustafaev and his daughter and grandson have not been registered to live in their own homes for fifteen years now. During this time Mustafaev and his daughter have experienced the full weight of repressive measures — arrests, trials, confiscation of property, physical violence, and so forth.

A similar fate befell the family of Fakhri Meschanov. Meschanov and his family went to the Crimea in October, 1976, but to this day they have not received permission to live in their own home. On three occasions he and his family have been expelled from the Crimea and their property stolen.

In September 1984 the family of Nariman Asanov, including five children, were expelled from the village of Dobroe in the Simferopol *rayon* of the Crimea. One member of the family suffered a broken arm at the time of the expulsion. Asanov's home was confiscated.

I could give hundreds more examples. Suffice it to say that over 700 unregistered Crimean Tatar families were living in the Crimea in 1978–9.

I shall use only one document to demonstrate the persecution of the Crimean Tatars on the basis of nationality. This document is a decision of the Crimean *oblast* court of 3 June 1976 concerning Musa Mamut and his wife Zekie Abdullaeva. The judgement states that 'Musa Mamut and Zekie Abdullaeva were found guilty and convicted in that in April 1975 they came from Tashkent *oblast* to the village of Donskoe, Crimea *oblast*, and there concluded a deal regarding the purchase of house no. 136 Komsomolskaya Street . . .' Having served two years of imprisonment, Musa Mamut returned once more to the Crimea. When on 23 June 1978 he was again arrested, Musa Mamut burned himself to death in protest.

Musa Mamut's tragedy is the tragedy of our whole people. The Crimean Tatars stated in their 'Declaration 1984' to the Politburo: 'The tragic situation of our people is the direct consequence of the existence of discriminatory legal acts . . . We regard it as essential that all anti-constitutional legal acts concerning our people be abolished. This is the sole means of liquidating the consequences of the cult of personality and restoring to it full national rights in its historic homeland in the Crimea.'

However, the Soviet government and Party are continuing to ignore the demands of the Crimean Tatar people and to conduct a policy of forcible settlement in our place of exile in Uzbekistan. The authorities in Uzbekistan have been given the task of settling the Karshi steppes with Crimean Tatars. Even unregistered families of Crimean Tatars from the Crimea are being forcibly transferred to the Karshi steppes in Uzbekistan.

In 1983 the editor of the newspaper *Lenin Bairagy* (the organ of the Central Committee of the Communist Party of Uzbekistan which appears in the language of the Crimean Tatars) received a new censorship instruction from the authorities — from then on the paper was forbidden to use previous Crimean Tatar designations for cities in the Crimea as well as the terms 'Crimean ASSR' and 'Crimean Radio Committee'.

Such measures are intended to liquidate the Crimean Tatars as a people as soon as possible. It is for the same purpose that repressive measures against activists of the national movement of the Crimean Tatars have been intensified. In 1982 Yura Osmanov and Nurfet Murakhas were arrested for a second time, while Mustafa Dzhemilev was arrested for the sixth time.

On 29 December 1975 the USSR Council of Ministers issued a new decree, no. 1067, 'On the Procedure for Awarding Scholarly Degrees and Scholarly Titles'. The Academy of Sciences of the Uzbek SSR cited this decree when depriving me of the right to defend my candidate's dissertation in history.

All changes in Soviet legislation between 1975 and 1985 relating to the Helsinki Final Act have been effected with the sole purpose of violating individual rights and religious and national rights.

CHAPTER 20

Rising Mortality in the USSR

ALLAN WYNN

The crude death rate (i.e. from all causes) in the USSR has risen progressively since 1966. In order to conceal this embarrassing development the USSR ceased in 1972 to publish its mortality data and to provide the World Health Organization with them. All other developed countries make these data public.

However, by using isolated and disparate Soviet sources — e.g. reports by special commissions, scientific journals, information provided by health authorities and the press — it is possible to formulate data with a high, but not certain, probability of accuracy concerning the crude and specific death rates since 1972.

The data reproduced in the following tables show that the life expectation of men in the USSR fell from about 66 years in 1966, when it peaked, to about 62 years in 1983. This figure compares with 71 years for men in the USA and a slightly lower figure for most of Western Europe. However, more important than the absolute level of life expectation is the greatly different trend of mortality. In the USA life expectation for men and women is rising steadily. In most of Western Europe it is also rising or remaining steady. The USSR and the other countries of Eastern Europe are alone in Europe in showing a consistent decline in life expectation, particularly in men; the same trend is present for women but it is not marked. The average life expectation for women in the USSR in 1983 was estimated to be 73.9 years compared with 78.7 years in the USA.

The causes of these mortality changes are complex and are not fully known. Judging from their published reports, the Soviet medical authorities place the blame on heavy and rising tobacco and alcohol consumption as well as inadequate diet, accidents and

TABLE 1
Crude Death Rate per 1,000 of Soviet Population, both Sexes

Republic	1960	1982
RSFSR	7.1	10.1
Ukraine	6.9	11.3
Byelorussia	6.6	9.6
Estonia	10.5	11.9
Georgia	6.5	8.4
Armenia	6.8	5.5

TABLE 2
Death Rate by Age and Sex per 1,000 of Soviet Population

Age Group	Male		Female	
	1964–5	*1973–4*	*1964–5*	*1973–4*
40–44	5.7	7.4	2.5	
45–49	7.5	9.7	3.5	3.7
50–54	11.9	13.9	5.4	5.8
55–59	16.5	19.5	7.4	8.2
60–64	26.2	28.7	12.6	12.6

TABLE 3
Age-Adjusted Death Rate from Coronary Heart Disease per 100,000 of Population in Selected European Countries among Men Aged 35-74, 1969–77

Country	Year		% of Change
	1969	*1977*	
Eastern Europe[a]			
Bulgaria	299.3	423.5	+ 41.5
Czechoslovakia	587.9	590.4[b]	+ 0.4
Hungary	441.6	499.2	+ 13.0
Poland	186.5	307.7	+ 65.0
Romania	170.5	237.3	+ 39.2
USSR	376.7	529.2	+ 40.6
Western Europe			
Austria	428.3	455.3	+ 6.3
England and Wales	662.1	671.7	+ 1.4
Finland	893.7	878.0	− 1.8
German Federal Republic	427.3	548.1	+ 7.2
Italy	313.0	309.6	− 1.1
Switzerland	290.4	312.7	+ 7.7
Yugoslavia	185.0	227.6	+ 23.0

[a] *data from East Germany are not available.*
[b] *1975 data.*

TABLE 4
Death Rate from Hypertension (High Blood Pressure) in USSR with Associated Cerebral Vascular Disease, per 100,000 of Population

Year	1960	1965	1966	1967	1968	1969	1970	1971	1972	1973
Death Rate	24.7	38.1	43.7	49.5	50.8	53.2	51.9	N/A	N/A	51.2

	1974	1975	1976	1977	1978	1979	1980	1981	1982
	50.7	53.1	54.4	54.0	55.7	56.6	56.7	56.1	55.1

work-related and other stress. They are probably correct. They do not mention medical care.

Heart disease mortality has risen strikingly in the USSR, especially in its European republics. In the USA it has fallen in the period of this review by 25 per cent. It is stationary or falling in most of Western Europe. Very striking is the increased mortality in the USSR from cerebral arterial disease ('strokes' associated with high blood pressure). This is in marked contrast to the experience of advanced industrialized countries, where there has been a considerable decrease in this cause of death. The Soviet experience almost certainly reflects inadequate medical care. A joint Soviet–American study has shown that in European Russia more than 30 per cent of the male population have high blood pressure compared with 11 per cent in a comparable population sample in the USA, and that the proportion receiving adequate medical care in the USSR is below 10 per cent, far fewer than in the USA.

The relation of these data to human rights issues is indirect. The standard Soviet response to alleged violations of human rights in the USSR and the socialist countries is that their peoples have surrendered individual rights for collective economic and social rights — the right to work, housing, education, medical care, etc. This argument cannot, in my view, be sustained: human rights are indivisible. The data concerning mortality in the USSR suggest that if indeed a bargain has been made, it is a very poor one.

1 M. Feshbach, 'Soviet Union: Population Trends and Dilemmas', *Population Bulletin*, vol. 37, no.3 (1982).
2 David E. Powell, 'The Emerging Health Crisis in the USSR', *Current History*, vol. 84 (1985), p. 325.

CHAPTER 21

The Control of Scientific Activity in the USSR

FRANTIŠEK JANOUCH

The Academy of Sciences plays a highly important role in Soviet society. It comprises a network of hundreds of institutes and laboratories employing tens of thousands of scientists using the most modern equipment to be found in the USSR.

The Academy enjoys a relatively high degree of autonomy owing to the fact that its role is essential to the Soviet authorities for the military, space and nuclear programmes, the development of modern computer technology, and the chemical and biological industries. Without progress in all these and related fields, the USSR cannot maintain superpower status.

In 1975, in connection with the two hundred and fiftieth anniversary of the founding of the Academy (publication of the book was delayed), there appeared a volume containing the full texts of the Academy's Statutes since its establishment.[1] A comparison of the Statutes for 1927, 1930, 1935, 1959, 1963 and 1977 reveals a consistent tendency on the part of the Soviet authorities to restrict the autonomy of the Academy.

The rights accorded the Academy by the 1927 Statute were indeed remarkable. The elections to the Academy were announced publicly and the lists of candidates had to be published in the central press. The election itself was conducted by secret ballot of the Academy's General Assembly. All sessions of the Academy were open. Only full members of the Academy were eligible to vote for the offices of president, vice-president and permanent secretary. The Academy also had the right to issue its publications without censorship, to receive foreign publications without restriction, and to purchase equipment and literature abroad duty-free.

The 1930 and 1935 Statutes contained only minor changes. But the Statute of 1959 included dramatic changes. The section on the Academy's special rights was now no more than a parody of the original. The Academy retained the right only to maintain its own archives and to exchange its publications with institutions in the USSR and abroad as well as with 'friendship' organizations. The rights to publish without censorship, to obtain or send publications abroad, and to make duty-free purchases abroad were abolished.

The 1963 Statute omitted a very important individual right of Academy members, that outlined in para. 30 of the 1959 Statute, to receive financial support for their own research. This right was important because it had enabled members to maintain their own laboratory or group in the Academy.

The Academy still retained one element of its autonomy — the secret ballot. This procedure made it more difficult for the Soviet authorities to ensure that people elected to the Academy's highest offices were sufficiently pliable. However, the 1977 Statute severely curtailed the publicity around the election, the aim being to ensure that the Academy would accept people of lower reputation and ability.

In another important change, the Academy's secretary could now be elected not only by full members but also by corresponding members. As it is now relatively simple to become a corresponding member, this change will no doubt result in the future in the election of a less independently minded individual.

It is of the greatest importance for scientists to receive scientific information. The major channel through which scientific information is provided is the scientific journals. In the 1950s and 1960s it was a fairly easy matter to obtain scientific journals in the USSR. The USSR was not a member of a copyright agreement and was thus not bound by any of the requirements of such an agreement. From the late 1950s onwards, the USSR was reproducing virtually all the important Western journals and distributing them throughout the country. Although these reprints were subject to strict censorship and came out with a delay of several months, the journals were easily available.

With Moscow's accession to the Universal Copyright Convention in 1973, the reprinting of Western scientific journals ceased. But a combination of the high subscription charges for these journals and the shortage of hard currency in the USSR led to a situation in which scientists in the smaller laboratories and provincial universities no longer had access to much scientific information. While this phenomenon may not be censorship in the usual meaning of the word, its consequences are very similar.

There can be no doubt that, in the scientific sphere, the USSR has been developing into an increasingly closed society.

Note
[1] *Ustavy Akademic nauk SSSR* (Statutes of the Academy of Sciences of the USSR) (Moscow, 1975).

CHAPTER 22

The Abuse of Psychiatry in the USSR

VICTOR DAVIDOV

We have all heard of the abuse of psychiatry in the USSR; it is a practice which began under Stalin. Before I was arrested, I too had heard of it. But when I entered a special psychiatric hospital in Kazan, I saw that everything I had ever heard about punitive psychiatry and about the conditions in the special psychiatric hospitals was not true — the truth was infinitely worse.

In my first days in the hospital I suffered a gigantic shock — a shock which destroyed any ideas I had ever had about humanity, justice, goodness and man's noble destiny. I watched sane people go insane and become mute animals. This was not an observation by an outsider but my own personal experience.

On the first day I entered the special psychiatric hospital I was given two injections for refusing to have my hair cut and my beard shaved off. These injections contained very small doses but for almost three days and nights I was in a state of total stupefaction, half-asleep, half-awake, completely unable to control my bodily functions, suffering physically. Then they gave me tablets, but at first there was no effect. I felt nothing. But soon, after perhaps a few minutes or a few hours, I once again lost control over my body, over my own mind. I could not stay in one place, I could not lie down or stand still. I felt a need all the time to move, to change my position, but I did not know why. I could not understand it, I could not control my body — my body itself controlled its own move-ments, its own thoughts. I was unable to concentrate on any one thing, my consciousness became a continuous flow, totally alien to my person.

In the first few days I was in this institution, I felt myself turning into a semi-human creature, a creature unable to think about anything except eating or sleeping. Then this feeling began to pass and there remained only apathy. A human being with his own intellect, hopes, soul and beliefs, had been transformed into an animal which says nothing and thinks nothing and is interested in nothing.

What I have said will not be new to those who have followed the practice of punitive medicine in the USSR. The abuse of psychiatry in the USSR began to experience a crisis when public opinion in the West as well as Western psychiatrists turned their attention to this phenomenon, i.e. from around the beginning of the 1970s. I entered a special psychiatric hospital in 1980 and stayed there until 1983. I would like to describe the improvement in conditions which took place in the 1970s.

Conditions improved in all respects. The hospital became far cleaner, the inmates were given better clothing — underwear, slippers, etc. — things which are very important for prisoners. At one time, one pair of slippers had been provided for an entire ward. Also, fewer people were now being declared insane. The protection people have through being known in the West — to Western correspondents and to public opinion — makes things difficult for Soviet psychiatrists.

At my first medical examination, in Chelyabinsk, I was given a clean bill of health despite the directive of the criminal investigator. The first and only question I was asked was who had been the doctor who had attended to me. I said it was Dr Voloshanovich and that he had examined me one month before I was arrested and had found nothing wrong with my mental condition. The name of Dr Voloshanovich had a magical effect on the doctors: they asked no further questions and let me go right away. I was recognized as being in a sound mental state, despite the investigator, thanks only to the fact that my case was known and that Dr Voloshanovich and the Working Committee for Investigating the Abuse of Psychiatry had taken up my case and appealed to the psychiatrists.

The second medical examination I had that was directed by the investigator was in the Serbsky Institute (the 'Institute of Fools' as it was called by Viktor Nikipelov, a member of the Moscow Helsinki Group). Here I was no longer protected as I had been in Chelyabinsk. Now the Working Committee for Investigating the Abuse of Psychiatry had been routed and the only members still at large were Irina Grivnina and Feliks Serebrov. They were unable to protect me and I was certified mentally ill. The diagnosis that was made — 'sluggish (*vyalotekushchaya*) schizophrenia' — a diagnosis applied only to dissidents, was invented by Soviet psychiatrists. It is schizophrenia without symptoms.

Later I was sent to the Kazan psychiatric prison and then to the Blagoveshchensk psychiatric prison. At the latter, precisely two months after my arrival, I became aware that the attitude towards me of the psychiatrists and other political prisoners, and especially ordinary prisoners, had changed. Political prisoners in psychiatric hospitals are normally given better conditions. However, I was picked out from the other political prisoners. At Blagoveshchensk, for instance, it was forbidden to keep a pen — pen and paper were provided once a week only for letters. But when I asked to be allowed to keep a pen, no objection was made. Also, I was prescribed a very small dose of medicines, about one-third of what I had had in Kazan. The general attitude of the doctors also indicated I was being given special treatment. They allowed me to wear my own clothes and to receive from home literature in foreign languages, even philosophic and atheistic literature denied to other patients.

It was six months before I realized why I was being given this special treatment. I received two letters from a group in Krefeld in West Germany who had adopted me as a political prisoner and prisoner of conscience. My special position was due to the fact that people in the West — human rights campaigners — were concerned about me and were disrupting the plans of the psychiatric executioners.

I was released a little over two years later. This is a record of sorts: no political prisoner had ever been freed from a psychiatric prison in under three years. Egor Volkov, for example, who had organized a workers' strike, had been in the Blagoveshchensk prison since 1968, i.e. for seventeen years. I was able to get out in this relatively short time solely because my name was known in the West. The Campaign against Psychiatric Abuse in the USSR, Amnesty International, the Internationale Gesellschaft für Menschenrechte — all were aware of my plight and appealed to the Soviet authorities and to the heads of the psychiatric prison.

Thus it can be seen how susceptible are the Soviet authorities in regard to the issue of prisoners of conscience as long as they are protected by human rights organizations in the West.

The Andropov regime introduced no changes regarding political psychiatry in the USSR. In May 1983 all political prisoners at the Blagoveshchensk prison were asked to sign a statement that they would henceforth abandon all political activity. Those who signed were freed. Also in spring 1983, a secret circular went out from the Serbsky Institute to the effect that as many prisoners as possible should be certified as mentally sound so that the number of prisoners could be reduced. This circular did have an effect on political psychiatry in the USSR in general: the number of inmates fell by 20 per cent.

But it is too soon to speak of the end of punitive medicine in the USSR. We are aware that people are still in psychiatric prisons, people are still suffering from terrible medicines and conditions and from being in the company of people who really are insane and are sometimes aggressive. There is, for example, the writer and critic Vladimir Gershuni, who is currently serving a second sentence in a psychiatric hospital; the Baptist Vladimir Khaylo; the dissident Nikolay Baranov, who has now spent fifteen years in a psychiatric prison; Lev Ubozhko, who has also spent fifteen years in a psychiatric prison; and the Ukrainian writer and poet Viktor Rafalsky — sixteen years. We must not forget them.

My experience is that efforts to rescue prisoners of psychiatry can succeed only if they are made with great pressure. We must not forget, or allow to be taken off the agenda, the question of the abuse of psychiatry in the USSR, a practice comparable with the experiments carried out in Hitler's death camps. This practice is a negation of our concept of civilization, and these crimes are especially vile in so far as they are carried out by persons whose calling it is to save human life. It is our duty to rescue those who are in psychiatric prisons in the USSR, to remove them from this nightmare.

CHAPTER 23

An Unusual Story

NIKOLAY PANKOV

On 25 March 1985 my wife, myself and our dog left the USSR. This sentence sums up four years of single-handed struggle with the Soviet authorities. We joined no organization, no group. No one suffered as a result of any connection with us. Ours is an unusual story. Very few people leave the USSR in the way we did.

My wife and I worked in the so-called special department of *Goskino*, the USSR State Cinema organization. This is where films shown to top Soviet Party and government officials are stored. The officials see the films (as far as I know) in their city homes and *dachas*. It was our task to show them to lower-ranking comrades, for example, to members of the Committee for Lenin Prizes; staff members of the journal *Kommunist*; members of the Institute of the USA and Canada; the late Sokolov, director of the Eliseev food store, etc.

There seems nothing unusual in this — a cinema is a cinema. But what *was* unusual was that these people preferred not to see films praised by the Soviet press, films awarded state prizes and on which Soviet youth are reared, but Western films! Not that they buy them — they simply steal them, have copies made, and then dub them into Russian and enjoy themselves watching them in closed screenings.

We provided a special service for delegates to the 26th Party Congress in 1981. During the day the delegates adopted the most magnificent plans; during the night they took time off from their grandiose planning watching Western films. One film they saw was about the sex life of a dentist. Most appropriate.

Not only did we provide a service for participants in the Congress: we were awarded a bonus for our effort. But my wife and

I did not make proper use of this bonus — we donated it to a fund for Soviet political prisoners. We felt this was putting money earned by Soviet prostitutes to the best possible use.

In 1982 we submitted an application to emigrate. We did not have the necessary invitation, from Israel or elsewhere. In accordance with Soviet law and the international legal instruments to which the USSR is a signatory, we insisted on our right to emigrate for political reasons. We made no secret of the fact that we detested the Soviet regime and socialism, in particular 'developed socialism'.

In a word, we said what was in our minds. We were later told this was dangerous. Of course, our applications to emigrate were rejected and we were dismissed from our jobs. The formal reason we were given for the dismissal was that a reduction in staffing levels was necessary. Then we went to court, claiming the dismissals were illegal, and the court restored my wife's job. But she was not allowed to work; she was paid for a time but then the payments ceased. We complained to the competent authorities, including the Procurator General. Before we eventually left, I totted up everything we had spent on correspondence in these few years. The total spent on postage came to a staggering 100 roubles! (A registered letter in the USSR costs ten copecks.)

In 1982 my wife entered hospital for gynaecological treatment. It was essential that she remain in bed for a period of time. But to our misfortune there were elections — these are a regular occurrence in the USSR — and, as we refused to vote, my wife was told to leave the hospital. For her to have done so under those circumstances would have had the most serious implications but, thankfully, friends in the US embassy in Moscow intervened and all turned out well.

On 7 September 1983 *Pravda* printed a Tass item from Washington stating that President Reagan had said something baseless about human rights in the USSR. We wrote to *Pravda* asking it to publish a retraction of this statement, claiming that Reagan was perfectly entitled to criticize human rights violations in the USSR and that our case was in itself one such violation. We wrote to President Reagan and sent copies of our correspondence to *Pravda* and we had a postal receipt proving that *Pravda* had received it. We claimed there were grounds for an appeal to the USSR Supreme Court and for initiating a law suit: the editor of *Pravda*, we said, was liable to five years' imprisonment and the director of Tass to seven years.

However, there was no reply and on 30 September I was summoned to the *militsiya* on a completely different pretext. I was bound and sent to psychiatric hospital no. 13 in Moscow. An accompanying document said I had wrecked the premises of the *militsiya* and murdered half their staff, that I had been confined in the Kashchenko psychiatric hospital a dozen times, I was classified as mentally ill, etc.

Luckily, I did not remain in the hospital for more than one night (I was there for fifteen hours altogether). That evening our French and American friends in Moscow protested to the hospital and the following morning a commission of competent psychiatrists headed by Fastov, one of Soviet psychiatry's brightest luminaries, was formed. The commission concluded that my mental functions were normal. My criticism of *Pravda* was said to have been 'highly logical'. In short, I should never have been put in the hospital. I was advised to be 'prudent'.

A few days later, my wife and I were invited to a commission headed by Pyatov, one of the leading psychiatrists in Moscow, to determine whether I should be held in a psychiatric hospital or merely kept under periodic observation. The commission's conclusion was unambiguous: neither my wife nor I required treatment in a psychiatric hospital, but, once again, we were advised to be 'prudent'.

But we were not 'prudent' because we still wanted to emigrate to the West. When the USSR Supreme Soviet election began we wrote to the central electoral commission suggesting that the media should pay attention to the negative personal attributes of Andropov and Tikhonov. When we received no response, we once again, fully in accordance with Soviet law, demanded that Andropov and Tikhonov be dropped from the electoral lists. We said that we had appealed on many occasions to the USSR Supreme Soviet to remove our Soviet citizenship but we had never received a single reply as to the merits of our request. Instead of inculcating discipline in the Supreme Soviet, we argued, Andropov had let things get out of hand — Supreme Soviet members were out doing their shopping instead of staying in their offices doing their duty in helping people to renounce their citizenship. It was Tikhonov's duty, as Chairman of the Council of Ministers, to see to it that the USSR fulfil both the provisions of its constitution and the international treaties and obligations it had undertaken to observe. Refusing to allow us to emigrate was one such violation. It was our considered view that such unworthy people as this should be replaced by more deserving candidates.

On 21 February both my wife and I were summoned to the 104th *militsiya* station and we were sent to the same psychiatric hospital, no. 1. At first the doctor at reception refused to admit us. He recognized me and said there was nothing wrong with either my wife or myself. Just at that moment the telephone rang. Then the doctor said: 'Forgive me but I must do my job.'

We spent only five days in this psychiatric hospital. From our first day there we were visited by US diplomats and the US embassy in Moscow protested about the illegal manner in which we had been treated. We had always been aware that we might eventually wind up in a psychiatric hospital and we had therefore made certain that we had witnesses. In Moscow there was a French psychiatrist and our friends, who were French diplomats, had arranged a report testifying to our sound mental health. These precautions made it very difficult for Soviet psychiatrists to take measures against us.

A doctor in the hospital later told us that we had been helped by the influenza epidemic and quarantine — one of the rare cases when a virus has served Soviet medicine. This was the formal reason why no visits had been permitted. All the same, we were told that we could not be prevented from meeting with foreigners and we were transferred to psychiatric hospital no. 5 at Stolbovaya Station, about fifty kilometres south of Moscow. This is not a special psychiatric hospital in the true sense of the word as it comes under the Ministry of Health. But it is also not a normal hospital as it has a number of special functions. It is intended for sick criminals, murderers, rapists and drug addicts, who are imprisoned there for long periods.

My wife and I were placed in the most difficult conditions. At first, we were not permitted visits. We were told we would spend the rest of our lives there if we did not abandon our desire to leave the USSR. The fact is that had the West not intervened we would still be there. There can be no doubt on that score.

Immediately our case was given publicity in the West, our circumstances improved. As far as I was concerned, the hospital claimed I was receiving strong medicine, Vitamin B and a single tranquillizer at night. But this was not the case where my wife was concerned. For a week and a half she was injected with Haloperidol, a very painful French drug which is frequently administered in cases where real mental illness is involved. But when it is administered to a healthy person it has the opposite effect and may bring about hallucinations and delirium. Even now my wife can feel the effects of this treatment. She has an unexpected hypertonic crisis, her hands shake, her hair has gone grey.

Following our release from the hospital, we conducted a struggle with the Soviet postal authorities. Also, we wrote large numbers of letters to the West — to heads of state and government, public organizations and the like. It would be interesting to find out whether any of these letters ever reached their destinations. We were given assurances by the Ministry of Communications that all our letters were received on time. We sent them with a certificate of delivery and demanded a notification with the addressee's signature. But this was not available. In accordance with Soviet law, we applied to the court for compensation for letters which never arrived. We sent fifty-one such notifications abroad.

On 13 February 1985 we received a telephone call from the OVIR[1], and the following day we met KGB Colonel Seryagin. Seryagin said that he was empowered to enable us to emigrate providing we left on an Israeli visa. We said we were ready to leave on any visa. A few weeks later, we emigrated.

Note
[1] Department of Visas and Registration of Foreign Citizens.

CHAPTER 24

Western Correspondents in the USSR and the Flow of Information

DAVID SATTER

To evaluate the performance of Western correspondents in the Soviet Union it is necessary to ask ourselves a basic question: who really controls the flow of information on which we base our impressions of the Soviet Union?

I was a correspondent for six years in Moscow from 1976 until 1982, and when I first began my work there, it puzzled me that the Soviet authorities tolerated the presence of foreign correspondents. I could not understand why they did not force them to paraphrase Tass releases from offices in Helsinki. It was only after working for a number of years in the Soviet Union that I began to realize that the Western correspondents in Moscow, far from being a problem for the Soviet authorities, were actually necessary to them and that, on balance, they serve the interests of the Soviet authorities and not those of their own readers.

The Soviet authorities do not want the Soviet Union to resemble China during the Cultural Revolution. They understand that the world distrusts a country about which there is no information. They want the West to have information about the Soviet Union, but they want it to be the type of information which will lead Western leaders and Western public opinion to draw consistently erroneous conclusions. And for this, they are heavily dependent on the unprofessionalism, inexperience and, occasionally, the corruption of Western correspondents.

Few people in the West read Russian newspapers or journals, or speak Russian. Few have the chance to meet Soviet citizens or to visit the Soviet Union. In other words, there are few sources of independent impressions. By successfully manipulating Western correspondents, the Soviet authorities can do a great deal to confuse Western public opinion as a whole.

The Soviet authorities make an enormous effort to disinform the West with the help of Western journalists and there are two reasons why their efforts are, in general terms, a success. The first is the enormous effort made by the Soviet authorities, who understand the uses of repetition and, emptying words such as 'peace', 'democracy', and 'imperialism' of their content, employ them like bludgeons, to drive out thought. The other is the constitutional inability of Western correspondents to deal with Soviet disinformation techniques and to take steps to guarantee their intellectual and journalistic independence.

Once a mendacious, Soviet propaganda position has been decided on — and all Soviet propaganda is, to a greater or lesser extent, mendacious — it is repeated in every newspaper, every radio broadcast and every television news programme, as well as in every official statement or speech by a Soviet leader and in every private 'chat' that a Soviet official may have with a Western journalist.

Official lies are repeated so often and presented in so many different ways (in magazines or pamphlets, published interviews or reports of speeches, with illustrations or simply text) that the average person can be forgiven, after a time, for assuming that somewhere there must be some truth in them.

After the invasion of Afghanistan, the authorities said that the Soviet Union had entered the country in response to a 'call for help' from the legitimate Afghan government, which was faced with a 'foreign invasion'. This explanation became the basis of various 'peace initiatives' in which the Soviets offered to withdraw their troops after the 'foreign interference' — in reality, the indigenous Afghan resistance — came to an end.

An American editor, demonstrating the numbing effect on his subconscious of this type of propaganda, reacted to one such Soviet 'peace' offer by asking his newspaper's correspondent in Moscow whether this meant that the Soviets had 'blinked', forgetting that aside from the Soviet army, there was never any 'foreign interference' in the first place.

The Soviet authorities, besides inundating Western correspondents with disinformation, try to ensure that disinformation is the only type of information which is available to them by arresting those who are ready to speak to Western journalists honestly. In my personal experience, the most striking example of this was the fate of Aleksei Nikitin, a coal miner, who accompanied me and Kevin

Klose of *The Washington Post* in Donetsk, where we spoke to coal miners about their lives. Shortly after we left Donetsk, Nikitin was seized and imprisoned in a series of psychiatric hospitals. He was tortured intermittently with injections and imprisoned in a series of psychiatric institutions where he remained until his tragic death from stomach cancer early in 1984.

The combination of a constant deluge of disinformation and the vacuum of truthful information created by a system which is organized to destroy anyone who tries to speak honestly has done a great deal to create the many misconceptions about the Soviet Union which flourish in the West. But the result is not the creation of the Soviet authorities alone. They could not have achieved what they have without the unwitting help of Western correspondents.

Faced with a country which requires an exceptional effort of analysis in order to be understood, Western publications traditionally send correspondents to Moscow who are completely unqualified. Only a minority of the correspondents speak Russian and there were times during my tenure in Moscow when the proportion of American correspondents who could not speak Russian reached 90 per cent. Dr Sakharov, for example, was frequently interviewed for UPI by the agency's Soviet translators, who were provided by the KGB. *Time* magazine sent their KGB-provided Soviet translator to interview Soviet citizens as an 'American correspondent'. It was common for non-Russian speaking correspondents to interview their KGB-provided maids in an attempt to obtain the reaction of the Soviet 'man in the street'.

Many Western correspondents arrived in Moscow knowing nothing of Soviet history or Soviet ideology and, from the beginning, made the most common and fatal error of all: they compensated for their lack of background by endowing Soviet society with the characteristics of the United States.

The work of Western correspondents in Moscow is also poorly structured. Almost all correspondents serve in the Soviet Union as part of a normal rotation and, sent to Moscow as they would be sent to Paris or Bonn and with exactly as much preparation, they arrive with the assumption that covering the Soviet Union is little different from covering a society where truthful information is readily available. The result is that, determined to be productive, they begin energetically to regurgitate Soviet disinformation.

With about ninety Western correspondents (including those from

Japan) to cover a country which is larger than the United States, almost every Western correspondent is expected to report on every government statement. The phenomenal duplication of effort is reflected in the high percentage of the total journalistic output which consists of nothing but paraphrases of articles in *Pravda* and Tass. Under these circumstances, a fierce struggle develops to see who can find 'high-level' Soviet sources whose inane and unattributable remarks are attributed to 'Soviet officials' and used by Western correspondents in an attempt to make a given Soviet position more 'life-like', in the process rendering Soviet official lies more plausible to the outside world.

In the end, the tremendous repetition in reporting from the Soviet Union under the existing system has the same deadening effect on the Western reader as constant repetition has on Soviet citizens. It becomes difficult to distinguish what is reality.

Most of the inadequacies of Western reporting from Moscow are the result of error, not bad intentions, but there are a number of personal factors which contribute to what is a deplorable situation.

In the first place, Western correspondents in Moscow are too inclined towards careerism. This careerism is easily manipulated by the Soviet authorities who understand how to use a correspondent's ambitions to further their ends. They can make themselves available when a correspondent's editor visits Moscow and in that way demonstrate the correspondent's 'access'. They can release routine information slightly in advance to favoured correspondents or reward the most cooperative of them — which frequently means the most corrupted — with interviews, even with the Soviet leader.

The Soviet authorities know the requirements of different types of correspondent. Wire-service reporters, for example, can be rewarded with information five or ten minutes before their competitors. The favouritism costs the Soviet authorities nothing and it means nothing for the Western reading public but it is a competitive advantage for which reporters are often willing to pay with their integrity.

The absurd result of Soviet-manipulated careerism is that Western correspondents in Moscow frequently compete fiercely to repeat mendacious propaganda and treat with barely disguised contempt those Soviet citizens who approach them with genuine information.

At the same time, every journalist in the Soviet Union is aware that if he refuses to cooperate, he may be the target of provocations. He may not be confident that, in the face of an accusation by the Soviet government, his newspaper would be ready to believe him and not the Soviets. Being honest means taking a risk.

It should also be noted here that, besides careerism, the behaviour of Western correspondents is sometimes influenced by money. There are certain types of soft black market activity which are available to correspondents and which, although technically legal, induce political caution in those who engage in them. One widespread activity is the purchase of cars for resale at four times their value in soft currency which can then be exchanged with the correspondent's company at the official rate. It is not surprising that the correspondents who were the most active in selling automobiles also tended to show the most professional scepticism towards the information supplied by dissidents and to attach the greatest importance to their official contacts.

If Western correspondents do not do their job, the West will lack the information it needs to make decisions. The information provided by dissidents, at great risk to themselves, sheds light on the fundamental nature of Soviet society but, if it is not reported, the dissidents' efforts are unavailing.

Among Western correspondents in Moscow it was typical to report on dissidents only when they were arrested. Of course, there was a need to report on them when they were arrested, but the deeper analysis of Soviet society which their detailed information would have made possible was rarely made because the information they provided was seldom reported and hardly ever seriously analysed.

This problem concerns all of us. It has not received enough attention and I was glad to be able to raise it at this Hearing.

CHAPTER 25

Economic Rights of the Soviet Population

IGOR BIRMAN

While I support wholeheartedly any attempts, including the Sakharov Hearings, to protect the human rights of Soviet citizens, I wonder why *economic* rights are rarely, if at all, mentioned. In my view, they are no less important, and have perhaps been subject to more frequent abuse than any other rights. As we approach the end of the twentieth century, it has to be said that if the citizens of this or that country do not enjoy a good living standard, then this is the result of their living under a non-democratic regime. Of course, the living standards of such democratic countries as the United States, Spain, Costa Rica and India are patently not identical; nevertheless, human beings have a right to live in accordance with the modern opportunities which are available. Indeed, this is a fundamental right, but a right subject to abuse in non-democratic societies, particularly the USSR.

I will attempt to discuss this extremely complex issue under the following categories: the economic organization of Soviet society; labour conditions; standard of living.

The economic organization of Soviet society

Under this heading, I have in mind primarily the prohibition in the USSR of private, non-governmental economic activity. According to Marxist dogma, private ownership of the means of production leads to the exploitation of man by man. It is for this reason that the means of production in the USSR belong to the state.[1]

The following results flow from this state of affairs. First, for decades now the USSR's state-owned economy has proved ineffective: the shamefully low standard of living in the USSR is a direct result of the state-run economy.

Secondly, by not permitting private ownership, the state compels individuals to work for *it*, not for themselves. In the view of Engels, labour created man (apes do not work). Perhaps this is true, but I would add: *freely chosen labour*. If you work for someone else your labour is not free — it does not humanize you. Many individuals in the West work for other people, but *by their own choice*. In the USSR, not working for the state may be considered a crime, punishable by exile and hard labour.

Thirdly, as the only employer, the state subordinates all its citizens to itself. In respect of human rights, the very fact that you are unable to make a living other than working for Big Brother is a major restriction on your freedom.

Fourthly, as the sole employer, the state forbids strikes. Workers are thus unable to protect their rights but are at the mercy of the state.

The declared purpose of prohibiting private property was to prevent exploitation. In fact, if we assume that the very notion of exploitation is valid, exploitation by man has been replaced by exploitation by the state.

Social inequality in the USSR is extraordinary: the official disparity in wages, without taking into account assorted perks, is about tenfold.[2]

A number of instruments exist in the USSR to compel workers to work harder. For example, most blue-collar workers are paid piece-rates and not by the hour. Also, the main task of Soviet trade unions is so-called socialist emulation, not increased pay or improved working conditions.

Soviet propaganda claims that one of the regime's achievements is to have removed unemployment. Three observations are in order. First, this simply is not true: in some cases, finding a job is difficult. According to Soviet publications, it takes on average thirty-five days to find employment. However, in some states in America, if you do not find work within two weeks you receive unemployment benefits. We are, of course, also aware of structural unemployment in the USSR.

Secondly, the apparent absence of unemployment in the USSR is not a particular achievement but a direct result of low labour productivity.

Thirdly, an unemployed American enjoys a far higher living standard than his Soviet counterpart. By my calculations, average *per capita* income in the USSR is lower than the official poverty level in the US.

Labour conditions

Regrettably, we have very limited data on this topic. The fact that information on the number of work-related accidents, illnesses, overtime work and the like are not published contrasts sharply with the practice in democratic countries. However, by using indirect data we are able to make a number of observations:

(a) While the USSR claims the greatest scientific achievements, and investment's share of the national product is impossibly high, about 40 per cent of all blue-collar workers are employed in manual labour.[3]

(b) In one area the USSR has attained equality of the sexes: the most difficult physical jobs are frequently performed by women.

(c) As mentioned above, we do not have data on occupational hazards but we do know that deaths at the work place are not exceptionally rare. A personal observation: I myself was impressed to see how well protected road and construction workers are in the West. In the USSR their position is very different.

(d) A further indirect indication of poor working conditions is the fall in the USSR's relatively low life expectancy. Poor working conditions are one of several factors which play a role here.

(e) In order to be as objective as possible, it should be said that the USSR is ahead of many Western countries in the retirement age — sixty years for men and fifty-five years for women.

Standard of living

The history of the twentieth century, as we have said, has demonstrated that a good standard of living for the masses is entirely feasible. We are perfectly entitled to declare that only in those countries with a poor social organization and an inadequate social structure does the standard of living not correspond to ours.

Human beings are rarely satisfied with what they have. And only in fairy tales do people in communist societies live in accordance with their wishes. It is impossible to determine the level of consumption that is objectively sufficient; this must be done on a comparative basis.

In my view, the most important comparison is between what is desired and what is obtainable. This may be illustrated by a pair of scissors: one blade represents what is desired, the other what is possessed. Where the scissors are or what the real level of consumption is are of less importance than how far the second blade is separated from the first, how wide the opening of the scissors is. The following observations may be made in regard to the post-war period of Soviet history. There can be no doubt that *per capita* consumption in the USSR in this period has grown far more slowly than has been officially reported. Soviet statistics show that real *per capita* income between 1940 and 1983 rose by more than sixfold,[4] but this is misleading and ridiculous for the following reasons:

(a) The rise began at an exceptionally low level. I would say that in food, clothing and housing the Soviet standard of living in 1950 was no higher than in Tsarist Russia in 1913.

(b) In 1950–60 the rise was very swift, but in the 1970s it was very slow. In my estimation, since the end of the 1970s, growth has ceased.

(c) In the early 1950s the gap between the blades of our scissors was very wide; Soviet citizens were told this was the result of the war. The gap later narrowed, but since 1970 it has been widening again. Although I am clearly unable to substantiate my statement, since no surveys of the Soviet population exist, I would claim that the Soviet people are now not at all satisfied with their consumption level. Three factors are of significance in this respect. First, growth has ceased. Even according to Soviet official data, in 1982 there was no improvement in the living standard. It is true that substantial growth was reported in 1983–4 but it is clear that all this 'growth' was in increases of money savings which, under current Soviet conditions, have no relevance. Secondly, the Soviet people are aware how far behind the West they are in this respect. Thirdly, the Soviet economy is in such a dreadful state that hope for improvement hardly exists.

The following table shows how many years are required for Soviet *per capita* consumption to catch up with the American, if we extrapolate the Soviet growth rate over the last twenty-three years for the future. It should be stressed that (a) official Soviet data are used and (b) the Soviet growth rate is slower now than during the entire period shown.

TABLE 1

In How Many Years Soviet Consumption Will be Equal to 1976 American Consumption

Consumption, per capita					Lag, years
	USA	USSR[b]			
	1976[a]	1960	1983	increment	
Meat, kg	118	40	58.4	18.4	74
Fruit, kg	103	22	44	22	62
Cars, sales, per 100	46	0.2	5.5	5.3	176
Housing, sq. metres	44	8.9[c]	13.8[c]	4.9	142
Telephones in private use, per 1,000	529	4[d]	61[e]	57	188
Roads, km per 1,000	23.6	1.3	2.9	1.6	298

[a] Data explained in I. Birman, *Ekonomika nedostach* (New York, 1983), pp. 252, 274, 309, 326, 327, 438.

[b] *Narodnoye khozyaistvo SSSR v 1922-1972*, p. 372; *Narodnoye khozyaistvo SSSR v 1983 godu*, pp. 6, 328, 342, 423, 441.

[c] Only urban population.

[d] Assuming 20 per cent of telephones in private use.

[e] Assuming 60 per cent of telephones in private use.

The Soviet people have been told for decades now that their low standard of living is due to the necessity for rapid economic development and a military build-up. Even if these reasons were true (and I do not believe they are), the question that must be asked is: how many generations of Soviet citizens will have low growth rates instead of butter and how many more sacrifices will have to be made in order to build newer and newer weapons?

Notes

[1] Exceptions are the so-called cooperatives. However, their separation from the state is purely formal. Suffice it to say that Soviet statistics report all cooperative activity together with that of the state. Another exception is the so-called collective farms. Formally, they belong to the farmers but in reality this is not the case at all. Only the agricultural plots are not state-owned but they are severely restricted and are not liquidated solely because the state could not otherwise feed the population.

[2] Indeed, the minimum monthly wage is 70 roubles, and there are those who make 700 roubles and more.

[3] See *Voprosy ekonomiki* no. 5 (1984), 47. According to *Ekonomika i organizatsiya promyshlennogo proizvodstva* no. 11 (1983), p. 24, the proportion of

workers in Soviet industry engaged in manual labour fell from 35.4 per cent in 1972 to 30.2 per cent in 1982. According to *Planovoe khozyaistvo* no. 9, 1982, 25, 60 per cent of workers in the Soviet construction industry are manual labourers.

[4] *Narodnoe khozyaistvo SSSR v 1983 gody* p. 37.

CHAPTER 26

The Effect of Western Pressures on Soviet Internal Policies

PETER REDDAWAY

It is a very difficult matter to determine the effect of Western pressure on the USSR's domestic policies. The Soviet government is not subject to public interrogation in a parliament or congress. I would, however, like to make a number of tentative general observations regarding Soviet policies on dissent and emigration:

(1) Western pressure cannot have a radical or irresistible effect but it *can* have an effect which is more than marginal, as was the case in 1974–9.
(2) This effect can be far more evident at some periods than at others, and it may also be 'reversible', i.e. Soviet policies may move in the direction opposite to that desired.
(3) When this 'reverse process' occurs, as it has in the years since 1979, Western pressure is equally important (if not more so) as in the previous period. This is for two reasons. First, Western pressure limits the extent of the Soviet reaction — it prevents the policies from being even more repressive than they might otherwise have been. Secondly, the pressure is even more important than before in terms of the morale of the dissidents and would-be emigrants. They become aware of these pressures from Western radio broadcasts and other sources and feel they are not being abandoned in their hour of trial.
(4) The Western pressures could, and should, be more intense, more resolute and more coordinated than has been the case up to now. We have more leverage than we may think — we should use it even though it may cost us something in the short run (in economic terms, for example).

Underlying these general observations are my estimate of the importance of the following factors: the Soviet regime's desire to increase its political power and influence at home and abroad; its desire for greater military strength, not only for reasons of national security but also as a potential source of political power; its desire to expand its empire geographically and to undermine the West; its realization that a strong economy is essential to achieve these objectives; and its realization that international prestige and status are prerequisites for achieving these ends.

This Soviet strategy has, however, a number of flaws. One major flaw is the weakness of the Soviet economy, a weakness which compels Moscow to rely on the West for large annual supplies of grain, a considerable amount of advanced technology, favourable credit terms and scientific know-how.

Another weakness is the regime's difficulty in attaining a high level of international prestige and status. This difficulty increases to the extent that the USSR's economic weakness and oppressive political methods — especially in the sphere of dissent and emigration — become more widely known. In so far as the West is in a position to draw attention to this economic weakness and these oppressive political methods, and to impose sanctions which will hurt the regime, it is evident that the USSR is to a certain degree dependent on the West. In my view, it is likely to remain so indefinitely, and probably to an increasing degree as time passes.

Before we consider how we are to take advantage of this relative Soviet dependence, in order, *inter alia*, to help bring about less repressive policies in the areas with which we are concerned here, it is necessary to clarify two points.

First, what are the Soviet regime's psychology and methods in pursuing its aims? To my mind, these still derive from Lenin's well-known dictum *Kto-kogo* — that is to say, who has the dominant power — political, economic and military — and the will to use it. This power–political approach involves hard-headed calculation, pragmatism, a readiness to bargain and a readiness to sell out an ally without hesitation should the need arise (as some communist parties loyal to Moscow have learned to their cost). This approach has been revealed in occasional statements by Soviet officials to dissidents and would-be emigrants. On one occasion in 1980, for example, a KGB colonel told a Pentecostal group which had been seeking to emigrate for a number of years: 'Don't compare yourselves with the Jews. They fetch a good price, but we get very little for you!'

Secondly, we ought to look at the record of the last fifteen years regarding Western pressure for improved Soviet performance in respect of human rights. The Western pressure first became strong in 1969–70, on the issue of Jewish emigration. The Soviets responded, early in 1971, by suddenly permitting Jewish emigration to rise from virtually nil to 13,000 in 1971, and to over 30,000 in 1972. The Soviet calculation appears to have been as follows. The détente that was emerging served their interests for the reasons outlined above. The USA, as the key Western negotiating partner, was pressing hard for Jewish emigration and was prepared to pay a price as part of a broad package of political, economic and military deals. In regard to dissent, Western pressures were growing at this time, although they were still relatively weak. Thus the regime did not suppress the dissident groups which had emerged in the late 1960s; rather, it took half-measures, seeking gradually to escalate them and hoping they would not attract international attention.

In 1973, in response to this escalation, Western pressures grew dramatically, partly in connection with the prominent role played by Dr Sakharov and Aleksandr Solzhenitsyn in the dissident movement. In 1973–4 the regime was concerned with pushing for the Conference on Security and Co-operation in Europe (CSCE), intending it, as it were, to crown the edifice of détente. But the West was insisting that provisions relating to human rights and emigration be included in the CSCE's final document. What the Soviets therefore did was to make considerable concessions. They agreed to the inclusion of some humanitarian provisions in the Helsinki Final Act and gradually reduced the number of arrests of dissidents. The number of arrests known to us declined dramatically from almost 200 per year in the early 1970s to 80 in 1975. It remained at about this level from 1975 to 1978. During this period, dissent grew more rapidly than before, both geographically and regarding diversification.

In late 1976 the Soviet authorities decided on a new crackdown on dissent as the CSCE review conference in Belgrade approached. We know of the actual Soviet policy at this time from a briefing given by a senior Soviet official for newspapers editors which was subsequently leaked to *samizdat*. The official said: 'Editors of newspapers and journals are receiving numerous demands from Soviet people finally to show firmness to the dissidents and silence them. It has been decided to imprison the fifty most active dissidents and deal severely with their associates. It is time to show strength and not pay attention to the West.' Although a similar decision was made with regard to cutting down drastically on emigration, both these new policies were sharply reversed in early 1977, when Jimmy Carter was elected President of the United States with a strong stand on the issues of human rights and emigration. The result was that the new wave of arrests petered out and Jewish emigration rose to the unprecedented figure of over 51,000 in 1979. Dissent continued to diversify.

But the briefly pursued policy of late 1976 and early 1977 was taken up again by the Soviet authorities from 1979 onwards. By 1983, as we know, emigration had been curtailed drastically while dissenting groups had mostly been suppressed or driven underground, where they remained active but far less visible to the outside world and consequently far less troublesome to the Soviet authorities.

The main reasons for this change of policy since 1979 are, in my view, as follows. First, these new, tough policies were used in subtle ways by Brezhnev's rivals in the power struggle against him: the implication was that Brezhnev was to blame for having allowed too much laxity regarding dissent and emigration. Secondly, the policies of the 1970s on human rights and emigration had, of course, certain negative aspects — or costs — from Moscow's viewpoint. For example, the USSR's prestige abroad had been damaged by the testimony of the dissidents and emigrants. Also, détente was beginning to sour in 1979 for a number of reasons and the Soviet invasion of Afghanistan virtually destroyed it.

The invasion of Afghanistan caused the USSR to be so widely criticized throughout the world, including the Third World countries, and subject to so many economic and other sanctions that the additional price the USSR would be obliged to pay for suppressing human rights and stopping emigration seemed likely to be a relatively small one and therefore worth paying.

And indeed that price has proved to be small. The CSCE review process has, of course, been used by the West to good, though diminishing, effect, and the campaign against the Soviet political abuse of psychiatry has led to a considerable decline in the level of such abuse and to the forced resignation of the USSR from the World Psychiatric Association.

In general, however, the Western pressures and sanctions have *not* been commensurate with the seriousness of the deterioration in the areas of human rights and emigration since 1979.

In my view, the West should now seek to bring the following pressures to bear on the USSR. First, it should regard an improvement of Soviet policies on human rights and emigration as an integral (if not formal) part of any broad new deals which may be struck with the Soviet leaders in the coming year or two, without any hesitation or apologia. The record shows that this demand is not unrealistic: the Soviets were able to live with the situation from 1974 to 1978–9 without the system showing signs of collapse.

Secondly, as regards bilateral relations between the West and the USSR, the Western countries must seek improved co-ordination of their policies so that each country can put human rights and emigration into an important and agreed position in their policies alongside the political, economic and military aspects of any broad improvement in relations with the USSR.

Thirdly, in international bodies, especially those pertaining to the United Nations, there has been an excessively defeatist attitude on the part of the Western countries to the effect that the USSR cannot be brought to task in these bodies. We should be bolder: international public criticism does indeed embarrass the Soviet leaders.

Fourthly, professional bodies should be more prepared to speak out and use sanctions in the way the World Psychiatric Association did on the issue of psychiatric abuse. Church bodies should do likewise regarding Soviet persecution of religious people.

Finally, the West should probably begin to threaten the USSR with breaking off the Helsinki process, and it should be prepared to carry out this threat if the USSR does not improve its performance. I believe it will never actually be necessary to *carry out* the threat because — provided it is made with conviction — I believe the Soviets *will* make concessions. At the least, they will return to the situation of the mid- and late 1970s. The fact is that the Helsinki process is an integral part of the Soviet conception of détente and the Soviets have never abandoned that process, even in the worst periods of the last five years or so. Of course, it is necessary that the Western powers seek to develop as united a front on this issue as possible and the forthcoming Ottawa meeting of human rights experts will hopefully provide a wealth of material showing the drastic nature of the deterioration in the human rights field over the last few years.

I do not believe that these suggestions for intensified pressure and a greater degree of coordinated action are unrealistic. Authoritarian empires have liberalized their procedures when the pressures became too great. The Soviet authorities did liberalize their procedures in a number of respects in the mid-1970s. But, in any case, this is the best chance we have for increased security in the world, for arms control, for disarmament, for a generally more peaceful world. After all, Dr Sakharov gained his Nobel Prize for demonstrating the intimate link that exists between human rights, arms control and world security. Liberalization in the USSR would, I believe, gradually put increased restraints on the Soviet military budget and would increase the curbs on Soviet aggressive intentions.

CHAPTER 27

Can the West Influence Soviet Internal Policy?

MIKHAIL VOSLENSKY

The fact that the USSR is a great power has two aspects to it. On the one hand, it is able to resist external pressure more easily than most other countries. On the other hand, by reason of its multi-faceted interests throughout the world and its links with various countries and political forces, it is unable to ignore governmental and public opinion in the West without jeopardizing these interests and links. Thus although the exertion of pressure on the USSR will not bring about radical results, it should by no means be regarded as a fruitless exercise.

Western pressure may be brought to bear on the USSR on the following basis:

(a) The USSR has a chronic and huge problem of underproduction as well as a technology which, even in the military sphere, tends to lag behind that of the West. The cause of this particular backwardness is the bureaucratic nature of 'real socialism', the problem, being systemic, cannot be overcome within the framework of the same system. The USSR thus has a need for normal economic relations with the West (where overproduction rather than underproduction is a problem).

(b) In order to facilitate its political expansion, Moscow requires a lessening of tension between the USSR and the West — i.e. 'détente', certainly on a unilateral basis.

Also, in order to facilitate this expansion, the USSR pays considerable attention to building support for itself on the part of as many influential circles in the West as possible. Moscow expects those who collaborate with it to pressurize governments and parliaments in the West in favour of unilateral concessions, and 'détente' and to condemn those who advocate 'cold war' or 'nuclear holocaust' policies.

For these reasons, the Kremlin seeks to create as favourable as possible an impression on the West. This is why it is possible in certain circumstances to obtain from the Soviet authorities individual concessions in the sphere of human rights.

The leverage is as follows. The *nomenklatura* leadership in the USSR, as in other communist countries, seeks to create the impression that it is a serious partner in international negotiations, i.e. that it fulfils the international obligations it has undertaken, including, of course, the various treaties and agreements it has signed. Thus the most successful means of exerting pressure on the Soviet leaders in human rights matters is to demonstrate each and every Soviet violation of its international obligations in the human rights area — in particular, violations of UN human rights pacts and the Helsinki Final Act. The logical conclusion will be that there is no point in signing new agreements with the USSR until it has fulfilled the obligations it has already undertaken. This perspective might lead Moscow to prefer to make some concessions on human rights.

There exists a theory in the West that it is more useful to discuss specific cases of the abuse of human rights behind closed doors. Practice does not bear out this theory, especially in the human rights sphere.

Of course, Soviet propaganda will attack with its customary vituperation every Western attempt at putting overt pressure on Moscow. This does not, however, mean that the *nomenklatura* leadership will not in fact make concessions. One revealing example of successful Western pressure is the Soviet decision to return to the arms limitation talks in Geneva. The Soviet leaders long declared these negotiations could not be renewed until the Pershing and Cruise missiles had been removed from Europe. But when it became clear that Western Europe was determined to go ahead with the installation of these weapons and that the Soviet refusal to negotiate was creating a negative impression in the West, the USSR returned to the negotiating table and Gorbachev even accepted a summit meeting on arms control and other issues — under the pressure of the SDI project.

Nothing I have said means that we should reject confidential negotiations with the USSR on human rights matters. It is, however, of the utmost importance that these negotiations be conducted in a businesslike manner.

A combination of pressure by governments and public opinion in the West on the Soviet leaders together with, if necessary, confidential negotiations would seem to offer the best possible results in efforts to overcome violations of human rights in the USSR and the other communist countries.

CHAPTER 28

Influencing Soviet Human Rights Policy

ELLIOTT ABRAMS

Everyone would agree that the human rights situation in the Soviet Union has deteriorated in recent years. The deterioration seems to be due to a number of factors, both internal and external. The Soviet leadership recognizes that the country faces serious problems at home and abroad and that there are no quick and easy solutions to these problems.

Prior to the election of Gorbachev as CPSU General Secretary in March 1985, the Soviet Union had gone through a period of prolonged leadership uncertainty. At times of such uncertainty, it is not surprising that a fundamentally repressive regime would seek relief from these problems by increasing control and repression at home, while trying to reduce or eliminate contact between their citizens and the outside world. The course of events in recent years appears to fit some such pattern. The Soviets have conducted wave after wave of arrests aimed at destroying or isolating those groups in Soviet society who refuse to submit to the controls of the state and who dissent from the tenets of Soviet ideology.

They have eliminated the ability of the average citizen to place direct-dial phone calls to the West, enacted more stringent customs regulations, made it more difficult to send package mail to the USSR, interdicted international mail, and established new penalties for unauthorized contacts with foreigners. They have also cut all forms of emigration dramatically — Jewish, German and Armenian.

In this context of generalized repression there have been renewed manifestations of antisemitism in the Soviet Union. We are not certain how to explain this phenomenon. One possibility might be that in cutting off the safety valve of Jewish emigration, the Soviet authorities have brought on themselves a new upsurge in religious and national consciousness in one of the USSR's most assimilated minorities, and are unsure of how to deal with it over the long term. In the short term, they have embarked since last July on a campaign of arresting and convicting teachers of the Hebrew language and others in the forefront of this new awareness and identity.

These arrests have been combined with other forms of intimidation, including a determined antisemitic campaign in the Soviet media. At the same time, Soviet treatment of other groups has hardly been better. Ukrainian human rights activists, as usual, have suffered particularly badly. And although Ukrainians number less than 20 per cent of the population of the Soviet Union, they account for over 40 per cent of its political prisoners.

Continued Soviet efforts to suppress religion are equally disturbing, with Ukrainian Greek Catholics, Lithuanian Roman Catholics, unregistered Baptists, Seventh Day Adventists, and Pentecostalists coming in for particularly severe repression. There has also been little progress on the cases of major human rights figures such as Dr Sakharov, Anatoly Shcharansky, Iosif Begun and Yury Orlov.

Recently, there have been some minor positive gestures on the Soviets' part. Quite frankly, we as yet see no definite signs of significant improvement in regard to human rights. Whether the arrival on the scene of a relatively young and presumably more durable Soviet leader will have a positive impact on Soviet human rights policy over time is impossible to say.

The current US administration took office in early 1981 at a time when the present deterioration in the Soviet human rights situation was already well under way. The administration quickly identified four agenda items as critical to US–Soviet relations — arms control, regional issues, bilateral issues and human rights.

There were a number of factors involved in identifying human rights as a critical agenda item. There was an awareness that the human rights situation was deteriorating. President Reagan and later Secretary of State Shultz both came to the job deeply concerned about that deterioration. They believed that any society that so abused the rights of its citizens was dangerous internationally precisely because it was corrupt and oppressive at home.

Soviet unwillingness to live up to the human rights provisions of the Helsinki Final Act also cast doubt on the reliability of Soviet commitments in other areas. There was also an appreciation that we and the Soviets are engaged in a struggle for hearts and minds. Systematic human rights violations occur in many countries.

But the Soviet Union is not just any country. It is a superpower which progressively markets its social and political system as a model for the rest of the world. Soviet propaganda has been all too effective in portraying the Soviet Union as a progressive, peace-loving society. They have won a sympathetic ear in parts of the Third World and among certain groups in the West.

While we know the grim reality that lies behind the sweet words of the Soviet propaganda machine, we need to ensure that those who might be tempted by Soviet propaganda also know that reality. The struggle for hearts and minds is a struggle we dare not lose. Making human rights a critical element of our overall policy approach to the Soviet Union has served the purpose of reminding those who might be tempted by Soviet words of the brutal reality of Soviet life.

In keeping with the critical importance attached to human rights in our relationship with the Soviet Union, our human rights policy towards the Soviet Union has taken on both multilateral and bilateral aspects. Over the past four years we have made human rights a prominent and enduring part of our bilateral exchanges with Soviet leaders. In virtually every high-level exchange we have had, we have detailed our specific human rights concerns and made clear their importance to the US–Soviet relationship.

We have told Soviet leaders again and again that there can be no overall improvement in relations without some significant movement on our human rights concerns. Although obviously we cannot go into the specific content of bilateral exchanges I can say that we routinely discuss general human rights issues of particular concern to us, and also raise the cases of particular human rights activists.

The Soviet response to our raising human rights concerns at bilateral exchanges has been predictable. They are visibly annoyed when we raise the subject and claim our interest in their human rights performance represents interference in their internal affairs.

On many occasions they have sought to avoid discussion of human rights issues on the grounds that these are not legitimate topics for discussion between governments. On the other hand, we believe that the Soviet authorities are coming to recognize and accept that human rights will remain a permanent component of the US–Soviet agenda. We do not expect to see miracles overnight.

The Soviet Union will remain a repressive society by Western standards for the foreseeable future. But there is no reason why the Soviet authorities cannot significantly lower the level of internal repression and re-open the door to significantly higher levels of emigration without endangering the leading role of the Communist Party.

Such actions could not help but have a positive effect on bilateral relations. This is a point we have repeatedly made to the Soviet authorities and which we shall continue to make until we get results. The Soviets tend to respond to this approach by reversing the equation. They have hinted on a number of occasions that we could expect an improvement in their human rights performance — and they often mention Jewish emigration here — in the wake of significantly improved bilateral relations. They argue that when relations are bad, as they have been in the recent past, they have no incentive to alter their internal policies. But when relations were significantly better, as was presumably the case in the mid-1970s, they were responsive to our concerns. That is one Soviet response.

We reject the kind of linkage suggested here. We are interested in their deeds, not in their words, and we see no reason to reward the Soviets for a hint of better times ahead. On the other hand, we recognize that there has been a noticeable improvement in the tone of US–Soviet relations recently — obviously, we will return to arms control negotiations in Geneva and are currently engaging the Soviets in discussion on a range of regional and bilateral issues. President Reagan has invited General Secretary Gorbachev to visit the United States. The presence of a relatively young and more vigorous man at the Soviet helm itself provides an opportunity to move forward across the board on relations. For these reasons, we believe now is the time for the Soviets to live up to the logic of their statements on the consequences of improved relations. They have certainly not done so yet. The relatively minor gestures they have made recently are simply that. Unless we see some significant progress soon we will have no choice but to conclude that a true overall improvement in relations is not going to be possible. We believe the Soviet Union does want to improve relations with the United States. We believe that recent developments in our bilateral relations have created a situation in which significant progress on human rights issues is possible.

The hope is that the new Soviet leadership will have the foresight and the confidence to seize this opportunity and we will be ready to reciprocate if they do.

Now let me turn to the multilateral side of this question — to the Conference on Security and Cooperation in Europe (CSCE). Obviously, there is plenty of room for scepticism about Western human rights efforts, even for pessimism. In the years since 1975, can we after all say that the human rights situation in the Soviet Union has improved? We cannot. Let us candidly admit that we do not know precisely what works and what does not in respect of Soviet behaviour. We can, I think, be sure of the exact relevance of overall East–West relations to Soviet internal affairs. After all, let us remember that de-Stalinization came at the height of the cold war. And then at the height of détente, emigration may have increased considerably. But there was no significant improvement in the Soviet internal situation at all.

We must always keep in mind that all outside stimuli pale in comparison with internal factors in determining the internal policies of the Soviet regime. This is not a counsel of doom, however. The Soviets still act rationally and we can think of our approaches to them in some sort of cost-benefit terms. Thus, for example, they have to ask themselves whether particular human rights improvements will gain them something in the West — a particular reaction on our part for a general improvement in their reputation. And, of course, that calculation will change depending on the context — whether it is, for example, the day after they invade Afghanistan — or ten years after they invade Afghanistan.

It is certainly fair to ask what we have gained from the CSCE process. I would suggest three responses. First, the issue of Soviet human rights violations has in the last ten years been thoroughly legitimized as a matter of diplomatic discourse.

For example, ten years ago it would have been impossible to think that the Soviets would come to an international human rights meeting in a Western country where their record would be repeatedly addressed, yet they will do precisely that in Ottawa[1] in a few weeks. And every Western government has accepted that discussion of Soviet internal affairs is in this sense now on the international agenda.

Secondly, and consequently, it has been possible to achieve a level of engagement on this issue that I think would have been unimaginable twenty years go. Every NATO and neutral government in Europe and the North Atlantic area is now engaged in the issue of Soviet human rights violations. It is now customary for senior officials to raise these issues when they visit the USSR or East European countries or when they receive visits from officials of those countries. It is customary to discuss them at international gatherings in and out of CSCE. Discussion of these issues is common in parliaments and in the press. Thirdly, the issue has proved to be one in which there is substantial unity among the free nations.

Thinking back to Madrid,[2] the harmony among the neutral and non-aligned and NATO countries on East bloc human rights violations was quite remarkable. There may be divisions on arms matters or political questions, but there are no divisions on Sakharov.

From this experience of ten years perhaps there are some lessons we can learn. Certainly, we have learned that pressure and attention are crucial: pressure and attention from governments and parliaments and press, from public groups, through international organizations, in every possible way. And certainly we have learned that joint pressure is much preferable. Joint pressure avoids making the human rights issue a matter of East–West tension, or bilateral tension, and it makes clear the issue is an unavoidable one for all the free nations. Certainly, we have learned that we must always keep human rights on our agenda with the Soviets. Perhaps if one thinks of carrots and sticks, one can be too literal. The fact is that the Soviets, as previous speakers have said, care a great deal about what we say about them. Too often, we think only in terms of linkage between human rights improvements and a variety of relations with the Soviets on trade matters, cultural affairs, scientific exchanges and the like. All of those are important. But let us never forget that our pressure on human rights issues is itself viewed as a stick by the Soviets, and any reduction in that pressure is itself a carrot. Or, if I may change the metaphor, one of the most important forms of linkage is between Soviet human rights performance, and what we say about Soviet human rights performance.

One of the great prices the Soviets pay day to day for their miserable repression is that we tell the world about it again and again. And there is obviously a direct link between how they behave and what we say about them. Let us pause for a moment on that 'we', for it would be a grave error to think only of relations between our governments and the Soviet government, and forget relations between our societies and Soviet society. One of our crucial goals and methods must be to mobilize private opinion in the West, so that Western scientists and doctors and writers carry on a campaign for human rights and progress themselves, personally and in their own organizations, and directly with their counterparts in the Soviet élites, for the human rights struggle is not primarily that of Western governments but that of Western societies.

It would be easy to be pessimistic but let us recall again the desire of the Soviet regime for acceptance and legitimization by the West. We speak of a regime whose ideology is discredited and unpopular and whose economy has never been made to function effectively except for the production of weapons. It craves the legitimacy that we in the West can confer. This gives us a great asset in holding firm to our standards of human rights. CSCE is a valuable forum for carrying on the human rights struggle between the free societies in which we live and those which, denying freedom, will forever be seeking from us the approval their repressive systems deny them from their own populations. While we err if we idealize CSCE, we would also be greatly mistaken if we were to fail to utilize it.

Notes

[1] Meeting of Experts on Human Rights and Fundamental Freedoms (CSCE process), Ottawa, 7 May–17 June 1985.

[2] CSCE follow-up meeting, Madrid, 11 November 1980–9 September 1983.

CHAPTER 29

Dealing with the USSR: Diplomacy and Human Rights

JOHN MACGREGOR

The British Government essentially responds to two pressures which emanate from Parliament. In the eighteen months I have been in the Soviet Department it has seemed to me that these pressures fell into two distinct categories. First, there is a very substantial parliamentary voice that responds to the very things that are being discussed at this meeting, i.e. a deep human concern related to the USSR — and to other countries too, of course, about the issue of human rights. The second pressure we are under, which stems in part from, for instance, a concern about nuclear weapons, is that we should have better and more active relations with the USSR. It is the lot of Foreign Offices that they must seek a way between these two pressures which are, in a sense, opposite poles.

There are those who believe that one might arrange some sort of boycott, that one might have nothing to do with the USSR — the carrot-and-stick approach, with the stick being very much in evidence. On the whole, this kind of linkage has proved ineffective in the past and efforts to tie specific human rights issues to entirely different issues of foreign policy have not had a particularly good track record. Perhaps the Carter administration made a more serious effort than any other since the war to link these issues, to make some kind of 'Benthamite' micrometer of human behaviour which would be applied right across the board to every country.

Unfortunately, the realities of life (as the Russians would say) impinged on this and, at the end of the day, I do not think this linkage did very much to further the cause of human rights. There may have been during that period a slightly more positive international scene than there is today but I do not think it was necessarily related to this policy and it may well have preceded it. I have in mind, for example, the very high level of Jewish emigration from the USSR throughout the 1970s.

I think the view that British ministers have come round to is that what might loosely be termed 'parallelism' is the only effective way of operating. This means that we do indeed, as the Prime Minister stated when she attended President Andropov's funeral last year, seek better relations, and more contacts, with the USSR. At the same time, we do not allow all the awkward issues to be swept under the carpet. There is no reason at all why you cannot have perfectly business-like relations with the USSR and, at the same time, not fail to mention issues like human rights, Afghanistan, or the Helsinki Final Act — issues which are of real concern to the government.

Most people will regard the short-term effect of such a policy as minimal. But the fact is that nothing in East–West relations is a short-term policy. You can achieve things only over the long term — in arms control, trade agreements, or human rights. You just have to work on the admittedly optimistic basis that, by raising these issues again and again, by not letting them slip into the background, you will have a sort of drip effect on the stone, and eventually bring about changes.

I would like to close by quoting from a speech Mr Malcolm Rifkind, Minister of State at the Foreign and Commonwealth Office, made in Parliament on this theme on 28 November 1984:

What can we do realistically to show our concern and to encourage more human practices in the Soviet Union? First, the Government will ensure that the issue of human rights and the Soviet Union's Helsinki and Madrid commitments are kept firmly on the agenda of our ministerial contacts with the Russians. . . . We must show that these questions have not been, and will not be, forgotten.

Secondly, as well as mentioning the wider issues, we should on occasion mention individual names of those we are trying to help. At times — and recent years have been such times — this may be without apparent result, but that does not make it worthless . . . would we have seen the strangely concocted films of Dr. Sakharov and his wife in Gorky if it had not been for the constant mention of his name by Western representatives?

Obviously we have to be selective about names. The names which are chosen must be in some sense representative of categories of human rights abuse. When my right hon. and learned Friend the Foreign Secretary met Mr. Gromyko in July, he mentioned Father Gleb Yakunin, a Russian

Orthodox priest, Dr. Koryagin, a Soviet psychiatrist, Anatoly Shcharansky . . . and the Sakharovs . . .

Thirdly, with respect to what can be done, I think that hon. Members themselves can join in this process. The Russians are more in evidence in social and political circles in London these days, which is something that we welcome. This gives hon. Members the opportunity to mention particular cases that have been brought to their attention by constituents when they meet Soviet diplomats. The point can be put over in moderate and reasonable terms. This would help to show that concern about human rights is something which not only the Government are concerned about. This would show that it is the concern of all hon. Members.

A question that is often raised is whether these approaches should be publicised or remain confidential? My experience leads me to believe that what is required is a carefully judged mixture of both. If these matters remain confidential, there will be little public pressure on the Russians for visible improvements. If everything is done in a blaze of publicity, the Soviet reaction will tend to be not to respond, out of pride and stubbornness. I think that it is right that Ministers should make clear to the House and the press that they have raised human rights issues with Soviet Ministers, but there will be occasions when the specific names mentioned will not be made public. And when we do make names public, we assure ourselves via those most closely connected with the persons concerned that the public mention of their names will not do them harm . . .

Meanwhile, over human rights as much as any other part of the East–West agenda, we must show patience and persistence. We must not allow the subject to slip out of sight as relations with the East improve. It is not part of the Government's policy of pursuing better East–West relations to avoid the awkward issues. The Soviet Union CSCE commitments remain, and we shall continue to remind it that we expect it to live up to these in their entirety. We shall continue to insist that progress must be made on all fronts, not simply selective ones. Advances on security or trade matters must not be at the expense of the human rights commitments. The fact that attention in the CSCE process this year has largely been on the conference on disarmament in Europe in Stockholm will be balanced next year by the undoubted considerable interest in this House and elsewhere in the human rights meeting in Ottawa. The latter will give the West good opportunity to make this principle clear in practice as well as theory . . .

. . . the Government will continue to plug away at this issue, to press for improvements in Soviet treatment of its Jewish community, and the other minority communities that suffer discrimination of one kind or another. We will do that not only because it is a most important part of the CSCE process that we should do so, and not only because common humanity compels us to do it. We shall continue to explain that the way that the Soviet authorities treat their citizens creates in itself a wider and real problem of trust and understanding in this country. If they wish us to accept the genuineness of their desire for peace and security, there would be no better earnest of their intentions than to show in the way that they treat their own citizens and especially those who wish to travel or to emigrate that their motives vis-à-vis their neighbours and the West are indeed peaceful and friendly.

CHAPTER 30

The Helsinki Process and Beyond

CATHY COSMAN

The Helsinki Final Act was dismissed by many as yet another arcane diplomatic exercise. Others denounced it as legitimizing Soviet territorial expansion. Yet others considered that at least its human rights provisions were of value.

Strangely enough, each of these perceptions has justification. Some would say that vagueness is precisely what is wrong with the Helsinki accords. I would argue to the contrary, not because I favour diplomatic vagueness but because such differing interpretations are what give the agreement its staying power.

The Helsinki Final Act is not a treaty. It does not therefore have the force of international law and the obligations accepted by the thirty-five signatory states are not binding. The Final Act is an expression of political intent.

A unique feature of the Helsinki accords is how it binds together many diverse aspects of inter-state relations. It spans everything from military security to trade to educational and cultural exchanges.

The Helsinki agreement sets up a framework of state-to-state relations in which each of the participating states has the right of veto over every aspect of every agreement within the 'Helsinki process'. Hence concluding documents hammered out during Helsinki review meetings tend to lack specificity and human rights criticism. This consensus rule also has a crucial positive effect: each country — ranging from tiny Luxembourg to the giant USSR – has an equal voice in the Helsinki proceedings.

The Helsinki accords promote a pan-European political consciousness. Under Basket One, 'Declaration on Principles Guiding Relations between Participating States', Principle I speaks of sovereign equality and respect for sovereign rights. Principle VIII is a pledge to respect the equal rights and self-determination of peoples. Principle II commits participants to refrain from the threat or use of force. Principles III and IV pledge the inviolability of frontiers and the territorial integrity of states. Principle X refers to obligations under international law. These pledges, taken together, form the basis of a long-term pan-European undertaking. The ultimate effect of these accords is to undermine the Yalta legacy of ideological and political blocs.

The Yalta legacy is rejected in the Helsinki accords in other ways. Principle VII of Basket One commits the participating states to promote human rights and fundamental freedoms. Freedom of thought, conscience, religion or belief is based on the inviolable dignity of the individual. In other words, it is the individual and not the state which is the final repository of all rights. And there are more specific pledges which promote the rights of religious believers and ethnic minorities. These pledges are amplified in Principle IX, which states that individuals as well as states and institutions have a positive role to play in the Helsinki process. Thus the Helsinki accords stress the equality of all participating states and ascribe unique importance not only to individual rights but also to the individual's role in the Helsinki process itself.

The important human rights pledges of Basket One are amplified in Basket Three, which spells out measures to make the East–West divide more permeable to people and ideas. There are pledges to promote family reunification across international boundaries. There are promises to ease access to various kinds of information from all the participating states. There are pledges to ease the working conditions of journalists. There are commitments to increase cultural and educational exchanges.

In the four years after the signing of the Final Act, Soviet performance in the area of human rights improved somewhat. Despite numerous arrests, human rights groups in the USSR increased in number and effectiveness. In the key year of 1979 Jewish emigration reached a record high level of 51,320. Soviet citizens had somewhat better access to Western radio broadcasts. Since late 1979, however, all this has changed. Several factors played a role in the hardening of the Soviet attitude to human rights matters. One factor was Western reaction to the Soviet invasion of Afghanistan. A second factor was the decision by a number of West

European countries to deploy American Pershing and Cruise missiles. A third factor was the turmoil in Poland.

I believe, however, that Soviet domestic considerations were paramount in the new all-out assault on dissent. The USSR was ruled by a succession of three old and mortally ill men. In this atmosphere of political instability the Party leaders and security forces came increasingly to fear dissent. After 1979, arrests of Soviet human rights activists tripled to a known average of 238 per year. Sentences became longer and the so-called offences were more broadly defined. Conditions of detention for the estimated 10,000 Soviet political prisoners deteriorated markedly. In 1985 nine political prisoners known to us died — a post-Stalin record. In January 1980 Dr Andrei Sakharov was summarily banished to the closed city of Gorky. At times thereafter he in effect disappeared behind a veil of officially imposed silence.

At the same time, the emigration of Jews, Germans and Armenians was curtailed sharply, harsh laws were passed to discourage free expression and contacts with foreigners, and Soviet jamming of radio broadcasts was greatly stepped up in the summer of 1980.

How were these myriad Soviet human rights violations reflected in the Helsinki review meetings? At the Belgrade review meeting in 1977 the United States delegation was the only one to mention the names of seven victims of Soviet repression. Other Western delegations touched on the issue of Soviet and other East European violations of human rights only gingerly. During the marathon review meeting in Madrid the United States delegation publicly mentioned the names of 130 victims of Soviet repression. Fourteen other Western countries also referred to the names of victims of human rights violations in the USSR during the course of the Madrid review meeting. Indeed, during the Madrid meeting the Soviet human rights record was subjected to the most thorough criticism by the West. Madrid proved a uniquely useful forum for increasing Western awareness of Soviet human rights abuses.

The Helsinki process is an essential part of the long-term process of forging a pan-European political consciousness. It represents the best hope for people on both sides of the East-West ideological divide. It is up to Western governments and publics to see that it serves as the most effective form possible in the tough real world of hard political choices.

CHAPTER 31

Proposals for the Ottawa Meeting of Human Rights Experts

GERALD NAGLER

I would submit the following proposals to the Ottawa meeting of human rights experts, which convenes in May this year in the framework of the Helsinki process:

Avoidance of abstract discussions

The meeting should confine itself to the discussion of specific violations and questions of implementation. The issues include: emigration, family visits and reunification; religious freedom; minority rights; torture and mistreatment of political prisoners; the abuse of psychiatry; freedom of expression. Specific cases should also be raised.

Release of individuals monitoring human rights abuses

Delegates should insist on the release of all the imprisoned members of the various Helsinki groups in the USSR, members of Charter 77 and the Committee to Defend the Unjustly Persecuted in Czechoslovakia, the Committee for Social Defence in Poland, and all other persons monitoring human rights, defence lawyers and editors of human rights publications. These groups and individuals have specifically monitored the implementation of the human rights provisions of the Helsinki accords and have prepared extensive documentation on violations. Imprisoned members of the Turkish Peace Association, founded in response to the security provisions of the Helsinki accords, must also be freed. Government authorities and security police must end the harassment of human rights advocates, including the activists in Yugoslavia who monitored the recent 'Belgrade Six' trial.

Legitimization of monitoring groups

The participating states must formally accept the notion that citizens, either individually or collectively, have the right to monitor government compliance with the human rights and other provisions of the Helsinki accords. Individuals or groups, both independent and sponsored by governments, must be permitted to investigate and report their findings about human rights abuses in their country to their own governments and to those of other participating states. They must be free from harassment and not subject to imprisonment for their monitoring activity.

Institution of reporting procedures

We urge the participating states to institute a reporting mechanism within the Helsinki process, specifically the formation of a body that would receive and compile allegations of human rights violations and the results of fact-finding missions. Submissions may be made by individuals, citizens' groups, or governments. Governments must ensure access to this reporting body by permitting contact in person or submission of reports by mail or other means of communication. Petitioners must be assured freedom from harassment after filing such reports.

Fact-finding missions

The reporting body must be permitted to examine allegations of human rights violations, allegations made by any participating state, private organization or individual, and to make its own investigations. This body would be given access to victims of abuse and allowed on-site inspection of places of mass disturbances, civil disobedience and demonstrations. This body would also be authorized to observe trials and report its findings, and would be encouraged to prepare reports for publication and presentation at future human rights experts' meetings or any CSCE review meeting.

Recognition that human rights advocacy is not interference in internal affairs

With the institution of the reporting mechanism, the participating states must formally accept the notion that other partners in the Helsinki process may (a) examine compliance with the human rights provisions of the Final Act and the Madrid Concluding Document by any participating state and (b) make statements about such violations at CSCE meetings. Furthermore, they should recognize that enquiries, fact-finding missions, observation of trials, or statements of concern regarding human rights abuses are made in the spirit of adherence to universal human rights standards acknowledged by all the participating states, and should not be construed as interference in the internal affairs of any state.

Access to participating countries by the Red Cross

The participating states must permit the International Committee of the Red Cross to give aid on their territories and, in particular, afford it access to persons incarcerated in prisons, labour camps and psychiatric hospitals.

Reviewing of human rights abuses in Turkey, Yugoslavia and Malta

At previous Helsinki review conferences human rights abuses in the following countries have been reviewed: Bulgaria, Czechoslovakia, East Germany, Hungary, Poland, Romania, the United States and the USSR. Violations of the accords have been documented in the last year in other countries, e.g. Malta, Turkey and Yugoslavia. We are particularly concerned with the mistreatment of political prisoners in Turkey and Yugoslavia, and with the infringement of various human rights in Malta. We urge that these issues be raised by the participating states at the Ottawa conference.

Reviewing of mistreatment of minorities

In view of the strengthened language in the Concluding Document of the Madrid Conference concerning the treatment of minorities and the protection of the rights of ethnic groups in the participating countries, we urge that representatives of the participating states raise the issue and take steps to resolve the crises of mistreated minorities, including, but by no means limited to: the Turks of Bulgaria; Hungarians in Romania and Czechoslovakia; the Kurds of Turkey; the Crimean Tatars and Koreans in the USSR.

Ratification of international human rights covenants

The Concluding Document of the Madrid Conference calls upon 'those participating states which have not yet done so, to consider the possibility of acceding to' the international human rights covenants. To our knowledge, eight of the participating states, including the United States, are not yet parties to the international covenants; twenty-four are not yet parties to the optional protocol to the International Covenant on Civil and Political Rights. We urge those participating states which have not yet signed these covenants to explain why ratification has been delayed in their countries and to indicate possible ways to expedite ratification.

CHAPTER 32

Resolution of the Panel
(11 April 1985)

The Panel notes with profound regret that the reports presented at the Fifth Sakharov Hearing indicate a considerable deterioration of the human rights situation in the USSR, as reflected both in its laws and in its practices. It appears to be worse now than in 1975, when the Helsinki accords were signed, particularly in view of the following:

(1) The increased persecution of Soviet citizens claiming the human rights and fundamental freedoms to which they are entitled under international law.
(2) A dramatic decrease in the level of emigration, indicating a serious violation of the fundamental human right to leave one's country of origin.
(3) The increasing persecution of religious and ethnic minorities.
(4) The increased jamming of Western broadcasts, and other actions which impede the free flow of information, carried out in direct violation of the pledge to increase the exchange of printed and broadcast information.
(5) The deterioration of cooperation in the cultural and scientific sectors.

While this deterioration cannot be attributed to any single factor, the Panel calls for greater persistence and determination on the part of the Western signatories to insist on compliance with the accords and with the Soviet Union's freely accepted legal obligations under the international human rights treaties.

The Panel recognizes that violations of human rights are not confined to the Soviet Union, and deplores these wherever they occur. It calls for an examination of all possible policy options, with a view to securing greater compliance with all human rights obligations, as well as with the provisions of the Helsinki Final Act by its participants.

The material presented at the Fifth Sakharov Hearing will be conveyed to the participants of the forthcoming meeting of 'human rights experts' in Ottawa. The Panel urges participants of the meeting in Ottawa to take all available steps to amend the deplorable trend of Soviet human rights policies.

Finally, the Panel calls on the governments of the West to use all possible means to secure the restoration to Andrei Sakharov and his wife of the human rights to which they are entitled, including their right to emigrate.

Dr Simon Wiesenthal,
Chairman of the Panel,
Fifth International Sakharov Hearing

CHAPTER 33

Biographical Notes on the Speakers

ELLIOTT ABRAMS, born 1948, United States. An attorney, his appointments have included: 1975, Assistant Counsel, US Senate Permanent Subcommittee on Investigations; 1975–76, Special Counsel to Senator Henry Jackson; 1977–78, Special Counsel to Senator Daniel Moynihan; 1981–85, Assistant Secretary for Human Rights and Humanitarian Affairs. He is currently Assistant Secretary of State for Inter-American Affairs.

LUDMILLA ALEXEYEVA, born in the USSR. She is a historian and was an editor at Nauka publishing house. Between 1967 and 1974 Mrs Alexeyeva signed petitions and letters in support of many dissidents including Ginzburg, Galanskov, Marchenko and Chalidze. She was interrogated in the cases of Pyotr Yakir and Viktor Krasin. She is a founding member of the Moscow Helsinki Monitoring Group.

IGOR BIRMAN, born 1928, Moscow. He graduated in economics from the Plekhanov Institute, Moscow. He held several senior appointments in planning institutes in Moscow and was a member of the Academy of Sciences' Scientific Council on Mathematical Economics. He emigrated in 1974. In 1979 he was a member of the East–West technology transfer advisory panel of the Office of Technology Assessment of the US Congress. In 1981 he became president of the Foundation for Soviet Studies and editor of *Russia* magazine.

REV. MICHAEL BOURDEAUX, born 1934, Cornwall. In 1960 he was ordained into the Anglican Church. After widespread studies and parish work, he founded the Centre for the Study of Religion and Communism (now Keston College) in 1969. He has visited the USSR seven times as well as Romania and Poland. In 1984 he was awarded the Templeton Prize for Progress in Religion.

CATHY COSMAN graduated from Brunel College in history in 1967. She took her Masters at Brown University in Slavic languages and literatures in 1969 and her PhD at Brown University in 1971. She was a Fulbright Scholar at the Free University of Berlin in 1973–74, and worked at the International Research and Exchanges Board and the all-Union Institute of Cinematography, Moscow, in 1974–75. Since 1976 she has been a Soviet specialist at the Commission on Security and Cooperation in Europe, US Congress, Washington DC.

VICTOR DAVIDOV, born 1956, Kuibyshev. He studied history at university there, and became involved in dissident activity as a student, taping and distributing extracts from the *Gulag Archipelago*. He and his friends became increasingly vocal in their opposition to the Soviet regime. He was classified as a schizophrenic, and in 1980 committed to a special psychiatric hospital. Prior to this he was examined by a Soviet psychiatrist, A. Voloshanovich (now resident in the UK), and pronounced sane. He was recently allowed to emigrate.

GEORGY DAVYDOV, born 1941, USSR. He graduated as a geological engineer from the Plekhanov Mining Institute in Leningrad. In 1972 he was arrested and charged with criminal conspiracy and circulation of *samizdat* writings, including the Programme for the Democratic Movement of the Soviet Union. He was sentenced to five years' strict regime camp and two years' exile. He was very active in support of fellow prisoners who were mistreated by the prison authorities, and in Vladimir prison he signed a statement of political prisoners to the Commission on Legislative Proposals of the USSR Supreme Soviet, setting forth principles for the legal regulation of political prisoner status. He declared himself a political prisoner. He was released in 1980 and emigrated the same year.

KEITH EDWARDS, born 1925, Plymouth. Formerly Assistant Chief Engineer, External Services of the BBC; he has recently retired. After twenty-five years' service in the BBC's External Services specializing in short-wave broadcasting he is accepted as one of the world's experts in this field. He was awarded the Queen's Silver Jubilee Medal in 1977 and the MBE in 1982. Responsibility for the operational management of the transmission services in the UK and at relay stations during a period of intense competition necessitated many developments to ensure continuing audibility of the BBC's External Services programmes throughout the world. Additional responsibility for the development and operation of the technical facilities of the BBC's Monitoring Service from 1970 led to greater interest in the receiving problems including a special interest in the problems created by jamming.

FERDINAND FELDBRUGGE, born 1933, The Hague. He studied law in Utrecht from 1950 to 1955. He has taught law in the Universities of Utrecht and Leiden. He has also taught at the Russian Institute, Columbia University, and the Russian Research Center at Harvard. Since 1973 he has been Professor of Soviet and East European Law and director of the Documentation Office of East European Law at Leiden.

SIDNEY HEITMAN, born 1924. Since 1977 he has been Professor of History at the University of Colorado, USA. He has been the recipient of many academic awards and fellowships and is a member of numerous associations and institutes for Slavic studies. He is also the author of many books, articles and reviews.

FRANTIŠEK JANOUCH, born 1931, is a professor of theoretical physics. In 1970 he was forbidden to work in his profession and to publish. In 1974 he was allowed to accept a guest professorship offered by the Swedish Royal Academy of Sciences. In 1975 he was deprived of Czechoslovak citizenship. He is the Chairman of the Board of the Charter 77 Foundation in Stockholm.

DINA KAMINSKAYA, born 1920, USSR, entered law school in 1937. She worked as a defence lawyer for thirty-seven years, and defended many dissidents. She was expelled from the College of Advocates, and was exiled from the USSR in 1977. She now lives in the United States.

CRONID LUBARSKY, born 1934, Pskov, USSR. An astrophysicist, he studied at Moscow State University and worked at the Chernogolovka Institute of Solid State Physics. He was arrested in 1972, accused of compiling and distributing anti-Soviet literature and sentenced to five years' strict regime camp. He emigrated in 1977. He is now editing *USSR News Brief*.

JOHN MACGREGOR, born 1946, educated Balliol College, Oxford. In 1973 he joined the Foreign Service. He served in India and as Private Secretary to Malcolm Rifkind MP, and is currently Assistant Head of the Soviet Department at the Foreign and Commonwealth Office.

GERALD NAGLER is President of Urania AG, Stockholm and Executive Director of the International Helsinki Federation for Human Rights, Vienna.

BOHDAN NAHAYLO is a British-born writer on Soviet affairs. A regular contributor to the *Spectator*, he has written for *The Times*, *Guardian*, *Observer* and *Wall Street Journal*. After postgraduate study at the London School of Economics, he worked for several years as Amnesty International's researcher on the Soviet Union, and during this time also wrote reports on several Soviet national minorities for the Minority Rights Group. He is currently a research analyst for Radio Liberty in Munich, and is working on books dealing with Soviet dissent and nationality problems.

VLADLEN PAVLENKOV, born 1929, Gorky, USSR. A teacher of history, he was dismissed from his university post in 1968 after the appearance of leaflets calling on people to follow the Czech example. He was arrested in 1969, tried in 1970 and found guilty of planning to found an anti-Soviet organization and writing and circulating anti-Soviet works. He was sentenced to seven years' strict regime camp. He was very active in support of human rights in the Soviet Union, with special regard to conditions of confinement for political prisoners. He emigrated to the USA and is now director of the Freedom of Communications Committee.

NIKOLAY PANKOV worked as a projectionist in *Goskino*. He applied to emigrate despite the fact that he belongs to no 'category' which might enable him to do so. He revealed the Soviet practice of showing illegally copied Western films. Following incarceration together with his wife in psychiatric hospitals, he was finally permitted to emigrate in 1985.

PETER REDDAWAY, born 1939. He graduated from Cambridge and has done extensive work in Soviet studies, including a period at Moscow State University. As senior lecturer at the London School of Economics, he was the recipient of many academic awards and in 1983 to 1984 was Visiting Fellow at the Woodrow Wilson International Center for Scholars in Washington. His book *Russia's Political Hospitals* (with Sidney Bloch) received the Guttmacher Award. He is the author of many articles concerning Soviet policy, especially in the field of dissent and the abuse of psychiatry for political purposes. He is now Secretary of the Kennan Institute for Advanced Russian Studies, Woodrow Wilson International Center for Scholars.

MARITE SAPIETS, born UK. She obtained her BA in Russian from Sussex University, where she also took an MA with a dissertation on Pasternak's poetry. She currently works as a researcher at Keston College, where her specializations are Roman Catholics and Seven-Day Adventists. She has published in *Religion in Communist Lands* and elsewhere.

DAVID SATTER, born 1947, United States, is a graduate of the University of Chicago and was a Rhodes Scholar at Balliol College, Oxford. He worked as a journalist on the *Chicago Tribune*, from 1972–76, and was Moscow correspondent for the *Financial Times* from 1976–82. He is currently writing a book on the USSR with the support of a Guggenheim Fellowship.

AISHE SEITMURATOVA, born 1937, is active in the Crimean Tatar movement. A graduate in history, she worked as a schoolteacher in Samarkand. In 1971 she was arrested and charged with preparation and dissemination of anti-Soviet literature and sentenced to three years' imprisonment. In 1974 she was refused re-admission to the Uzbek Academy of Sciences' Institute of History to complete her postgraduate course. She now lives in the United States.

LOUISE I. SHELLEY, born 1952, New York. She is Associate Professor at the Schools of Justice and International Service, the American University, Washington. At present she is on a Guggenheim Fellowship writing on Soviet justice.

PAUL SIEGHART is active in the work of the International Commission of Jurists, and is chairman of the executive committee of its British section, Justice. He is also a governor of the British Institute of Human Rights, a trustee of the European Human Rights Foundation, and the author of *The International Law of*

Human Rights (Oxford University Press, 1983), described by Lord Gardiner as 'the last word on the subject for years to come'. His new introduction to human rights laws, *The Lawful Rights of Mankind*, was published in April 1986 by Oxford University Press. Mr Sieghart was a member of the panel at the Fourth International Sakharov Hearing in Lisbon in October 1983.

NINA STROKATA, born 1925, Odessa. A microbiologist, she graduated from Odessa Medical Institute, where she was employed, 1950–52. In 1971 she was dismissed from her job and not permitted to defend her doctoral thesis. In 1972 she was charged with disseminating *samizdat* literature and sentenced to four years' imprisonment in a strict regime camp. She now lives in the United States, where she is a Western representative of the Ukrainian Helsinki Group, of which she was a founding member.

VLADIMIR TOLZ, born 1944, USSR. He worked as a historian and was one of the editors of '*V*', a *samizdat* news bulletin, and for several years was a major source of information for the *Chronicle of Current Events* and *News from the USSR*. He emigrated in 1982 and now lives in Munich, where he does research into contemporary Russian history and writes a series on history for Radio Liberty.

MIKHAIL VOSLENSKY, born 1920, USSR. He studied at Moscow State University. He served in the Allied Control Commission in Germany before becoming vice-director of the Information Service of the World Peace Council. He was senior researcher at the Soviet Academy of Sciences before being promoted to the Chair of History at Lumumba University, Moscow. From 1950 until he emigrated in 1972 he occupied high positions, including the post of secretary to the Disarmament Commission of the Soviet Academy of Sciences and vice-president of the Soviet–East German Historians' Commission. His work brought him into close contact with the apparatus of the Central Committee of the Communist Party of the Soviet Union. Since 1972 he has taught in German and Austrian universities and since 1981 he has been director of the Institute for Contemporary Soviet Studies in Munich. He is the author of five books and over 450 articles and reviews.

SIMON WIESENTHAL, born 1908, Poland. He worked as an architect until the Second World War. He was a prisoner in Nazi concentration camps and has been active since the end of the war in searching for Nazi war criminals and in assisting former victims of persecution. He has been widely honoured for his humanitarian work and selfless pursuit of justice. He is the director of the Jewish Documentation Centre in Vienna.

ALLAN WYNN graduated in medicine from Melbourne University, was elected a Fellow of the Australian College of Physicians and practised as a consultant physician in Melbourne. He took up residence in London in 1972 and became aware of the abuse of psychiatry for political purposes through contact with the late David Markham. He joined the committee for the release of Vladimir Bukovsky and acted as chairman for the Working Group on the Internment of Dissenters in Mental Hospitals. He joined the committees for the release of Pyotr Grigorenko and Aleksandr Ginzburg. In 1983 he became a member of the Board of the Sakharov Institute in the USA and, in 1985, chairman of the Executive Committee for the Fifth International Sakharov Hearing.

EFREM YANKELEVICH, born 1950. In 1972 he graduated as a radio engineer from the Institute of Communications in Moscow. He is the son-in-law of Elena Bonner, wife of Andrei Sakharov. In 1973 he was offered a scholarship at the Massachusetts Institute of Technology but was denied a visa to go to the United States from the Soviet Union. He wrote a letter to the authorities on the occasion of the trial of S. A. Kovalev, requesting an end to closed trials. In December 1975 he travelled to Vilnius with Sakharov for Kovalev's trial, was not admitted, and lost his job. He emigrated in 1977 to the United States. Andrei Sakharov has appointed him his official representative in the West.

APPENDIX I

The Jewish Problem in the USSR

HAROLD STONE

According to the Soviet census of 1979 there was a total of 1,810,876 Jews in the USSR. However, many observers believe the true figure to be between 2 million and 2.5 million. The Soviet Jews are predominantly an urban population and they inhabit mainly the USSR's Slavonic republics.

The rights of Soviet Jews, both collectively and individually, continue to be infringed by the Soviet authorities, in violation both of the international obligations undertaken by the USSR — including the humanitarian provisions of the Helsinki Final Act — and of Soviet domestic legislation.

Jewish emigration from the USSR seems essentially a function of Soviet–US relations. In line with the deterioration of relations between the superpowers since the beginning of the 1980s, the emigration of Soviet Jews has steadily dwindled from a total of over 51,000 in 1979 — the peak year of the emigration of the 1970s — to an annual average of around 1,000 by the mid-1980s.[1]

Despite numerous assertions by Soviet spokesmen in general, and representatives of the official Anti-Zionist Committee of the Soviet Public in particular, to the effect that virtually all Jews who wish to emigrate from the USSR have already done so, abundant evidence indicates that this is far from being the case. On the contrary, all the indications are that the desire for emigration among Soviet Jews remains great. According to Israeli statistics, almost 650,000 invitations (*vyzovy*) were sent to Soviet Jews by relatives in Israel between 1968 and mid-1985; since about 266,000 Jews were able to obtain an exit permit by the end of 1985, there was clearly a great excess of invitations over visas granted.

It should also be stressed that, in a situation where minimal emigration is permitted and harassment of potential emigrants is a regular practice of the authorities, many Soviet Jewish citizens seem likely to be deterred from applying to emigrate. Applicants for emigration face a variety of forms of harassment. These include:

(a) loss of job — the often highly qualified 'refusenik' is frequently fired from his job and compelled to accept any form of unskilled labour;
(b) the 'refusenik' or his children may be expelled from higher education institutions;
(c) vilification in the Soviet media;
(d) interference with correspondence and loss of telephone;
(e) physical violence;
(f) criminal prosecution — at the beginning of 1986 eighteen 'Prisoners of Zion' (i.e. emigration activists) were serving sentences after having been convicted on a variety of charges, in particular Article 70 of the RSFSR Criminal Code ('anti-Soviet agitation and propaganda') and Article 190–1 of the RSFSR Criminal Code ('defaming the Soviet state'). The harshest sentence, seven years labour camp and five years exile, is currently being served by Iosif Begun, a Hebrew-language activist who first applied to emigrate to Israel in 1971. Also at the beginning of 1986, a total of twenty-two former 'Prisoners of Zion' remained in the USSR, unable to obtain exit permits.

There are at present in the USSR almost 1,200 known 'refuseniks' who have been seeking to emigrate for at least ten years. There is also a total of almost 7,400 'refuseniks' who have been waiting to emigrate for between five and ten years.

The officially recognized national language of the Jews of the Soviet Union is Yiddish. It is estimated, however, that only just over 13 per cent of Soviet Jewry are proficient in this language: Russian is the language used most commonly by Soviet Jews. Yet even such Yiddish cultural facilities as exist are inadequate.

The restrictive policy regarding, for example, Yiddish books is striking if one examines the number of books published in the languages of other Soviet nationalities which, according to the 1979 census, were of a size similar to that of the Jewish minority. Thus in 1980, 1981 and 1982 the number of Polish books issued was, respectively, 79, 95 and 86. The corresponding numbers of Yiddish books was 20, 8 and 6.

The Soviet authorities also make propagandistic use of the existence of the so-called Jewish Autonomous *oblast* of Birobidzhan as the place where Jewish culture can 'legitimately' be enjoyed. But, according to the census of 1979, only 10,166 Jews — i.e. 0.5 per cent of Soviet Jewry — lived among the *oblast*'s total population of 188,710.

There can be little doubt that Soviet cultural policies towards the Jews must ultimately lead to the extinction of the Jewish minority, i.e. cultural genocide — a concept recognized by the Soviets. Anxious to preserve their national heritage, some Soviet Jews have, fully in accordance with Soviet law, resorted to educational activities of their own. They have organized in private apartments informal seminars and study groups on Jewish cultural matters and issued *samizdat* publications.

The Soviet authorities have paid special attention to the harassment of Hebrew-language activists. Hebrew cannot be taught or studied in the USSR as a foreign language except in the most restricted framework. Soviet officials do not attempt to justify the virtual ban on Hebrew, which is entirely illegal.

There exist in the USSR no facilities in regard to Jewish religious education. Soviet spokesmen point out that parents may educate their children religiously but, in so far as there is no more than a skeletal framework of Jewish religious life in the USSR, the parents often do not possess the necessary knowledge to do so.

Soviet official sources frequently give a figure of about ninety functioning synagogues in the USSR. The true figure, however, seems to be closer to fifty. Even if one were to accept the figure of 60,000 Jewish believers in the USSR, a statistic provided by Soviet official and semi-official sources, the total of fifty synagogues is entirely insufficient. Moreover, the figure of 60,000 Jewish religious believers excludes, for instance, those Jews who visit synagogues irregularly or adhere selectively to Judaic rituals.

The handful of Soviet students permitted to study at the Rabbinical Seminary in Hungary falls far short of the number of rabbis needed in the USSR. Also, there has for a long time been a shortage of Jewish prayer books, bibles, calendars and similar publications. Moreover, Jewish religious artefacts can neither be manufactured in the USSR nor easily imported.

There is a general shortage of burial space for religious Jews in the USSR. In Moscow the situation is especially critical. In an appeal to the authorities in early 1984, Moscow Jews claimed that the authorities had repeatedly rejected requests that a new Jewish cemetery be built in the capital or even that a plot of land be set aside for Jewish burials in non-Jewish cemeteries.

Judaism in the USSR suffers particular discrimination in that it is denied a framework for the organization of Jewish religious life. Furthermore, the Jewish religion remains the only recognized denomination which is not permitted to maintain regular links with co-religionists outside the USSR.

There is considerable evidence of anti-Jewish discrimination in regard to political appointments and employment. However, the best documented case of discrimination is in admissions to institutions of higher education. In particular, a group of Moscow mathematicians conducted a *samizdat* investigation of the admission in the years 1979, 1980, 1981 and 1983 of students from five leading physics and mathematics schools of Moscow, partly to the Mathematics and Mechanics Department of Moscow University and partly to the Moscow Institutes of Physical Engineering and of Physics and Technical Engineering. It appears that the investigation was prompted by the fact that there were only 2 Jewish students among the 425 successful applicants to the Mathematics and Mechanics Department. The authors of the investigation concluded that there was 'no doubt concerning the purely racist standards of the Enrolment Commission'.

There has been no abatement of the pervasive, long-lasting campaign of anti-Zionist propaganda in the Soviet media, a campaign which has often assumed classical antisemitic forms. Perhaps the most frequently recurring theme of this propaganda is the equation of Zionism with racism, Fascism and Nazism.

Many Jews in the USSR tragically find themselves in a position where they can neither assimilate nor emigrate.

Note
[1] These and other data in this paper are taken mainly from the following reports which were prepared for recent 'Helsinki process' meetings at Ottawa, Budapest and Berne respectively:
The Position of Soviet Jewry: Human Rights and the Helsinki Accords, 1985 (London, 1985); *The Problems of Jewish Culture* (London, 1985); and *Human Contacts, Reunion of Families and Soviet Jewry* (London, 1986).

APPENDIX II

The Helsinki Process: A Balance Sheet

EDWARD KLINE

On 1 August 1985, the thirty-five participating states met in Helsinki to commemorate the tenth anniversary of the Final Act of the Conference on Security and Cooperation in Europe (CSCE).

The 'Helsinki process' has failed to capture the attention of the American public. But it has stirred up clashing assessments inside the foreign policy establishment.

Critics complain that 'the Helsinki process spreads a fog of false, but soothing assumptions', that the discussion of human rights with Soviet officials entangles us in complicity with evil. Others claim that the Final Act confirmed the Soviet hegemony over Eastern Europe mistakenly conceded at Yalta.

Supporters of the Helsinki process range from persons who believe that the negotiations and meetings can be useful, to cynics who argue that a pretence of dialogue is necessary for NATO unity and to placate American public opinion. Max Kampelman, head of the American delegation at the Madrid CSCE Meeting, insists that the exposure of Soviet misconduct and obstinacy outweighs any connotation of Soviet respectability.[1]

Many points at issue between critics and supporters can be decided by a review of the record.

Anxious to receive confirmation of post-war European frontiers, the Soviet Union in 1954 suggested a European conference which could produce some substitute for a peace treaty. The Soviet proposal made no headway while Konrad Adenauer remained Chancellor and persistently blocked Western recognition of East Germany. The Bucharest Declaration on Strengthening Peace and Security in Europe adopted by the Warsaw Pact in July 1966 revived the idea of a pan-European conference. The initiative was stalled briefly by the 1968 Soviet invasion of Czechoslovakia. It regained momentum after Willy Brandt came to power in 1969 and began seeking openings to the East.

Germany — its frontiers, the relations between East and West zones, and the status of Berlin — had remained the focus of post-war tensions. The West was anxious to work out more stable and satisfactory arrangements for Germany and for Berlin in particular. West Germany signed treaties with the USSR and Poland in 1970. In talks conducted between 1970 and 1972, West and East Germany negotiated a series of agreements on the status of Berlin, traffic, mail and telephone links, and visits. The Four Power Agreement in Berlin, which the West had made an explicit precondition for opening negotiations on a European conference, was drafted in August 1971 and signed on 3 June 1972.

The USSR had often used the vulnerable position of West Berlin to exert pressure on the West. Since 1972 the Soviet Union has respected the Four Power Agreement and this has bolstered the Europeans' sense of security. (A poll taken in October and November 1984 reported that only 13 per cent of West Europeans believed that a world war would break out in the next ten years.) The Berlin agreement was the first achievement of the CSCE process and probably justifies the entire cost of CSCE. Henry Kissinger, however, used Soviet eagerness for a European conference to gain one more concession: that negotiations between NATO and the Warsaw Pact on the reduction of military forces in Europe would open in Vienna in November 1973. While the talks on Mutual and Balanced Force Reductions (MBFR) have dragged on for more than ten years without agreement, they have reduced pressure for unilateral US troop withdrawals from Europe and also helped to ease fears of war.

With these preliminaries settled, negotiations opened in Helsinki on 22 November 1972. Representatives of thirty-two European countries, the United States and Canada participated. (Monaco was invited at a later stage.) The preparatory sessions of CSCE lasted until July 1973, when a negotiating agenda was agreed upon. From September 1973 until July 1975 diplomats from the participating states met in Geneva to work out the provisions of the Final Act. The Soviet Union succeeded in incorporating the principles of 'non-intervention in internal affairs' and 'inviolability of frontiers'. (The West, however, managed to insert a provision that 'frontiers can be changed, in accordance with international law, by peaceful means and by agreement.')

The inclusion of Principle VII ('Respect for human rights and fundamental freedoms, including the freedom of thought, conscience, religion or belief') was a signal accomplishment. Among the specific provisions of Principle VII are the 'freedom of the individual to profess and practice, alone or in community with others, religion or belief...'; 'full opportunity for the actual enjoyment of human rights and fundamental freedoms' by persons belonging to national minorities; confirmation of 'the right of the individual to know and act upon his rights and duties in this field'; and a pledge by the participating states to 'fulfil their obligations as set forth in the international declarations and agreements in this field, including *inter alia* the International Covenants on Human Rights'. (Valery Chalidze has remarked on the inclusion in the legally non-binding Final Act of the odd stipulation that the participating states will fulfil their obligations under the legally binding Covenants. This is merely acknowledgement that political interests and decisions carry more weight than legal texts in relations between sovereign states.)

The Soviets' proposal would have limited CSCE and the Final Act to two sections — one covering general principles and security and one covering trade and cultural cooperation. But again, several European countries, led by the Netherlands, took advantage of Soviet eagerness for a positive outcome and gained agreement in April 1973 to include a 'Third Basket' in the Geneva negotiations. The Third Basket contains useful provisions on family reunification, travel, access to information, working conditions for journalists and cultural exchanges, thanks to skilful bargaining by a few European countries in the face of Soviet hostility and American indifference.

After more than two years of negotiations, the 40,000-word Final Act was completed in July 1975:

In a very real sense, the nature of CSCE had changed significantly from the original Soviet aim to consolidate the USSR's own position on Eastern Europe and to inhibit Western cohesion ... The CSCE in fact became a negotiation about the manner and pace of breaking down the division of Europe and alleviating the human hardships engendered by it.[2]

As statesmen travelled to Helsinki later that month to sign the Final

Act, the suspicion spread that the West had been outmanoeuvred by the crafty Russians. President Ford complains in his memoirs:

'no trip I made during my Presidency was so widely misunderstood. "Jerry, don't go" the *Wall Street Journal* implored, and the *New York Times* called the trip "misguided and empty" . . . I didn't expect the outrage the trip would provoke among Americans of East European descent. A sampling of my White House mail showed 558 letters against the Helsinki agreement and only thirty-two in favor of it.'

Ford, however, left for Helsinki believing that we should 'make good use of the European Security Conference to get a commitment from leaders of closed and controlled countries to permit greater freedom of movement for individuals and freer flow of information and ideas. The conference also promised to set a standard by which the world could measure progress.'[3]

George Kennan, a seasoned diplomat sceptical of vague, multi-lateral agreements, was surprised by the public reaction to the Final Act:

'The Western powers were immediately attacked for having assented, in this document, to the thesis that the existing boundaries of Europe should not be altered by force. This, it was claimed, was equivalent to a formal abandonment of all Eastern Europe, including Eastern Germany, to permanent Soviet domination, and was thus a major, unwarranted, and unrequited concession to the Soviet Union.

'Actually, none of the Western powers had the faintest idea of attempting to alter any of these boundaries by force or any other way, even in the absence of such a declaration; the very thought of any sort of removal of the division of Europe was in fact abhorrent to them. The supposed concession was therefore not a very real one. The Russians, on the other hand, subscribed in at least three places in the Helsinki communiqué to sentiments which, under even the most perfunctory standards of observance, would have ruled out a repetition of the action taken in Czechoslovakia in 1968. They also accepted language relating to human rights which was at least misleading when taken in relation to their established practices. These latter provisions turned out to be somewhat embarrassing to the Soviet government in the months that followed — so much so that it could well be said that if anyone lost the semantic battle which the Helsinki negotiations actually amounted to, it was the Soviet side and not the West.'[4]

Why did the Soviet Union so doggedly pursue a European conference if they paid a substantial price for illusory benefits? Arkady

Shevchenko in his recent book *Breaking with Moscow*[5] attributes Soviet persistence to Brezhnev's sponsorship:

'The Soviet commitment to the European security talks had been made a matter of Brezhnev's personal prestige . . . At the Twenty-Fourth Party Congress in 1971, a sweeping peace program formally made the convening of the European conference an article of Communist faith. After that declaration of policy there could be no turning back. Leonid Brezhnev had come to see himself as the prime mover behind the European security campaign.'

Shevchenko also suggests a second, tactical reason for Soviet behaviour: 'Given the increasing tension with China, the Soviet Union wanted and needed a maximum of calm and good relations with Europe. The value of the security negotiations with the Europeans rested heavily on the insecurity which marked dealings between Moscow and Peking.'

A more fundamental reason for Soviet interest in the CSCE process — an interest which has survived Brezhnev's death — is Russia's enduring ambition to be recognized as a European country and an integral part of European civilization. (The Final Act's preamble refers to the 'common history' of the participants.) The Soviet leaders evidently regard concessions made on human rights and other issues as a reasonable fee for joining the European 'club'.

Before reviewing the sparring over the implementation of the Final Act which began at the Helsinki summit and continues to this day, tribute should be paid to the CSCE's role in unblocking European diplomacy. Until the CSCE negotiations, the USSR in effect handled foreign relations for the Warsaw Pact countries. By its specific reference to the 'Sovereign equality and individuality' of all participating states as well as by encouraging them to 'implement the provisions of the Final Act . . . bilaterally, by negotiations with other participating states', the Helsinki agreement sanctioned direct contacts between the Warsaw Pact countries and the other participating states. The USSR can still veto specific initiatives such as Erich Honecker's proposed 1984 visit to West Germany, but the East European countries have significantly expanded their diplomatic and cultural contacts with Western Europe and the United States under the CSCE umbrella. The Final Act has inspired the ruled in East Europe as well as their rulers to assert themselves. Charter 77 in Czechoslovakia, Solidarity in Poland and the autonomous peace movement in East Germany differ in character and purpose, but all were nourished by the Helsinki climate.

A remarkable collection of leaders met at Helsinki from 30 July to 1 August to sign the Final Act: Gerald Ford, Leonid Brezhnev, Harold Wilson, Giscard d'Estaing, Helmut Schmidt, Aldo Moro, Pierre Trudeau, Josip Tito, Edward Gierek, Gustav Husak, Nicolae Ceausescu, Olaf Palme, Archbishop Makarios and other presidents and prime ministers. They made the Helsinki meeting the visible culmination of détente. (The Final Act's preamble notes the CSCE's potential 'to make détente both a continuing and an increasingly viable and comprehensive process'.)

Beneath the superficial comity, however, détente was already floundering in difficulties. Congress had adopted the Jackson— Vanik and Stevenson amendments in late 1974 making most-favoured-nation tariff treatment for the USSR dependent on its emigration policy and limiting the amount of Export–Import Bank credit available to the USSR.

The Politburo retaliated by cancelling the 1972 Soviet–American Trade Agreement. This was more than a propaganda ploy. The Jackson—Vanik amendment offended Soviet leaders by its implication — however accurate — that they were willing to sell Soviet citizens, and the Stevenson amendment reduced the price offered. (The Soviets' own actions had contributed to the passage of the Trade Act amendments. Imposition of an 'education tax' on prospective emigrants suggested that ransom was desired. And major unannounced Soviet purchases in 1972 of government-subsidized American wheat, which triggered a sharp increase in American food prices, angered Congressmen and gained votes for the amendments.)

A persistent Soviet arms build-up coupled with aggressive Soviet behaviour in Angola, South Yemen and other Third World trouble spots alarmed the United States. The Yom Kippur War, the energy crisis, Nixon's resignation, and the fall of Saigon strained the framework of Soviet–American relations.

Brezhnev and Ford still used the rhetoric of détente in their Helsinki speeches, but the differences in their interpretations of the Final Act were plain. Brezhnev said on 31 July 1975:

'The Soviet Union regards the outcome of the Conference not merely as a necessary summing up of the political results of World War II . . . The results of the Conference represent a carefully weighed balance of the interests of all participating states and, therefore, should be treated with special care . . . The understandings reached cover a wide range of the most topical problems relating to peace, security and cooperation in various fields . . . The main conclusion which is reflected in the Final Act is this: no one should try, from foreign policy considerations of one kind or another, to dictate to other peoples how they should manage their internal affairs. It is only the people of each given state, and no one else, who have the sovereign right to decide their own internal affairs and establish their own internal laws. Any other approach would be precarious and perilous ground for the cause of international cooperation.'

President Ford responded on 1 August:

'We will spare no effort to ease tensions and to solve problems between us, but it is important that you realize the deep devotion of the American people and their government to human rights and fundamental freedoms and thus to the pledges that this conference has made regarding the freer movement of people, ideas, information. History will judge this conference not by what we say here today but by what we do tomorrow — not by the promises that we make but by the promises that we keep . . . The American people are still dedicated . . . to life, liberty, and the pursuit of happiness for all peoples everywhere.'

Disputes over interpretation and implementation of the Final Act continue and have themselves become a source of Soviet–American tensions. The frequent use of subjective terminology such as 'appropriate measures' or 'to examine in a favorable spirit' introduces an unusual amount of ambiguity into the Final Act, which was negotiated as an expression of political intent and not as a legally binding treaty.

Was the Soviet Union ever prepared to implement the humanitarian and Third Basket provisions of the Final Act? I believe that Brezhnev did make a serious effort until 1979 to fulfil Soviet commitments as he understood them. The West failed to recognize Brezhnev's resolve because conflicting definitions of key words meant that no meeting of minds was achieved at Geneva despite the concensus reached on the text of the Final Act. (Soviet perversion of the vocabulary of politics and human rights, so well described by Orwell, was originally a means of deceiving others. Now it often misleads the Soviet leaders themselves.)

The Soviet Union took many substantive actions after the

opening of the CSCE negotiations to accommodate Western expectations:

— The Soviet Union in 1973 ratified the International Covenants on Human Rights.

— Soviet jamming of the Russian-language services of the Voice of America, the BBC and Deutsche Welle was suspended in September 1973, one week before the CSCE negotiations opened in Geneva. (Jamming re-commenced in August 1980. Jamming of Radio Liberty was never discontinued.)

— After the 1975 Helsinki meeting, the Soviet Union took a number of measures to promote cultural and scientific exchanges. Two examples: An international book exhibition was held in Moscow in September 1975. Biennially since September 1977, International Book Fairs have been held in Moscow.

In 1976 a law was adopted by the USSR providing that: 'Historical and cultural monuments owned by foreign states, organizations or persons and temporarily brought into the USSR for cultural exchange within the framework of appropriate agreements shall be protected by the state.'

— In June 1976 the Presidium of the USSR Supreme Soviet issued a decree providing that 'ministries and departments of the USSR and the Union Republics, central organs of public organizations and their officials may have direct dealings with foreign journalists in the manner determined by the legislation of the USSR.' The USSR concluded an agreement with the USA in 1975 providing for reciprocal issue of multiple entry and exit visas for accredited journalists.

— The fee for a Soviet exit visa was reduced from 400 to 300 roubles effective from 1 January 1976, and to 200 roubles in 1978. Some of the paperwork required for exit visas was simplified, and the period in which a new application could be filed after a rejection was shortened to six months.

Soviet Jewish emigration, which had declined from 34,000 in 1973 to 13,000 in 1975 (a decline often attributed to the dispute over the Jackson—Vanik amendment), rose steadily after the signing of the Final Act to 14,000 in 1976, 17,000 in 1977, 29,000 in 1978, and peaked at over 51,000 in 1979.

Ethnic German emigration to West Germany reached 9,000 in 1976 and remained near that record rate until 1979.

— Elena Bonner, the wife of Andrei Sakharov, was permitted to travel to Italy for medical treatment in 1975, 1977 and 1979 [also in 1985–6 – ed].

— Arrests of prominent dissidents declined during the initial period of the Helsinki process.

The *Chronicle of Current Events* lists no arrest of a well-known dissident after 18 April 1975 (Andrei Tverdokhlebov) until the arrests of Ginzburg, Tykhy, Rudenko and Orlov in February 1977.[6]

Peter Reddaway supplies the following figures for documented arrests of dissidents by year: 1972 – 196; 1973 – 182; 1974 – 122; 1975 – 81; 1976 – 93; 1977 – 81; 1978 – 94; 1979 – 145; 1980 – 257.[7] While such figures cannot be precise in the absence of official Soviet statistics, the trend is clear.

— After publication abroad of *The Gulag Archipelago*, Aleksandr Solzhenitzyn was arrested on 12 February 1974, and charged with treason. He was, however, stripped of Soviet citizenship and expelled to West Germany on 13 February.

In January 1976 Ukrainian human rights activist Leonid Plyushch, who had been tried for anti-Soviet agitation, was released from Dnepropetrovsk prison psychiatric hospital and allowed to emigrate with his family.

On 18 December 1976, Vladimir Bukovsky was released from Vladimir prison and flown to Zurich airport where he and Luis Corvalan, former General Secretary of the Chilean Communist Party, were simultaneously freed.

Dr Mikhail Stern, an endocrinologist convicted on bribery charges after his sons applied for emigration, was released from a labour camp in March 1977 (he soon emigrated), one week before the International Stern Tribunal was to conduct hearings on his case in Amsterdam.

On 20 April 1979, two months before the Carter–Brezhnev Vienna summit, five prisoners who had been convicted in connection with the 1970 Leningrad 'hijacking' case — Anatoly Altman, Hillel Butman, Leib Khnokh, Boris Penson and Volf Zalmanson — were released fourteen months before the expiration of their ten-year terms. All emigrated to Israel.

On 27 April 1979, Mark Dymshits, Aleksandr Ginzburg, Eduard Kuznetsov, Valentin Moroz and Georgy Vins were released from confinement and flown to New York, where they were exchanged for two convicted Soviet spies.

— After the signing of the Final Act, many prominent dissidents were permitted — or forced — to leave for the West. Emigrants included: Natalya Gorbanevskaya and Vadim Delone in 1975; Andrei Amalrik, Anatoly Gladilin, Ernst Neizvestny, Aleksandr Nekrich and Vitaly Rubin in 1976; Ludmilla Alexeyeva, Mark Azbel, Petr Grigorenko, Cronid Lubarsky, Mark Popovsky, Valentin Turchin, Boris Vail, Efrem Yankelevich and Aleksandr Zinoviev in 1977 and 1978.

— Many other Soviet actions were linked by Soviet spokesmen to the Helsinki process.[8] However, the most convincing evidence of Brezhnev's intentions and his regard for the Final Act was the inclusion in the new Soviet Constitution adopted on 7 October 1977 (the 'Brezhnev Constitution') of Article 29, which reads:

The USSR's relations with other states are based on observance of the following principles: sovereign equality; mutual renunciation of the use or threat of force; inviolability of frontiers; territorial integrity of states; peaceful settlement of disputes; non-intervention in internal affairs; respect of human rights and fundamental freedoms; the equal rights of peoples and their right to decide their own destiny; cooperation among states; and fulfilment in good faith of obligations arising from the generally recognized principles and rules of international law, and from the international treaties signed by the USSR.

Article 29 is an exact recapitulation of the ten 'Principles Guiding Relations between Participating States' contained in the Helsinki Final Act.

The Final Act called for periodic follow-up meetings allowing the participating states to exchange views 'on the implementation of the provisions of the Final Act' and 'on the deepening of their mutual relations, the improvement of security and the development of cooperation in Europe, and the development of the process of détente in the future'. The Final Act specified that a preparatory meeting would be held in Belgrade on 15 June 1977, to decide on the date, duration and agenda of the first follow-up meeting.

The Moscow Helsinki Watch Group issued a pre-Belgrade report[9] which remains an excellent summary of the virtues and deficiences of the Final Act.

The report first addressed the question: 'Is the Soviet government observing the human rights obligations outlined in the Final Act?'

The report maintained that 'the Soviet government does not intend to fulfil its international human rights obligations'. Earlier documents of the Helsinki Group had detailed gross and persistent Soviet violations of: the right to emigrate and travel abroad; the national rights of the Crimean Tatars; and the right to exchange information and ideas. The report termed the arrests of Helsinki Group members on the eve of the Belgrade follow-up conference 'a demonstrative refusal by the authorities to fulfil their human rights obligations and proof of their determination to punish those citizens who supply information about these violations'.

The second issue addressed by the report was: 'the influence of the Helsinki accords on human rights in the USSR and the East European countries'. The report stated that

. . . the signing of the Final Act gave citizens grounds to demand that their governments respect fundamental human rights. It also gave them reason to count on the support of Western public opinion and government officials . . . The gross and flagrant violation of the human rights commitments undertaken by the Soviet Union has evoked widespread indignation in Western countries and has opened people's eyes to the gravity of the human rights situation in the Socialist countries and to the absence of any sort of progress in this regard.

The third issue addressed by the report was: 'The outlook for the Belgrade conference'. One possibility discussed in the report was that

. . . due to the absence of formal criteria governing observance of the humanitarian commitments in the Final Act, Western representatives, if they so choose, could pretend to be 'pretty well satisfied' with the state of affairs and could express the hope that 'isolated incidents' of violations of the humanitarian commitments would be corrected in the near future. It would be sheer hypocrisy to take such a stand in the face of the obvious truth. To do so would do irreparable injury to the cause of human rights as well as to European security.

Another possibility discussed in the report was that

. . .Western countries may conclude that the idea of linking human rights to international relations has failed . . . and may repudiate the Helsinki agreements since they have not been observed by the opposite side. That would aggravate international tension, increase military expenditures and diminish the chances for a stable peace and genuine international cooperation.

A third possibility discussed in the report — and the option favoured by the Helsinki Group — was that

...the Western countries will detail Soviet violations of humanitarian commitments and will conclude that the only means of preserving the Helsinki accords would be the establishment of agreed criteria for evaluating the facts ... If the Soviet Union refuses to accept concrete, measurable criteria for the evaluation of the facts, then its action will have the force of a unilateral destruction of the Helsinki accords ... Establishing verifiable criteria for implementation of the Final Act implies the creation of international bodies to collect and analyze pertinent information. Taking into consideration the limited opportunities at the disposal of citizens of the USSR and Eastern Europe, representatives of such bodies should be able to visit those countries and accept statements from individual citizens.

The leaders of most European countries and most American diplomats favoured the first possibility outlined by the Helsinki Group report — a cursory review of implementation depending primarily on self-reporting, with emphasis on the positive achievements and future amplification of détente. Pressure from the US Commission on Security and Cooperation in Europe[10] seconded by National Security Adviser Zbigniew Brzezinski resulted in the appointment of Arthur Goldberg as head of the US delegation a few weeks before the 4 October opening of the Belgrade meeting. During the review of implementation, Ambassador Goldberg cited specific names — Orlov, Shcharansky and others — and expressed

...deep concern about repression of Jews in the Soviet Union, about measures taken against religious observers, and political and cultural dissidents there and in other Eastern European countries, about the jamming of radio broadcasts, about the failure to permit adequate dissemination of Western newspapers, books, and religious materials, and about the harassment of the Nobel Prize winner and esteemed scientist and champion of human rights, academician Andrei Sakharov.[11]

Notes

1. Max Kampelman, 'Negotiating with the Russians', *Encounter*, February and March issues, 1985.

2. *First Semiannual Report by the President to the Commission on Security and Cooperation in Europe* (Washington DC, December 1976).

3. Gerald Ford, *A Time to Heal* (New York, 1979).

4. George Kennan, *The Cloud of Danger* (Boston, 1977).

5. Arkady Shevehenko, *Breaking with Moscow* (New York, 1985), pp. 264–7.

6. Several explanations have been offered for the resumption of arrests immediately after Jimmy Carter's inauguration and only four months before the preparatory meeting of the Belgrade Conference. The Soviet journalist Victor Louis reported in the London *Evening News* on 10 January 1977, that an 8 January bomb explosion in the Moscow subway, which had killed several passengers, was probably the work of Soviet dissidents and that the Soviet public was demanding retribution. This incident may have been used by the KGB to obtain permission from the Politburo for the arrests of key dissidents. On 30 January 1979, TASS announced that three members of the underground Armenian National Unity Party had been arrested in November 1977, tried and executed for the subway bomb explosion.

7. Peter Reddaway, 'Soviet policies on dissent and emigration: the radical change of course since 1979', Kennan Institute Occasional Paper, (Washington DC, 1984). Cited with the permission of the author.

8. *From Helsinki to Belgrade: The Soviet Union and the Implementation of the Final Act* (Moscow, 1977) contains documents and articles expounding the Soviet point of view.

9. *A Chronicle of Human Rights in the USSR*, no. 26 (April–June 1977), pp. 26–35.

10. The US Commission on Security and Cooperation in Europe (Helsinki Commission) is a mixed body composed of senators, representatives and officials from the State, Defense and Commerce Departments. The Commission was established by Act of Congress in 1976 on the initiative of Representative Millicent Fenwick after a visit to Moscow where Soviet dissidents urged the need for effective monitoring of the Helsinki accords. The Helsinki Commission has been the most consistent and effective body engaged in promoting the human rights provisions of the Final Act. In April 1985 Senator Alfonse D'Amato succeeded Representative Dante Fascell as chairman of the Commission.

11. Arthur Goldberg, 'Human Rights and the Belgrade meeting', *Vanderbilt Journal of Transnational Law*, nos. 2–3 (1980).

APPENDIX III

The Political and Social Thinking of Andrei Sakharov

COMPILED BY EFREM YANKELEVICH

The following extracts from Dr Sakharov's writings were collected in order to present a summary of his views on subjects of current interest.

Some of Dr Sakharov's views have changed significantly since the publication, in 1968, of his first well-known political essay 'Progress, coexistence, and intellectual freedom', while others have remained essentially unrevised. There will be no attempt, however, to discuss the evolution of Dr Sakharov's political views.[1]

The extracts in this compilation have been chosen to present Dr Sakharov's views in their most current form. Some earlier statements which I believe still reflect his thinking have also been included.*

Convergence and East–West détente

Dr Sakharov has commented extensively on détente. His views remain relevant to current foreign policy debates. Although pronounced dead on many occasions, détente is very much alive in Europe and, to a lesser extent, in the United States. The word 'détente' still has a positive connotation for the public, and possibilities for 'returning to détente' are regularly discussed in the press. The machinery of détente is largely intact — in the form of bilateral and multilateral commitments. (Several Soviet–American agreements of the détente era were renewed recently by the Reagan administration.) Probably the most cherished and recognized accomplishment of détente, the Helsinki Final Act, has spawned a series of follow-up meetings on security and cooperation in Europe, to which all thirty-five participating states are still committed. A Conference on Confidence and Security-building Measures and Disarmament in Europe is currently in session in Stockholm.

The evolution of détente in the early 1970s coincided with the increasing involvement of Dr Sakharov with social and political issues.

To appreciate Dr Sakharov's position on détente, it is helpful to recall his advocacy in his 1968 essay of convergence between 'socialism' and 'capitalism' as the only alternative to global destruction. While Dr Sakharov may now view differently the processes that can cause East and West to converge, his belief in convergence as the only viable option remains the core of his global outlook. In his 1983 article 'The danger of thermo-nuclear war', he re-affirmed his view that 'Genuine security is possible only when based on a stabilization of international relations . . . openness and pluralization in the socialist societies, the observance of human rights throughout the world, the rapprochement — convergence — of the socialist and capitalist systems . . .'

The earliest known expression of Dr Sakharov's views on détente are the remarks he made in August 1973 at the first press conference he gave. The press conference was called in connection with his summons to the First Deputy Procurator General of the USSR.

May I ask you about your essay Progress, Coexistence, and Intellectual Freedom, *which was published five years ago? If you think back to the analysis of world prospects you then presented, how has the situation in fact evolved, in your view?*
I discussed the possible evolution of events in terms of certain time spans, and these should be viewed as allegorical. But my premise still holds true, namely that the world faces two alternatives — either gradual convergence with democratization within the Soviet Union, or increasing confrontation with a growing danger of thermonuclear war. But reality has turned out to be trickier, in the sense that we now face a very specific issue: Will rapprochement be associated with the democratization of Soviet society or not? This new alternative, which at first sight may seem a halfway measure, better than nothing, in fact conceals within itself a great internal danger.

What alternative are you now referring to?
I mean rapprochement without democratization, rapprochement in which the West in effect accepts the Soviet rules of the game. Such a rapprochement would be dangerous in the sense that it would not really

solve any of the world's problems and would mean simply capitulation in the face of real or exaggerated Soviet power. It would mean an attempt to trade with the Soviet Union, buying its gas and oil, while ignoring all other aspects. I think such a development would be dangerous because it would have serious repercussions in the Soviet Union. It would contaminate the whole world with the anti-democratic peculiarities of Soviet society. It would enable the Soviet Union to bypass the problems it cannot resolve on its own and to concentrate on accumulating further strength. As a result, the world would become disarmed and helpless while facing our uncontrollable bureaucratic apparatus. I think that if rapprochement were to proceed totally without qualifications, on Soviet terms, it would pose a serious threat to the world as a whole.

In what way?
It would mean the cultivation and encouragement of a closed country, where everything that happens may be shielded from outside eyes, a country wearing a mask that hides its true face. I would not wish it on anyone to live next to such a neighbor, especially if he is at the same time armed to the teeth. I think that most of the political leaders in the West understand the situation, at least the Helsinki Conference seemed to suggest an awareness that rapprochement must be associated with simultaneous liquidation of [Soviet] isolation. Adoption of the Jackson Amendment [by the United States Senate, linking easier trade to unrestricted emigration from the Soviet Union] strikes me as a minimal step that would be significant not only by itself, but also as a symbolic expression of the view that rapprochement must involve some sort of control to insure that this country will not become a threat to its neighbors.[2]

Events of the succeeding seven years proved Dr Sakharov's apprehension concerning détente to be justified, at least to some extent. Meanwhile, he continued to elaborate on the dangers and promises of détente. Advocacy of a 'true' détente became a major theme of his public statements.

In his statement to the 1977 AFL-CIO convention, Dr Sakharov formulated his definition of détente. (Dr Sakharov was invited to the convention and attempted, unsuccessfully, to secure an exit visa in order to attend.)

Détente is not only the attempt, through establishing contacts, trade, and technological and cultural ties, to weaken the threat of universal destruction. It is also the complex, many-sided antagonism of two systems against each other, at the basis of which lies the contradiction between totalitarianism and democracy, between violations of human rights and their observance, between the striving to close society and the striving to open it. On the outcome of this struggle depends the convergence of our societies — which is the alternative to the collapse of civilization and to general destruction.[3]

In his article 'Alarm and hope', written in 1977 at the request of the Nobel Prize Committee, Dr Sakharov discusses a range of subjects pertinent to détente, including the origins of the Soviet policy of détente, détente and disarmament, and détente and the opportunity it offers to 'open up' Soviet society:

Is the totalitarian order capable of independent, harmonious, and gradual development within its own frontiers? This system apparently requires expansion, isolation from information, demagogic self-praise — particularly with respect to the 'shining future' of its global historical mission — as well as the use of the fruits of the scientific and technical progress of the capitalism it attacks. Having encountered substantial difficulties both in domestic development and in relations with the outside world, the system's leaders have been finally forced to modify their tactics and appearances, although without initial changes in the system's ultimate goals. The original tactics, which could be called the 'Comintern phase', went through several interim stages before being replaced by détente.

The term 'détente' is not new; at one time (1933–39) it was used to define relations between Western countries and Hitler's Germany. I have no wish to suggest that détente is purely a trap for the West. Tactical changes have in fact acquired such substance that they have brought on important changes at deeper levels. It is especially important that détente opens new possibilities for mutual influence and a chance to lead humanity out of a difficult predicament, a change which under no circumstances should be let slip. But détente carries with it a new danger, that totalitarian–socialist expansion has merely adopted a camouflage which makes it even more insidious.

What policy should the West adopt in its relations with the socialist countries under these new, more complex conditions? I am convinced that the main goal of détente is to guarantee international security. Essential to this goal are: disarmament, a strengthening of international trust, the surmounting of the closed nature of the socialist system, the defense of human rights around the world. These elements are not independent. Although disarmament occupies a certain priority, security cannot be attained by being limited to the purely military aspects of détente. Western leaders must not create the appearance of success in disarmament negotiations without real achievements; doing so, they would deceive their countries and — worst of all — provoke a unilateral disarmament. This danger is real because of both the tight secrecy in the socialist countries and the shortsightedness and domestic political maneuvering of certain Western politicians, who are prepared to jeopardize the delicate global balance for transitory political situations at home.

Disarmament negotiations are possible only from a position of equal strength. It is not only the West that is truly interested in disarmament and the USSR that compromises only in exchange for economic benefits, political and ideological concessions. In fact, the deeper interests of the USSR, gasping from overmilitarization, require decreases in military expenditures, and cutbacks in the army and in the military/industrial sector, to a much greater extent. In the actual conduct of diplomatic negotiations, it is essential to remember that the concept of disarmament has become central in Soviet propaganda; it cannot be ignored as easily as a trade agreement. Therefore, I believe the fear in the West that statements in defense of human rights may harm arms negotiations is unfounded.

Moreover, it is no less important to keep in mind that, without a true détente and the internal reform which it ideally requires, the actual scale of disarmament will be insignificant. The moral strength of the Western democratic tradition expresses itself in a calm, firm defense of human rights throughout the world. Supporting human rights in the socialist countries has the additional virtue of opening up the socialist system. Trade, scientific, and cultural contacts are important in their own right (especially for the socialist countries) as a means of continuing détente. But within reasonable limits they can also be used to bring indirect pressure towards reaching the basic goals of détente — disarmament and the guarantee of human rights.[4]

How is this pressure to be applied?

As to the possible forms of pressure appropriate in securing human rights, we must bear in mind that a specific human-rights matter can be solved only when it has become a political problem for the leaders of a violator country. Détente creates various levers for exerting pressure which, without threatening to exhaust its potential, nonetheless brings specific human-rights questions as well as general problems to the attention of top policymakers. These levers are controlled not just by governmental and legislative bodies. There is a role for nongovernmental organizations and private citizens involved in exchanges — business firms, scientific associations, trade unions, workers, scholars, authors, and artists. I am not suggesting blackmail, of course, but rather the adjustment of interests which is a normal part of the process of eliminating confrontation. Such measures as a partial and temporary boycott of scientific or cultural contacts, a temporary embargo on certain specialized equipment, or a dock workers' embargo, do not threaten détente. Another example of a more general sanction is the Jackson—Vanik Amendment. Its goal is to prevent the violation of the crucial right to emigrate; since this is an amendment to the American law on trade, it cannot be deemed interference in the internal affairs of other countries or as a threat to détente.

Speaking of trade, industrial, and general economic relations, Soviet propaganda usually stresses their mutually profitable nature. These assertions should be analyzed with care. Of course, once a particular company or Western country has got ahead of its competitors, it may gain temporary benefits, but on the whole it is the USSR and the countries of Eastern Europe which are vitally interested in acquiring technology and credits. It will be totally unforgivable if the West fails to use this leverage to open up Soviet society.

I do, however, consider it morally impermissible to use food relief as a means of pressure. This comment does not extend to cases where such aid is used for speculative purposes or to stockpile reserves for possible military mobilization.

I also consider it intolerable to impose conditions on arms negotiations; they should have absolute priority.[5]

In the same article, Dr Sakharov returns, for the first time since 1968, to the idea of convergence, presenting his revised views on that subject:

Marx and his disciples contended that the capitalist system had long ago exhausted its potential and that socialism's advantages in industrial organization, labor productivity, workers' living standards, and full citizen participation in all aspects of government would lead to the displacement of capitalism. Reality has proved otherwise. Socialism, at least in its totalitarian form, has indeed expanded, but not at all because of its advantages and progressive nature.

Over the same period, the capitalist system has also proved its capacity for development and transformation. In countries of the West, a standard and 'quality' of life unprecedented in the history of mankind have been achieved; there have been great advances in social welfare. Today's capitalist society, with a few reservations, can be called 'capitalism with a human face.' The great achievements of science and engineering, which I view as the root of this material progress, have created a profusion of consumer goods which in itself has alleviated the problem of the distribution of material wealth. But the *ideas* of social justice, human rights and democracy which have permeated social consciousness — originating in Christianity and other religious doctrines, and developing over the past 100–150 years through socialist thought, including Marxism — play no less significant a role in capitalist society. We can expect that over the next decade the West will make progress in solving other problems as well as the depletion of natural resources, population control, nationality questions, urban problems, crime, drug addiction, etc. — and will do so democratically without mass restriction of personal freedom.

We can also assume that socialist ideas, in their pluralistic, anti-totalitarian form, will continue to play a definite role in Western social development. This will in fact be the movement of the West toward convergence with the socialist world.

I feel less certain of a reciprocal evolution of totalitarian socialism toward pluralism. That will depend on many internal and external conditions, the most important of which is to overcome the 'closed' aspect of totalitarian–socialist society. Of course, these serious problems are not instantly resolved. Inevitably, we will have to deal with those who prescribe quick cures which are in fact more dangerous than the disease. But in the democratic West, with its wide-ranging, open discussion of critical issues, the influence of such extremists will, in the last analysis, I hope, be neutralized.[6]

It is plain now that the American policy of détente was motivated by a set of goals and assumptions completely different from those advanced by Dr Sakharov. As noted by some observers, including the architect of détente, Secretary Kissinger, détente was motivated primarily by the perceived inability of the USA to sustain the policy of containment in its traditional form. Among the principal reasons which prompted the Americans to adopt a policy of détente were: the Soviet military build-up which resulted, according to Secretary Kissinger, in the 'fateful combination of nuclear equality and conventional inferiority' for the USA; the lack of domestic support for active American involvement abroad and for the expansion of defence programmes; the fear that Europe might embrace neutrality if the USA were to lose the 'race to Moscow' to its NATO allies. These were the origins of détente, or the concerns détente was to address.

Due to Congressional pressure (such as the Jackson—Vanik Amendment), these defensive concerns were later complemented, to some degree, by the positive goals advanced by Dr Sakharov.

The Helsinki process

In August 1975, after two years of negotiations, representatives of thirty-five nations concluded the Conference on Security and Cooperation in Europe by signing the Helsinki Final Act (Helsinki accords).

In the chapter of the Final Act entitled 'Co-operation in

humanitarian and other fields' (the so-called 'Third Basket'), the participants declared their intention to facilitate reunification of families and travel, promote exchange of information, both printed and broadcast, improve working conditions for journalists, etc. In the Declaration on Principles Guiding Relations between Participating States the participants pledged 'to respect human rights and fundamental freedoms' and to 'promote and encourage the effective exercise of civil, political, economic, social, cultural and other rights and freedoms'. The Soviet Union also confirmed its obligations as a party to the International Covenants on Human Rights.

It is believed that the Soviet Union accepted these broad human rights provisions in exchange for the recognition of the postwar European borders and the promise of expanded East–West trade. Earlier, however, in 1973, the Soviet government had ratified the International Covenants on Human Rights without a specific *quid pro quo*.

It is not clear whether Western participants expected even minimal Soviet compliance with the human rights provisions of the Final Act. Although most observers believe that the Soviet government did not sign the Act in good faith, the period immediately following the Helsinki meeting witnessed the lowest level of political repression of the Brezhnev era. However, 1977 began with the arrests of members of the unofficial Moscow Helsinki Watch Group, founded in May 1976 to monitor Soviet compliance with the accords. Members of the Ukrainian and Georgian Watch Groups were also arrested in early 1977.

In October 1977, on the eve of the opening in Belgrade of the first Follow-up Meeting on Security and Cooperation in Europe, Dr Sakharov appealed to 'the Parliaments of all Helsinki-Signatory States':

Two years ago, the Final Act of the Helsinki Conference on Security and Cooperation in Europe was signed. Its historical significance was the proclamation of an inseparable bond between international security and an open society — that is, freedom of conscience, the free exchange of information, the freedom of people to move across state borders.

Is the West prepared to defend these noble and vitally important principles? Or will it gradually, in silence, acquiesce in the interpretation of the principles of Helsinki, and of détente as a whole, that the leaders of the Soviet Union and of Eastern Europe are trying to impose? . . .

Every person serving a term in the hell of the present-day Gulag for his beliefs, or open profession of them — every victim of psychiatric repression for political reasons, every person refused permission to emigrate or travel abroad — represents a direct violation of the Helsinki Accord . . .

The monstrously cruel sentences imposed this year . . . are not simply routine violations of the right of freedom of conscience, but a defiant act by the Soviet authorities — a test of the West's resolve to insist on the fulfillment of the principles of Helsinki.

To ignore this challenge would be a faint-hearted capitulation to blackmail. It is hardly necessary to add that this would probably have further negative consequences in all aspects of East–West relations without exception, including the fundamental issues of international security.

I believe Western parliaments should insist that their delegations to the meeting opening in Belgrade carry the sort of official instructions which would preclude any such surrender. It is essential to insist on the immediate release of those convicted or arrested for the expression of criticism, on the facilitation of emigration and foreign travel, and on the free sale of books, newspapers, and magazines published abroad. These are prerequisites for the successful conduct and conclusion of the Belgrade Meeting.

I am appealing especially to the Congress of the United States. President Carter, supported by the great power and influence of his country and guided by the express will and traditions of a freedom-loving people, proclaimed that the defense of human rights throughout the world is the moral foundation of United States policy. Now it is essential to give these principles energetic support.

We are living through a period of history in which decisive support of the principles of freedom of conscience, an open society, and the rights of man is an absolute necessity. The alternative is surrender to totalitarianism, the loss of all precious freedoms, and political, economic, and moral degradation.

The West, its political and moral leaders, its free and decent peoples, must not allow this.[7]

Later, Dr Sakharov repeated his belief that the arrest of those monitoring Soviet compliance with the Helsinki accords was a deliberate challenge to the Western participants, who were confronted

. . . with the painful dilemma of either defending the Helsinki principles with uncompromising demands for the liberation of all those arrested — thereby risking heightened tension with the East — or capitulating, backing off from the challenge and thus weakening their positions not only in human-rights matters, not only at Belgrade, but in all aspects of détente.

As an added benefit — even if the ploy were a partial failure — the Soviet authorities could count on these 'fresh' repressions to draw attention away from the other, massive and permanent human-rights violations in the USSR.[8]

Reflecting on the results of the Belgrade Meeting, Dr Sakharov wrote:

The closing of the Belgrade Meeting brought one episode of the Helsinki drama to an end. This is not the place for a detailed evaluation of its effect on the socialist and Western countries and of the Meeting's overall significance. The flabby stance taken by a number of major European states on the human-rights issue at Belgrade and the lack of any direct mention of the problem in the concluding document were certainly disappointing. Nevertheless, I view the session as an enormously important event with far-reaching consequences. For the first time, specific human-rights violations were discussed at such a representative international level, and the discussion attracted the attention of the press, public figures, and world opinion. Despite some slip-ups and compromises, the West in general made it very plain that observance of human rights is a matter of fundamental significance and will remain a central issue. The permanence of human-rights concerns was a key feature of the decision of the delegates to meet again in Madrid in 1980.

In this new phase, on the eve of the next series of trials of Helsinki Watch Group members, I now again call on society, Western political leaders, and those involved in cultural, scientific, trade, and technological contacts with the USSR and Eastern Europe to follow closely the reports on human-rights violations there and do all in their power to prevent and correct them. It is essential to employ all possible leverage — discreet and public diplomacy, the press, demonstrations and other means that strike at prestige, boycotts, cancellations of cooperative activities in one field or another, legislative limitations on trade and contactss similar to the Jackson—Vanik Amendment, prisoner exchanges — to save the individual victims of tyranny and lawlessness and entire categories of people suffering injustice and discrimination, to reverse the practice of arbitrary rule.

I must again emphasize the importance of defending all the arrested members of the Helsinki Watch Groups. Under the circumstances, their defense is the touchstone of Western resoluteness and perseverance as well as a test of the good faith and reasonableness of the Soviet side. This is a major international affair. In all the campaigns of support it is terribly important not to divide the arrested and convicted into separate categories — the important ones for whom it is easy to generate backing and publicity and the secondary figures whom the authorities count on dealing with in silence at their pleasure. I appeal for the creation of a unified international committee to defend all Helsinki Watch Group members, to bring together the forces of several groups already at work.[9]

The 1977 arrests of the Helsinki monitors were followed by a full scale crackdown on dissent (coming in two waves, the second wave starting in the fall of 1979).

Nevertheless, Dr Sakharov opposed a boycott of the second Follow-up Meeting at Madrid, which opened in November 1980. Addressing the conference from his place of exile in Gorky he urged the Meeting to 'further a political settlement in Afghanistan'.

I cannot agree with those who consider the Soviet invasion of Afghanistan to be an event unrelated to security in Europe. I also cannot agree with those who suggest a boycott of the Madrid Conference as a response to Soviet actions in Afghanistan or to the increased repression of dissenters. I believe that the participating States should use the opportunity offered by the Madrid Conference to further a political settlement in Afghanistan, which must provide for the withdrawal of Soviet troops and international guarantees of peace, neutrality and free elections. The participating states should also promote the release of prisoners of conscience in the USSR and Eastern Europe, and in Western countries as well, if persons are imprisoned there who have not used or advocated violence.

The critical international situation requires that the Western participating States coordinate their tactics and pursue their goals with more determination and consistency than at Belgrade. The Helsinki Accords — like détente as a whole — have meaning only if they are observed fully and by all parties. No country should evade a discussion of its own domestic problems, whether the problems of Northern Ireland, the Crimean Tatars, or Sakharov's exile (here I am speaking objectively). Nor should a country ignore violations in other participating States. The whole point of the Helsinki Accords is mutual monitoring, not mutual evasion of difficult problems.[10]

The Moscow Helsinki Watch Group announced the suspension of its activities in September, 1982, a year before the conclusion of the Madrid meeting. The announcement was signed by the three members of the Group remaining at liberty (the only founding member of the Group among them was Elena Bonner, Dr Sakharov's wife). By that time all members of the Ukrainian Helsinki Watch Group, formed after the Moscow Group, were already in prison or in exile. The Lithuanian Watch Group, as well as most other independent associations, had been crushed and silenced, sometimes losing their entire membership to the labour camps.

The crackdown on dissent has been accompanied by curtailment of postal and telephone communications and, in general, by vigorous attempts to reduce the flow of information across the Soviet borders. In 1980 jamming of all Russian-language Western broadcasts was resumed. The number of emigration visas issued has dropped sharply every year since 1979.

The two Follow-up Meetings on Security and Cooperation in Europe — in Belgrade (October 1977–March 1978), and in Madrid (November 1980–September 1983) — were expected to have a restraining effect on Soviet internal policies. Both meetings failed to reverse, or even slow down, deterioration of the human rights situation in the USSR.

The situation in most matters covered by the humanitarian provisions of the Helsinki accords has deteriorated sharply as compared to the pre-Helsinki period of détente.

Meanwhile, the 'Helsinki process' itself has been departing from the 'Sakharov doctrine' — the indivisibility of peace and human rights. The Madrid meeting has apparently reinforced this trend. Its participants agreed to hold a conference on the military aspects of security, the ongoing Stockholm Conference on Security-Building Measures and Disarmament in Europe, separately from limited meetings on human rights and 'human contacts'.

Arms control and the prevention of nuclear war

Dr Sakharov's public involvement with arms control dates back to 1957, when he wrote an article on the danger of nuclear testing in the atmosphere. His opposition to nuclear testing soon brought him into conflict with his superiors, including Khrushchev himself, but ultimately helped to conclude the 1963 Moscow Partial Test Ban Treaty.

Dr Sakharov's background and his role in the development of the Soviet H-bomb might have concentrated his attention on the technical aspects of arms control, but these aspects, in fact, are not the focus of his concern. He never viewed problems of arms control as self-contained, able to be solved by purely technical and diplomatic means, or separable from other global problems. While arms-control issues are often discussed in his articles, few, if any, deal exclusively with arms control *per se*.

Dr Sakharov's views are relevant to the current arms-control debates. His ideas, however, are very much his own, and do not fit in neatly with any particular camp.

Dr Sakharov summarized his thoughts in his address to a meeting of Nobel Prize Laureates convened at the Sorbonne in October 1983:

Today, no one — neither the West, nor the Socialist camp — can rely on the prudence of their potential opponent. For decades the West has stuck with a strategy of nuclear deterrence. It is unrealistic as well as immoral, however, to rely for too long on weapons which *must not be used*. The practically unavoidable escalation of a limited nuclear war would result in collective world suicide. Moreover, the superiority of the West in nuclear weapons has vanished. In Europe the nuclear balance has been tipped by Soviet SS-20 missiles. On the global front, the balance has been upset by hundreds of powerful Soviet silo-based missiles which are objectively first-strike weapons.

The restoration of parity in conventional weapons is necessary. That is the realistic road toward renunciation of the nuclear weapons which threaten our existence. During a transition period, until parity on conventional weapons has been attained and so long as nuclear weapons exist, the West — and possibly the USSR in certain categories — will still have to add to its nuclear arsenal. These additions will serve a dual purpose. They will assure the stability of nuclear parity. And even more important, they can spur the successful conclusion of disarmament negotiations. I call for serious and continuing negotiations, conducted with firmness but also with a readiness to adopt far-reaching and bold measures if the other side — East or West — shows itself prepared for realistic compromise.[11]

Dr Sakharov touches in this Sorbonne address upon most of the themes he developed in his article 'The danger of thermonuclear war' and in some of his earlier writings (the Szilard Award acceptance speech, 1983; his open letter to the Pugwash Conference, 1982; 'How to preserve world peace', *Parade*, 1981).

The origins of Dr Sakharov's position can be traced back to the concept of 'detailed parity' he advocated in the mid-1970s.

'What would be the ideal international agreement on disarmament on the technical plane?' he asked in 1975, in his Nobel Peace Prize lecture.

I believe that prior to such an agreement each side should issue an official declaration — though not necessarily publicly in the initial stages — disclosing statistics on all aspects of its military potential (ranging from the number of nuclear warheads to forecast figures on the number of draftees). The declaration should specify a tentative allocation of military resources among all regions of 'potential confrontation'. The first step would be to ensure that for every single strategic area and for all sorts of military strength an adjustment would be made to iron out the superiority of one party to the agreement in relation to the other. (Naturally this is the kind of pattern that would be liable to some adjustment.) This would in the first place obviate the possibility of an agreement in one strategic area (Europe, for instance) being utilized to strengthen military positions in another area (e.g., the Soviet–Chinese border). In the second place, potential imbalances arising from the difficulty of equating different weapons systems would be excluded. (It would, for example, be difficult to say how many batteries of the ABM type would correspond to a cruiser, and so on.)

The next step in disarmament would entail proportional and simultaneous de-escalation for all countries and in all strategic areas. Such a formula for 'balanced' two-stage disarmament would ensure continuous security for all countries, an interrelated equilibrium between armed forces in areas where there is a potential danger of confrontation, while at the same time providing a radical solution to the economic and social problems that have arisen as a result of militarization.[12]

In 1975, Dr Sakharov still entertained hopes for the realization of this 'ideal' disarmament process:

The new phase in international relations which has been called détente, and which appears to have culminated with the Helsinki Conference, does in principle open up certain possibilities for a move in this direction.[13]

In later statements, Dr Sakharov placed special emphasis on parity in conventional forces, while expressing growing apprehension about the strategy of mutual assured destruction.

Perhaps mutual nuclear terror is still keeping the world from World War III, but this distorted and wasteful balance of fear is becoming increasingly unstable. Political errors, new technological achievements by one side or the other, and the spread of nuclear weapons threaten to upset that balance at any moment. We must achieve a balance of power without the factor of nuclear terror by limiting ourselves to conventional weapons — whatever that might cost in economic and social terms — and public opinion must be mobilized in support of those efforts.[14]

He further elaborated on these themes in an open letter to his American friend and colleague, Dr Sidney Drell:

I am convinced that the following basic tenet of yours is true: *Nuclear weapons only make sense as a means of deterring nuclear aggression by a potential enemy*, i.e. a nuclear war cannot be planned with the aim of winning it. Nuclear weapons cannot be viewed as a means of restraining aggression carried out by means of conventional weapons.

Of course, you realize that this last statement is in contradiction to the West's actual strategy in the last few decades. For a long time, beginning as far back as the end of the 1940s, the West has not been relying on its 'conventional' armed forces as a means sufficient for repelling a potential aggressor and for restraining expansion. There are many reasons for this — the West's lack of political, military, and economic unity; the striving to avoid a peacetime militarization of the economy, society, technology, and science; the low numerical levels of the Western nations' armies. All that at a time when the U.S.S.R. and the other countries of the socialist camp have armies of great numerical strength and are rearming them intensively, sparing no resources. It is possible that for a limited period of time the mutual nuclear terror had a certain restraining effect on the course of world events. But, at the present time, the balance of nuclear terror is a dangerous remnant of the past! In order to avoid aggression with conventional weapons one cannot threaten to use nuclear weapons if their use is inadmissible. One of the conclusions that follows here — and a conclusion you draw — is that it is necessary to restore strategic parity in the field of conventional weapons . . .

The restoration of strategic parity is possible only by investing large resources and by an essential change in the psychological atmosphere in the West. There must be a readiness to make certain limited economic sacrifices and, most important, an understanding of the seriousness of the situation and of the necessity for some restructuring. In the final analysis, this is necessary to prevent nuclear war, and war in general. Will the West's politicians be able to carry out such a restructuring? Will the press, the public, and our fellow scientists help them (and not hinder them as is frequently now the case)? Can they succeed in convincing those who doubt the necessity of such restructuring? A great deal depends on this — the opportunity for the West to conduct a nuclear arms policy that will be conducive to the lessening of the danger of nuclear disaster . . .

In conclusion, I should stress especially that a restructuring of strategy could of course be carried out only gradually and very carefully in order to prevent a loss of parity in some of the intermediate phases.[15]

Dr Sakharov apparently perceives his major difference with Drell as concentrated on the question of what constitutes a reliable deterrent, on whether capability to deal a retaliatory strike (the core of mutual assured destruction doctrine) is sufficient to prevent nuclear war:

Is it actually possible when making decisions in the area of nuclear weapons to ignore all the considerations and requirements relevant to the possible scenarios for a nuclear war and simply limit oneself to the criterion of achieving a reliable deterrent — when that criterion is understood to mean an arsenal sufficient to deal a devastating blow in response? Your answer to this question — while perhaps formulating it somewhat differently — is positive and you draw far-reaching conclusions.

There is no doubt that at present the United States already possesses a large number of submarine-based missiles and charges carried by strategic bombers which are not vulnerable to the U.S.S.R. and, in addition, has silo-based missiles though they are smaller than the U.S.S.R.'s — all these in such amounts that, were those charges used against the U.S.S.R., nothing, roughly speaking, would be left of it. You maintain that this has *already* created a reliable deterrent — independently of what the U.S.S.R. and the United States have and what they lack! . . .

Your line of reasoning seems to me very strong and convincing. But I think that the concept presented fails to take into account all the complex realities of the opposition that involves two world systems and that there is the necessity (despite your stance) for a more specific and comprehensive unbiased consideration than a simple orientation toward a 'reliable deterrent' (in the meaning of the term as formulated above, i.e., the possibility of dealing a devastating retaliatory strike). I will endeavour to explain this statement.

Precisely because an all-out nuclear war means collective suicide, we can imagine that a potential aggressor might count on a lack of resolve on the part of the country under attack to take the step leading to that suicide, i.e., it could count on its victim capitulating for the sake of saving what could be saved. Given that, if the aggressor has a military advantage in some of the variants of conventional warfare or — which is also possible *in principle* — in some of the variants of partial (limited) nuclear war, he would attempt to use the fear of further escalation to force the enemy to fight the war on his (the aggressor's) own terms. There would be little cause for joy if, ultimately, the aggressor's hopes proved false and the aggressor country perished along with the rest of mankind.

You consider it necessary to achieve a restoration of strategic parity in the field of conventional arms. Now take the next logical step — while nuclear weapons exist it is also necessary to have strategic parity in relation to those variants of limited or regional nuclear warfare which a potential enemy could impose, i.e., it is really *necessary* to examine in detail the various scenarios for both conventional and nuclear war and to analyze the various contingencies. It is of course not possible to analyze fully all these possibilities or to ensure security entirely. But I am attempting to warn of the opposite extreme — 'closing one's eyes' and relying on one's potential enemy to be perfectly sensible. As always in life's complex problems, some sort of compromise is needed.

Of course I realize that in attempting not to lag behind a potential enemy in any way, we condemn ourselves to an arms race that is tragic in a world with so many critical problems admitting of no delay. But the main danger is slipping into an all-out nuclear war. *If* the probability of such an outcome could be reduced at the cost of another ten or fifteen years of the arms race, then perhaps that price must be paid while, at the same time, diplomatic, economic, ideological, political, cultural, and social efforts are made to prevent a war.[16]

Dr Sakharov's position, in the terms of current strategic nuclear policy debates, appears to be rather close to the doctrine of 'flexible response'. The extract above also contains echoes of Dr Sakharov's earlier concept of 'detailed parity'.

Dr Sakharov had expressed similar views in his Szilard Award acceptance speech:

Of course, in all the intermediate stages of disarmament and negotiations, international security must be provided for, *vis-à-vis* any possible move by a potential aggressor. For this in particular one has to be ready to resist, at all the various possible stages in the escalation of a conventional or a nuclear war. No side must feel any temptation to engage in a limited or regional nuclear war.[17]

'The danger of thermonuclear war' received considerable attention in both Western and Soviet media. (*Izvestiya* published an article, signed by four members of the Soviet Academy of Sciences, who accused Sakharov of calling for 'nuclear blackmail directed against his own country'.) Most commentators noticed neither Dr Sakharov's endorsement of the 'flexible response' doctrine, nor even his conditional acceptance of 'another ten or fifteen years of the arms race'. Most attention was given to Dr Sakharov's qualified support for the MX missile programme.

Dr Sakharov provisionally supported the MX programme as a 'bargaining chip' to be traded for Soviet heavy land-based missiles. For many years, he has viewed such missiles as destabilizing, first-strike weapons. In 1975, criticizing the Vladivostok agreement on the framework for a SALT 2 treaty, he outlined a first-strike scenario involving heavy MIRVed missiles.[18] He enlarged on this scenario in his letter to Dr Drell, and continued:

In view of this [destabilizing character of powerful silo-based missiles], it seems very important to me to strive for [their abolition] at the talks on nuclear disarmament.

While the U.S.S.R. is the leader in this field there is very little chance of its easily relinquishing that lead. If it is necessary to spend a few billion dollars on MX missiles to alter this situation, then perhaps this is what the West must do. But, at the same time, if the Soviets, in deed and not just in word, take significant verifiable measures for reducing the number of land-based missiles (more precisely, for destroying them), then the West should not only abolish MX missiles (or not build them!) but carry out other significant disarmament programs as well.[19]

Dr Sakharov's attitude towards disarmament negotiations is, perhaps, the most distinctive feature of his position on arms control. In his letter to Drell, he wrote:

On the whole I am convinced that nuclear disarmament talks are of enormous importance and of the highest priority. They must be conducted continuously — in the brighter periods of international relations but also the periods when relations are strained — and conducted with persistence, foresight, firmness and, at the same time, with flexibility and initiative. In so doing, political figures should not think of exploiting those talks, and the nuclear problem in general, for their own immediate political gains but only for the long-term interests of their country and the world. And the planning of the talks should be included in one's general nuclear strategy as its most important part — on this point as well I am in agreement with you.[20]

At the same time, Dr Sakharov questions the results disarmament negotiations can achieve. He remarked once, in 1977, that 'without a true détente and the internal reform, which it ideally requires, the actual scale of disarmament will be insignificant'.[21]

In 1978 he ascribed to the disarmament talks a relatively modest role in diminishing the chances of confrontation:

Disarmament negotiations have their own substantive significance. The fact that they are underway diminishes to some extent the likelihood that a major war will break out. They cannot, however, eliminate the reasons for politico-military opposition. When they bring about some limitation on military outlays, that is important, but unfortunately such limitation appears to be a reality mainly in the West. Until now no agreed restraints, as far as I know, have been able to compel the Soviet military-industrial complex to renounce even one projected weapons system or cut back the numerical strength of its army, air force, tanks, artillery, and strategic missiles. I am speaking here of real reductions, not so-called ceilings on forces. In these circumstances the West must complement arms negotiations by a concern for strengthening its armaments. The situation is especially dangerous in Europe, where the imbalance of forces is promoting a subtle economic and political dependence on the USSR . . .

No matter how important arms-control discussions are, they can produce decisive results only when they are joined to the resolution of broader and more complicated problems of military-political and ideological confrontation, including questions of human rights. The freedom to exchange information at home and across international borders, the freedom to move at home and to travel or emigrate abroad, all rank as prerequisites of international trust, basic to the process of diminishing hostility. As long as a country has no civil liberty, no freedom of information, and no independent press, then there exists no effective body of public opinion to control the conduct of the government and its functionaries. Such a situation is not just a misfortune for citizens unprotected against tyranny and lawlessness, it is a menace to international security.[22]

Despite Dr Sakharov's belief that the ultimate success of disarmament negotiations depends on progress in other fields, notably in human rights, he rejects the concept of 'linkage':

I . . . consider it intolerable to impose conditions on arms negotiations; they should have absolute priority.[23]

Later, in 1979, he repeated this position in an article written for *Trialogue*, the magazine of the Trilateral Commission:

In the Western press the thought has sometimes been expressed that the strategic arms limitation talks, in whose success the Soviet Union is interested, as is the entire world, have opened up possibilities of applying pressure on the USSR on the question of human rights. In my opinion, such a viewpoint is not correct. I believe that the problem of lessening the danger of annihilating humanity in a nuclear war carries an absolute priority over all other considerations . . . Consequently, the strategic arms limitation talks must be considered separately; and considered separately, we must ask ourselves whether it will lessen the danger and destructive power of a nuclear war, strengthen international stability, or prevent a one-sided advantage for the USSR or a consolidation of its already existing advantages. Such a separate, practical approach does not negate, of course, the undoubted fact that a durable international security and international trust are impossible without the observance of the basic rights of man, specifically political and civil rights. It should also be pointed out that the West should not consider the cutting of military expenditures as the main goal of arms limitation. The basic goals can only be international stability and the elimination of the possibility of a nuclear war.[24]

As well as direct linkage, Dr Sakharov also rejects 'reverse linkage', the idea that some concerns, including concern for human rights, should be sacrificed to improve prospects for arms negotiations.

For example, Dr Sakharov did not view Soviet rejection of the arms reduction proposals brought by Secretary Vance to Moscow in early 1977 as the result of the Carter administration's human rights policy. Nor did he attribute subsequent progress in the SALT II discussions to the apparent shift of American interest away from human rights issues:

Not long ago, we in the Soviet Union heard radio broadcasts of the comments of several American and European papers on the results of Secretary Vance's visit to Moscow in April 1978. A majority of the commentators agreed that a year before, President Carter's firm human-rights policy had been the main reason for the breakdown of the SALT talks with Foreign Minister Gromyko and that the progress achieved (the scale of which was unknown, but the comments cited the optimistic tone of official statements) was somehow the result of a 'softening' or 'erosion' of Carter's position . . .

As I said in the April 4 1977 interview with Swedish radio, the complications which showed up in the SALT negotiations last year are profound issues which could not be sidestepped. They are linked to fundamental flaws in the Vladivostok agreement, to traditional peculiarities of Soviet politics, and to certain technical issues — but not in any way to the problems of human rights.

Then and now I perceive the 1977 negotiations as in no sense a failure of American policy; they clearly demonstrated the dynamic and constructive character of the U.S. position, contributed to a degree in delivering the West from certain dangerous illusions, and created the basis for further talks and major decisions. It seems obvious to me that a firm policy on human rights could not and cannot 'spoil' anything. On the contrary, it shows that the West will not succumb to blackmail, feelings of weakness and uncertainty, that it will resolutely defend the principles which hold such fundamental significance for our common future. Weakness or excessive 'flexibility' on human-rights matters immediately undermines the Western positions all along the détente 'front'.[25]

Despite Dr Sakharov's stand against the use of nuclear forces to counter a conventional attack, his endorsement of a 'no first use' policy is tentative and qualified. He lists certain conditions to be met before that policy can be adopted:

The halting of expansion, the regulation of conflicts through negotiations, the creation of an atmosphere of trust and openness, the restoration and maintenance of a balance of conventional weapons — only under these conditions can there be progress in reducing conventional and nuclear weapons and in reducing the danger of war. Under those conditions, it will be possible to take the exceedingly important step toward removing the threat of thermonuclear annihilation from mankind. That step would be taken by concluding a treaty against any first use of nuclear weapons. In the long run, all this should lead to the complete banning of nuclear weapons. This is what we must strive for.

A quarter of a century ago, the explosions above the Pacific Ocean and the Kazakhstan Steppe marked mankind's entrance into a paradoxical epoch of mutual thermonuclear terror. But only equilibrium based on reason — not on fear — is the true guarantee of the future.[26]

The ideology of human rights

Perhaps the most complete expression of Dr Sakharov's political credo can be found in his article 'The human rights movement in the USSR: its goals, significance, and difficulties':

The sociological ideology which gives first priority to human rights is, in my opinion, the most reasonable in many aspects, if considered within the framework of the relatively narrow set of problems which it places before itself. I am convinced that ideologies based on dogmas or metaphysical precepts, or those which rely too heavily on the contemporary makeup of their societies, cannot be responsive to the complexity, sudden changes, and unpredictability of human development. The imperative and dogmatic concepts of all types of world reformers, as well as the irrational mirages of nationalism and national socialism, have so far been realized by violating the internal freedom of human beings and inflicting direct physical harm — embodied in the twentieth century in the horrors of genocide, revolutions, international and civil wars, anarchistic and state-inspired terror, and the hells of Kolyma and Auschwitz.

Communist ideology, with its promise of creating a world society based on social harmony, labor, material progress, and future freedom has, in fact, been transformed by governments which call themselves socialist into an ideology of a party-bureaucratic totalitarianism, leading in my view to the deepest historical dead end.

Moreover, at the present time there no longer exists a pragmatic capitalist philosophy of reasonable individualism, at least not in its pure form. The various upheavals of the twentieth century, such as the Great

Depression, destructive wars, and the specter of an ecological and demographic catastrophe, have demonstrated its inadequacy.

I believe that technical-economic progress is a supremely positive factor in our social life which to a large measure lessens the problem of distributing material wealth. At the same time, however, I acutely feel the dangers which are tied to this kind of progress, and recognize the inadequacy of a technocratic ideology in solving life's many-faceted complex of problems.

In contrast to the imperative nature of the majority of political philosophies, the ideology of human rights is in essence pluralistic, permitting various possible forms of social organization and their coexistence. It also offers the individual a maximum freedom of choice. And I am convinced that precisely this kind of freedom, and not the pressure exerted by dogmas, authority, traditions, state power, or public opinion, can ensure a sound and just solution to those endlessly difficult and contradictory problems which unexpectedly appear in personal, social, cultural, and many other aspects of life. Only this kind of liberty can give people a direct sense of personal happiness, which after all comprises the primal meaning of human existence. I am likewise convinced that a worldwide defense of human rights is a necessary foundation for international trust and security; it is a factor which can deter destructive military conflicts, even global thermonuclear conflicts which threaten the very existence of humanity . . .

The ideology of human rights is probably the only one which can be combined with such diverse ideologies as communism, social democracy, religion, technocracy, and those ideologies which may be described as national and indigenous. It can also serve as a foothold for those who do not wish to be aligned with theoretical intricacies and dogmas, and who have tired of the abundance of ideologies, none of which have brought mankind simple human happiness. The defense of human rights is a clear path toward the unification of people in our turbulent world, and a path towards the relief of suffering.[27]

Notes

1 Such a discussion can be found in the excellent, though now dated, article by Peter Dornan, 'Andrei Sakharov: the conscience of a liberal scientist', in Rudolf Tökes (ed.), *Dissent in the USSR* (Baltimore, 1975).
2 'Interview with Western correspondents', *Sakharov Speaks* (New York, 1974), pp. 203–5.
3 Andrei Sakharov, *Alarm and Hope* (London, 1979), p. 166.
4 *Alarm and Hope*, pp. 104–5.
5 ibid., pp. 108–9.
6 ibid., pp. 102–3.
7 ibid., pp. 157–9.
8 ibid., p. 177.
9 ibid., pp. 178–9.
10 *A Chronicle of Human Rights in the USSR*, no. 39 (New York, 1980), p. 25.

[11] Khronika Press, *Information Bulletin*, 26 October 1983.

[12] *Alarm and Hope*, pp. 12–13.

[13] ibid., p. 13.

[14] Andrei Sakharov, 'How to preserve world peace', *Parade*, 16 August 1981. Reprinted in Alexander Babyonyshev (ed.), *On Sakharov* (New York, 1982), pp. 268-9.

[15] See Andrei Sakharov, 'The danger of thermonuclear war', *Foreign Affairs*, summer 1983.

[16] ibid.

[17] *Bulletin of the Atomic Scientists*, June–July 1983.

[18] Andrei Sakharov, *My Country and the World* (New York, 1975), pp. 71–2.

[19] 'The danger of thermonuclear war'.

[20] *Alarm and Hope*, pp. 12–13.

[21] 'The danger of thermonuclear war'.

[22] *Alarm and Hope*, pp. 172–3.

[23] ibid., p. 109.

[24] Andrei Sakharov, 'The human rights movement in the USSR: its goals, significance, and difficulties', *Trialogue*. Reprinted in *On Sakharov*, pp. 256–7.

[25] *Alarm and Hope*, pp. 171–2.

[26] *On Sakharov*, p. 269.

[27] ibid., pp. 244–6.

* The translation of some of the extracts has been slightly amended (ed.).

INDEX